TROUBLE *at the* BAR

TROUBLE
at the
BAR

AN ECONOMICS PERSPECTIVE

ON THE LEGAL PROFESSION

AND THE CASE

FOR FUNDAMENTAL REFORM

CLIFFORD WINSTON
DAVID BURK
JIA YAN

BROOKINGS INSTITUTION PRESS
Washington, D.C.

The Brookings Institution is a private nonprofit organization devoted to research, education,
and publication on important issues of domestic and foreign policy. Its principal purpose is
to bring the highest quality independent research and analysis to bear on current and emerg-
ing policy problems. Interpretations or conclusions in Brookings publications should be un-
derstood to be solely those of the authors.

Library of Congress Control Number: 2020952504

ISBN 9780815739111 (pbk)
ISBN 9780815739128 (ebook)

9 8 7 6 5 4 3 2 1

Typeset in Garamond Premier Pro

Composition by Elliott Beard

CONTENTS

Acknowledgments   *vii*

ONE
INTRODUCTION   1

TWO
RETURNS TO LAW SCHOOL BEFORE   9
AND AFTER THE GREAT RECESSION

THREE
A BRIEF ASSESSMENT OF   51
THE MARKET FOR A LEGAL EDUCATION

FOUR
LAW FIRMS   59

FIVE
SELF-SELECTION OF GOVERNMENT LAWYERS   71
AND THE EARNINGS PENALTY

SIX
RESOURCE CONSTRAINTS FOR   107
LAWYERS IN GOVERNMENT

SEVEN
JUSTICE IDEOLOGY AND SUPREME COURT DECISIONS 129

EIGHT
A SYNTHESIS 169

NINE
POLICY REFORMS TO IMPROVE 179
THE LEGAL PROFESSION AND
BENEFIT THE NATION

References 193

Notes 209

Index 235

ACKNOWLEDGMENTS

We are grateful to Joan D. Winston for invaluable contributions that made this book possible. We also received useful comments and suggestions from Stephanie Aaronson, Robert Crandall, Jesse Gurman, Janna Johnson, Quentin Karpilow, Amanda Kowalski, Ashley Langer, Robert Litan, Vikram Maheshri, Kyle Rozema, and Michael Simkovic.

David Lampo carefully edited the manuscript, Cecilia González managed the editorial process, and Angela D. Miccinello created the index.

Funding for this research was generously provided by the Searle Freedom Trust.

ONE

INTRODUCTION

The legal profession occupies a special and vital role in American society. Its valuable social contributions include, for example, developing and applying the rule of law, enabling people to settle disputes peacefully, and promoting social justice for everyone in the country.

As pointed out by Bonica (2017), the profession has dominated American politics and public policymaking since at least 1840, when Alexis de Tocqueville wrote *Democracy in America*, and it continues to do so today. Of the roughly 1.3 million lawyers in the United States, about 7.5 percent of them (more than one hundred thousand) work in all levels of state and federal government. They lay claim to an entire branch of government, the courts, and they are heavily over-represented in the ranks of public officials; for example, there are more lawyers than any other occupation in Congress. Since 1789, lawyers have also accounted for nearly 60 percent of the presidents, 70 percent of the vice presidents, and 63 percent of cabinet members.[1]

Lawyers exert an enormous influence on public policy, even in areas where government employees trained in other disciplines have expertise. For example, the U.S. Department of Justice (DOJ) employs more than fifty economists in the Economic Analysis Group that works in the antitrust division, but it's the lawyers in the DOJ who decide whether or not to bring an antitrust case, and they determine the strategy to win it (Crandall and Winston 2003). The U.S. Department of Transportation does not have an economics division, but lawyers who influence national transportation policy occupy important policy-

1

making positions. There are other important government entities, such as the U.S. Federal Reserve, that are led by economists, not lawyers. However, attorneys at the Federal Reserve play a vital role by counseling the board on banking law and other issues and by administering the board's statutory responsibilities in consumer credit protection.

Hadfield (2020) succinctly summarizes law's importance from an economics perspective by pointing out that markets are defined by law, and policy is implemented with law. Law, therefore, forms the basic operating system, the transactional platform of all economic and social activity.

To the best of our knowledge, no one has offered a comprehensive overview of the legal profession's pervasive influence in the policy arena, which, in our view, has created two important social problems. First, the legal profession has been able to create a powerful self-aggrandizing position in the United States. In a widely seen segment on *60 Minutes* in 2014, attorney Mark Koplic went as far as to say that "we [lawyers] make the laws and we make them in a way that is advantageous to the lawyers."[2] Knake (2019) points out, for example, that the legal profession has, in particular, been able to preserve certain anticompetitive features such as the states' requirements that lawyers obtain a license to practice law and the American Bar Association's (ABA) regulation of the legal profession. Both features constitute barriers to entry that increase lawyers' earnings and reduce employment in legal services.

Economists have opposed occupational licensing in general (Kleiner and Vorotnikov 2018) and in the legal profession in particular on cost-benefit grounds (Winston, Crandall, and Maheshri 2011; Winston and Karpilow 2016). Barriers to entry that raise the cost of and limit employment in legal services do not address any alleged problems of imperfect information for consumers or improve the quality of legal services. On the contrary, Hadfield (2020) argues that the high price of legal services and the lack of innovation that could lower costs and increase quality are instead a consequence of the industry's self-regulation that has prevented competition that could transform its inefficient business model.

The legal profession has taken some tentative steps to allow alternative suppliers of legal services, such as LegalZoom, a company that enables its customers to create certain legal documents without hiring a lawyer. A few states have approved a new category of nonlawyer licensees, known as limited license legal technicians in Washington State, licensed paralegal practitioners in Utah, and legal paraprofessionals in Arizona and Minnesota, who have not yet passed the bar and are not full-fledged lawyers, to provide a limited range of legal services at low cost. Other states, like California and New Mexico, have established task forces to explore whether nonlawyers could provide some legal services. But high barriers to entry for would-be legal service providers still exist, and the ABA aggressively prosecutes the unauthorized practice of law (UPL) by individuals.[3] In addition, Hadfield (2020) reports that some state bar associations have used UPL actions to stop innovative firms such as LegalZoom from operating.

The second social problem caused by lawyers that merits attention is that the inefficiencies of the legal profession not only impose costs on consumers and would-be and actual suppliers of legal services but also contribute to a mindset that, given the legal profession's influence in government, decreases the efficacy of public policy more broadly. The most obvious examples are policies that directly increase business for lawyers at a higher cost to consumers. Matter and Stutzer (2015) find that lawyer-legislators are significantly less likely than other legislators, for example, to support tort-reform legislation that could reduce expenditures on liability disputes, and Bonica (2017) argues that lawyer-legislators have created tax loopholes that helped to develop the "income defense industry," which caters to high-net-worth individuals looking to minimize their tax liability. At the same time, lawyers themselves have not been subject to provisions in banking and financial legislation to improve transparency and avoid tax evasion, money laundering, failure to comply with regulations, and fair accounting.[4]

By enabling barriers to entry to persist and preventing nonlawyers and business entities that are not law firms from providing legal services, the legal profession, aided by policymakers, has restricted the public's access to legal services. Hadfield (2010) argues that compared with other advanced market democracies, the United States devotes fewer resources to legal markets and institutions to help individuals with their everyday legal relationships. Juetten (2018) characterizes the law profession's legal monopoly as failing the public because it does not serve 80 percent of the known market and continues to build barriers for people to access legal services. As indicated by the Legal Services Corporation (2017), a government-funded organization established by Congress that promotes equal access to legal services, the problem is particularly acute for low-income Americans because 86 percent of their civil legal problems have not been addressed with adequate or professional legal help. Strikingly, Judge Richard Posner abruptly retired from the U.S. Court of Appeals for the Seventh Circuit in 2017 to focus on litigation finance because he came to believe that the courts have failed to treat litigants who lack financial resources fairly.

The legal profession's role in restricting access to legal services clearly indicates its harmful effects on public policy. However, we argue that its harm is even more extensive. Because lawyers dominate public policymaking, their influence (and by implication, the legal profession's influence) is likely to be associated with the vast inefficiencies in government policies (Winston 2006; Schuck 2014; and Winston 2021b). Lawyers' training and career development have occurred in an environment shaped by regulations that have reduced competition and innovation and that have fostered status quo bias—a factor that has compromised government policymaking. In addition, legal training and practice does not encourage policymakers to acknowledge and correct their policy failures by subjecting decisions to rigorous retrospective cost-benefit analyses.

Commentators on the legal profession have identified several distinctive features of lawyers' training and approach to problem solving that compromise their ability to be an effective force for efficient and equitable policies. For example, Howard's (2019) critique of the legal profession points out that lawyers share a philosophy of the technical correctness of the law, such as compliance with a rule, regardless of the law's actual economic and social effects. Such legal rigidity also encourages status quo bias because any new, superior approach could be nixed because some lawyers claim it conflicts with some rule somewhere. At the same time, a focus on "correctness" also encourages legal advocates to find ambiguities in a law that they can exploit for their own benefit.

Gibney (2019) argues that the law fails to effectively confront social problems because law school graduates as practitioners demonstrate a slavish deference to authority, a belief in the normalcy of American law, an obsession with the past, and an unshakeable belief in the power of rules. To be fair, the stability in rules does provide a favorable climate for investment, and, given the separation of powers built into the Constitution, it can be difficult for policymakers to enact huge and potentially disruptive policy changes.

Still another serious flaw with the legal profession is that lawyers have well-defined ideological biases that are reflected in their policy positions (Posner 2008; Bonica, Chilton, and Sen 2016). Those biases have a powerful influence because lawyers have not been trained to develop an analytical approach, such as cost-benefit analysis, to carefully assess public policies.[5] For example, Chief Justice Roberts' response to statistical evidence that showed Wisconsin's voting districts had been warped by political gerrymandering was to dismiss it as "sociological gobbledygook," when, in fact, it was a conclusion based on basic mathematical methods (Liptak 2018).[6] Cohen and Yang (2018) found that Republican-appointed judges, all else equal, gave longer prison sentences to Black defendants than did Democratic-appointed judges. If future research corroborates that finding, would the judiciary look into the matter, or would it follow Roberts and dismiss the research as "sociological gobbledygook?"

Finally, Kronman (1993) laments the decline of lawyers as public-spirited statesmen who have practical wisdom. He argues that many lawyers have lost their ideals and their motivation for a career in law, which is an ominous sign for the country because a disproportionate share of America's political leaders have always come from the legal profession. Those future leaders will be less qualified than lawyers in the past and therefore less likely to be effective. Kronman blames institutions for the decline of the ideal of the lawyer-statesman, including American law schools, where legal thought does not stress that ideal; law firms, whose commercial culture downgrades it; and the courts, whose bureaucratization stymies it.

In this book, we join forces with lawyers who are concerned about their profession by taking an economic approach, one that provides a critical assessment of the legal profession that raises concerns about its self-regulation, how it limits the public's access to justice, and its role in the persistent inefficiency of government policy. Our approach focuses on the adverse effects created by barriers to entry in the practice of law and suggests that they appear in various ways throughout a lawyer's lifecycle: from law school through job choice and up to, in some cases, filling important elected or appointed positions in government. In our analysis, we investigate empirically important issues that arise during the lifecycle of lawyers' careers, beginning with law school and culminating, for some, in partnerships at major law firms or in positions at the highest levels of government. The issues that have significant implications for the legal profession and for social welfare, and our primary conclusions, include:

- *The economic returns from attending law school*: In chapter 2, we find that the monetary reward from an investment in time and money to obtain a law degree may have declined markedly since the Great Recession, and the value proposition of attending a low-tier law school has become increasingly difficult to justify.

- *The current state of legal education and the training a lawyer receives*: In chapter 3, we suggest that the private and social benefits of a legal education may have been reduced and the private and social costs increased by the excessive time and out-of-pocket costs of attending law school. There are now limited curriculum for students and job opportunities for graduates, and the quality of law school faculty, as suggested by their research accomplishments, is in question.

■ *Private law firms*: In chapter 4, we raise several concerns about private sector law firms, which are important because they are a potential breeding-ground for many lawyers who assume high-level policymaking positions in government. We argue that those lawyers are not imbued by their law firm experiences with the merits of efficient and compassionate public policy.

■ *Lawyers' self-selection to work in the public or private sector*: In chapter 5, we explore how lawyers' choices to work for the government or the private sector may be affected by an earnings penalty that is associated with working for the government. We find that the earnings penalty is large, consistent with evidence that the government is not able to attract and retain lawyers of the same ability, as measured by law school attendance and grades, as the private sector can attract and retain. We suggest that this allocation of legal talent may adversely affect government performance.

■ *Critical issues at the highest levels of government*: In chapter 6, we study the performance of the U.S. Department of Justice's Office of the Solicitor General, providing empirical evidence that even when the government can attract highly capable lawyers, the effectiveness of those lawyers may be reduced by the government's organizational and workplace constraints. And in chapter 7, we provide empirical evidence based on the outcome of business cases of growing ideological polarization among justices on the U.S. Supreme Court.

Some of the chapters develop new empirical evidence using econometric models. We provide a nontechnical summary of our analytical approach and the main findings, which enables nontechnical readers to skip the mathematical development of the models and to turn directly to an in-depth discussion of the findings and their implications. We then synthesize the empirical evidence that we develop here with other evidence to present a strong case that lawyers' performance in the public and private sectors could be improved substantially by deregulating the legal profession to spur competition and innovation in the private sector and to increase the quality and preparation of lawyers who occupy policymaking positions in the public sector.

Instead of self-regulation, members of the legal profession would have the freedom to acquire licensing credentials by attending accredited law schools and passing a bar examination, for example, or to not acquire any credential at all. Licensing would be a free-market outcome, and consumers would determine if it leads to higher-quality services that they are willing to pay for. We envision that licensing would be valued and reflected in higher rates for clients who seek a licensed lawyer to represent them, for example, in complex business litigation or in a case before the Supreme Court. Clients would be much less likely to pay licensed lawyers a higher rate for other legal services such as drafting a will or reviewing a simple contract. Even if licensed lawyers were generally of higher quality than unlicensed lawyers, consumers would be able to afford more, and have much greater access to, legal representation for all types of services.

We do not believe that the legal profession is likely to deregulate itself, but we suggest that the recent decline in the number of lawyers who are attracted to government positions and the public's disenchantment with elected officials conducting business as usual may lead to an influx of public officials who do not have allegiance to the legal profession and who would therefore be willing to eliminate its monopoly status and licensing requirements. Lawyers could therefore obtain training and experiences to optimize their career goals in the private or public sector and expand the public's access to justice. When lawyers are in a policymaking position, we suggest that their improved training and experiences could contribute more effectively to enabling America to become a fairer and more efficient society.

As this book goes to press, the United States and the entire world is engaged in a stressful battle to control and eradicate the novel coronavirus and its associated disease, COVID-19. In the final chapter, we argue that this challenging period is creating serious challenges for the American public, some of whom are in need of legal assistance, as well as for current and prospective law students, law schools, and law firms. At the same time, we argue that on closer examination, the global pandemic is also strengthening the case for deregulating the legal profession to improve its efficiency and equity, and consequently benefit society in general and its most vulnerable members in particular.

TWO

RETURNS TO LAW SCHOOL
BEFORE AND AFTER
THE GREAT RECESSION

Prospective lawyers in most states must attend and graduate from a law school accredited by the American Bar Association (ABA) and also pass a bar examination to obtain a license to practice law.[1] Although we are not aware of many formal academic studies, investing time and money in a legal education has been considered to be a sound, long-term investment because the vast majority of individuals who graduated from an accredited law school, passed a state bar exam, obtained employment as a lawyer, and paid back any law school loans in a timely fashion, probably earned more income over their working lives than they would have earned in most other professions.

But the Great Recession appears to have changed the terms of the law school investment decision because the recent growth in jobs that require a law degree has been slow, new lawyers' wages are stagnating, and the rising cost of law school is burdening many graduates with large debts.[2] Burk, Organ, and Rasiel (2019) point out that the problems facing law schools began in the aftermath of the Great Recession as the number of unique applicants to accredited law schools fell 35 percent from 2010–2011 through 2016–2017. Importantly, the reduction in applications is largely attributable to stronger prospective students, based on conventional qualifications, not applying to law school because LSAT scores were 15 percentile points lower at all but the strongest schools. The decline in the quality of recent law students has also been reflected in a decline in first-time bar examination pass rates (most states give aspiring lawyers three chances to pass the bar exam). For example, the first-time pass rate of the California bar examination in February 2020 was 26.8 percent—an all-time low. Other states also reported sharp declines in their bar examination pass rates.[3] Applications to law schools have rebounded somewhat since 2017, and the quality of applicants based on LSAT scores is also improving, but the strongest students' interest in law school is far below their peak interest.

Although we argue that some legal practitioners could satisfy the public's demand for certain legal services without obtaining a law degree based on a costly and time-consuming three-year course of study, the future of the legal profession depends to a significant extent on whether a law school degree is still a sound investment that is capable of attracting students who enable the legal profession to provide a full range of legal services. Thus, in this chapter, we estimate the economic returns that accrue from a J.D. degree for law students who graduated from law school before the Great Recession, balancing the direct and opportunity costs of obtaining a J.D. with the benefits it offers an individual over the course of his or her working life in order to test the belief that attending law school was, in fact, a good long-term investment. Given concerns that the Great Recession may have affected the terms of the law school investment, we then determine whether obtaining a J.D. is still a good investment in the postrecession environment. Our analysis takes the state of law school education and the regulations governing it as given, but in the next chapter, we assess legal education and consider how the profession could potentially attract more individuals to provide valued legal services.

Analyzing the returns to education, but not specifically to law school, has a long history in economics. As pointed out by Becker (1964), schooling can be analyzed as an investment decision—costs are paid initially, and rewards are reaped in the future. An optimal schooling decision, from the perspective of income maximization, generates a higher rate of return than any other available investment. Card (1999) provides a survey of empirical estimates of rates of return for different types of colleges, macroeconomic settings, and individual characteristics, placing the economic return on college attendance at around 10 percent.

Notwithstanding the extensive research on the returns to a college education, there is very little empirical work on returns to graduate or professional education.[4] Oyer and Schaefer (2009) estimated the returns to the quality of the law school attended *conditional* on attending law school, and found significant premiums associated with attending a top-tier law school relative to other law schools. But their work does not account for the decision to attend law school in the first place. McIntyre and Simkovic (2013) explored whether law school is indeed a wise investment, but they do not adequately address the issue of selection bias that arises because of unobserved variables that influence individuals' choices to attend law school, nor do they explore the effect of the quality of the undergraduate or law school, as indicated by ranking, on individuals' returns.[5] If a disproportionate share of workers who have the potential, based on their ability, to earn high incomes choose to obtain J.D.s—as appears to be the case—then failing to appropriately account for this behavior would produce upward biased estimates of the J.D. premium.

We combine data from large-scale surveys of lawyers and college graduates, which have detailed information on schooling and labor market outcomes, to estimate the returns on a J.D. as of 2002, 2007, and 2011 for lawyers who passed the bar in 2000; thus, our estimates are based at several important junctures of a lawyer's career as it evolved both before and after the Great Recession, which officially began in 2007 and ended in 2009. We also address the potential selectivity bias in those estimates that arises because individuals who choose to attend law school differ in many ways from individuals who comprise the general population. We then indicate how the characteristics of law students who entered and graduated from law school after the Great Recession differ from the characteristics of previous law students, and we assess how their returns may have changed.

We find that the cohort of lawyers who graduated from law school before the Great Recession, even expensive law schools that are ranked in the lowest-quality tier, earned sizable returns, and we also find that those lawyers were able to maintain the value of their law degree after the recession ended. By contrast, we find that the average quality of lawyers who graduated from law school *after* the Great Recession declined notably from the average quality of previous law students. Importantly, we conclude that this change, combined with changes in the market for lawyers, is likely to have had significant adverse effects on the returns from a law degree, which creates uncertainty as to whether an investment in a law school education is a sound one unless an individual graduates from a first-tier law school.

As pointed out by Dale and Krueger (2014), higher ability students may signal their ability by attending more selective colleges, or they may learn skills at more selective colleges that make them more productive workers. Dale and Krueger, for example, find that highly selective colleges provide access to networks for Black and Hispanic students that otherwise would not be available to them. Similarly, elite law schools can increase their graduates' returns by opening networks to the leading law firms that pay the highest salaries and tend to hire predominantly from such schools. We find that law school graduates' earnings increase by going to a higher-tier law school even when we control for self-selection.[6]

THE MARKET FOR LAWYERS

While claims abound in the popular press about the stagnation of the legal labor market, commentators have failed to look at the legal profession in relation to its long-term trends and in relation to other professions. Indeed, 2006, just prior to the recession, was a boom year for lawyers' earnings and employment, which made the subsequent decline in the market appear all the more pronounced. We provide context for our estimates of the returns to law school by using the Current Population Survey (CPS; administered by the Bureau of Labor Statistics) to provide a brief overview of the market, wages, and employment for lawyers and new law school graduates over time. We discuss the impact of COVID-19 on the market for lawyers in chapter 9.

Earnings

Lawyers' real and relative wages have increased dramatically during the last fifty years and have slowed only recently. CPS data indicate that college graduates earned, on average, $66,000 annually for the years 1995 to 2007 (in 2011 purchasing power parity, or PPP). During the same period, lawyers earned, on average, $158,000, which amounts to a premium of 140 percent. As reported in Rosen (1992), the premium during the years from 1967 to 1987 was 63 percent.

Of course, those raw averages do not account for the fact that lawyers have different characteristics than people who do not obtain a law degree. For example, as we study in detail for a particular cohort of lawyers, it's clear that lawyers have stronger intellectual abilities and work more hours than do college graduates who did not obtain a law degree. Private sector lawyers work approximately 10 percent more hours a week than nonlawyer college graduates, while public sector lawyers work about the same average number of hours as nonlawyer college graduates.

We take a more systematic approach by estimating an adjusted wage premium for lawyers. We ran a regression in logarithms of the wage on education dummies, hours of work per week, years of work experience, gender and race dummies, regional dummies, and year dummies, and we present the estimated wage premium for lawyer occupation in figure 2-1. Although the wage premium could be affected by other variables that we cannot control for, it is notable that we find that the premium generally ranged from between 20 percent and 30 percent throughout our sample period. Not surprisingly, it dropped moderately during the Great Recession, from 2007 through 2009, before rebounding over the next few years. Figure 2-2 shows the difference between the average wage of private sector lawyers, public sector lawyers, and nonlawyer college graduates, and indicates that the wage premium was relatively stable during and after the recession. At the same time, private sector lawyers earned a much greater wage premium than other lawyers and college graduates did.

The distribution of wages among new lawyers varies considerably. Data from the National Association for Law Placement indicate that it is characterized by a bimodal distribution with new lawyers working for large, corporate law firms in New York City and Washington, D.C., earning an annual base salary of $160,000 since 2007, and new government lawyers earning an annual salary of approximately $65,000, on average.[7]

FIGURE 2-1. Lawyers' Earnings Premium, Controlling for Demographic Characteristics

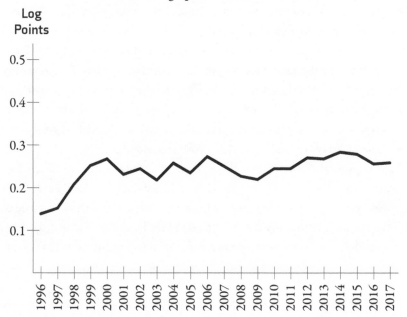

FIGURE 2-2. Lawyers' Earnings Relative to Other College Graduates, by Sector

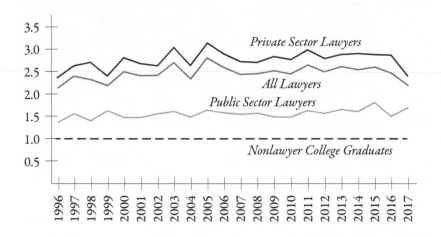

Employment

The changes in lawyers' wages have been accompanied by a fairly steady increase in the employment of lawyers, according to both the CPS and data from the Occupational Employment Statistics survey (OES; administered by the Bureau of Labor Statistics). Despite many reports in the popular press that legal hiring has stagnated, those data sources indicate that net growth in the legal services sector has continued even through the Great Recession. According to CPS data, the average annual growth rate in the number of lawyers since 1965 has been about 3 percent, with annual growth during the 1970s exhibiting a strong 6.5 percent before returning to 3 percent during the 1980s and early 1990s. Since 2008, growth has been more modest, but still positive, at about 1.5 percent per year. Figure 2-3 shows that although the legal sector's postrecession growth rate is slower than its prerecession rate, the sector appears to have weathered the recession quite well relative to college graduates as a whole. Notably, it grew faster than financial services did in the wake of the recession.

An important subset of overall employment growth is the rate of employment growth for new lawyers, but the CPS and OES data do not explicitly identify new lawyers because they include both new lawyers and the departure of existing lawyers to construct the growth rate of the legal sector. It is likely, however, that the growth in new lawyers exceeds the overall growth rate of the legal sector because some seasoned lawyers retire from the labor force.

FIGURE 2-3. Level of Employment Relative to 2008
for Lawyers and Various Industries

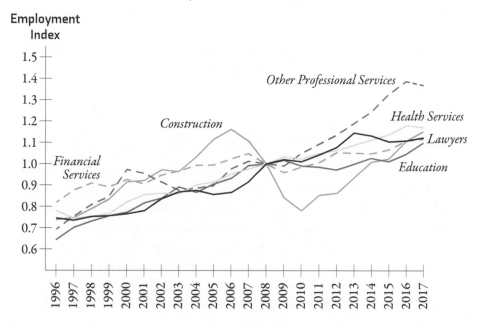

An Over-Production of Lawyers

As noted, entry barriers to the practice of law raise lawyers' earnings and enable law schools to charge higher tuitions than they would be able to in a deregulated environment. The higher cost of a legal education, however, has not prevented law schools from producing more graduates than the available jobs where one can practice law. For example, Norberg (2018) points out that graduates from ABA-accredited law schools have outpaced the number of full-time bar passage-required jobs by more than 30 percent every year since 2001. An increasing portion of new law school graduates have responded to the insufficient demand for full-time work in the legal sector by taking jobs in other sectors. However, it is not clear that their legal education is also beneficial for their work in those nonlegal sectors.

In sum, the aftermath of the Great Recession has created more uncertainty about the market for lawyers as individuals consider attending law school and whether they will be able to obtain a job that values their law degree above and beyond the job market's value of their college degree. The demand for lawyers has not returned to its prerecession level, especially as corporations attempt to curb their spending on legal services (Kiser 2019), and it is growing more slowly than it was before the recession. However, an investment in law school may still be justified from a financial perspective even if it takes some time before new law school graduates can find employment as a lawyer. In addition, new graduates may have an advantage over unemployed and underemployed would-be lawyers because they have no history of failing to find a job in the law sector and they would not be forced to signal that they were not sufficiently attractive for employment when the market was tight.

ANALYTICAL FRAMEWORK

We develop a simple choice-theoretic framework to determine the economic value of a J.D. where college graduates choose whether to go to law school or enter the labor market. We derive an empirical expression that compares the present value of what college graduates would earn over their lifetimes if they went to a three-year law school, but paid tuition and did not earn an income during law school, with the present value of what college graduates would earn if they did not go to a three-year law school, including the income that they would have earned while working instead of attending law school and the tuition that they would not have paid. After deriving the expression, we then estimate its empirical components.

An important technical consideration is that we control for the selectivity bias that may arise from the decision to attend law school. That is, highly intelligent individuals may attend law school and subsequently have higher earnings than college graduates who did not attend law school, but they may have had higher earnings than other college graduates regardless of whether they went to law school. In the remainder of this section, we explain our analytical approach. Nontechnical readers can skip this section and continue with the discussion of the data that we use to perform the analysis and the empirical findings.

Formally, a college graduate may go immediately to work, earning w_t^{nonJD} for each year t of a T year career, or may attend law school for three years, at a cost of tuition and foregone income each year, before beginning a working career of $T–3$ years with a salary of $w_t^{JD} = p_t + w_t^{nonJD}$, where p_t is the salary premium associated with a J.D. Thus, the economic value of a J.D. to the college graduate is the difference between the net present value of income earned during a working life with and without a J.D., $\text{NPV}_{JD} - \text{NPV}_{nonJD}$, where for a given interest rate r:

$$NPV_{JD}(w_t^{JD}, r, T) = -\sum_{t=1}^{3} \frac{tuition_t}{(1+r)^{t-1}} + \sum_{t=4}^{T} \frac{w_t^{JD}}{(1+r)^{t-1}}$$

$$= -\sum_{t=1}^{3} \frac{tuition_t}{(1+r)^{t-1}} + \sum_{t=4}^{T} \frac{p_t + w_t^{nonJD}}{(1+r)^{t-1}} \tag{1}$$

$$NPV_{nonJD}(w_t^{nonJD}, r, T) = \sum_{t=1}^{T} \frac{w_t^{nonJD}}{(1+r)^{t-1}} \tag{2}$$

Substituting those expressions, the difference $NPV_{JD} - NPV_{nonJD}$ can be written as

$$\left(\sum_{t=1}^{3} \frac{-tuition_t}{(1+r)^{t-1}} + \sum_{t=4}^{T} \frac{w_t^{JD}}{(1+r)^{t-1}} \right) - \sum_{t=1}^{T} \frac{w_t^{nonJD}}{(1+r)^{t-1}}$$

$$= -\sum_{t=1}^{3} \frac{tuition_t + w_t^{nonJD}}{(1+r)^{t-1}} + \sum_{t=4}^{T} \frac{w_t^{JD} - w_t^{nonJD}}{(1+r)^{t-1}} \tag{3}$$

The first summation term in equation (3) represents the costs of law school, including both the direct costs, namely tuition, and the opportunity costs, namely the forgone wages, while the second summation term represents the benefits of law school, namely the annual wage premium enjoyed by an individual with a J.D. We determine the returns to law school by measuring all the components of equation (3).

Unlike tuition, which we determine from descriptive, aggregate data, and the interest rate, which we determine based on a plausible assumption, we must estimate the J.D. and non-J.D. incomes. We specify those in logs for each year t over an individual i's career as:

$$\log w_{it}^{JD} = \alpha^{JD} + \beta^{JD} x_i + f^{JD}(t) + \varepsilon_{it}^{JD}$$

$$\log w_{it}^{nonJD} = \alpha^{nonJD} + \beta^{nonJD} x_i + f^{nonJD}(t) + \varepsilon_{it}^{nonJD} \tag{4}$$

where w_{it}^{JD} and w_{it}^{nonJD} are the annual wages individual i would earn as a J.D. or as a non-J.D., α is a constant level of wages, x_i are observed individual characteristics, t is time measured as the number of years since college graduation, and $\varepsilon_{it}^{JD}, \varepsilon_{it}^{nonJD}$ are the effects of unobserved variables on the incomes and perhaps the effect of a stochastic idiosyncratic income shock. Accordingly, β reflects the effects of characteristics x on wages, and $f(t)$ is a function that describes how the J.D. and non-J.D. wages evolve over time since college graduation.

Of course, for any given individual i, we never observe both w_{it}^{JD} and w_{it}^{nonJD} at a given point in time t. Instead, if we let JD_i take on a value of 1 if an individual obtains a J.D. and 0 otherwise, then we observe a wage conditional on J.D. status, which we express without a superscript:

$$\log w_{it} = JD_i * \log w_{it}^{JD} + (1 - JD_i) * \log w_{it}^{nonJD}. \tag{5}$$

We are interested in determining the premium from obtaining a J.D.; thus, substituting equation (4) into equation (5) yields:

$$\log w_{it} = \alpha^{nonJD} + \beta^{nonJD} x_i + f^{nonJD}(t)$$

$$+ \left(\alpha^{JD} - \alpha^{nonJD} + f^{JD}(t) - f^{nonJD}(t) + \varepsilon_{it}^{JD} - \varepsilon_{it}^{nonJD} \right) JD_i$$

$$+ (\beta^{JD} - \beta^{nonJD}) x_i \times JD_i + \varepsilon_{it}^{nonJD}$$

We make the simplifying assumption that J.D. and non-J.D. wages respond identically to an individual's observed characteristics x, that is $\beta^{nonJD} = \beta^{JD}$. (Indeed, in our empirical work, we tested the assumption and failed to reject it.) Rewriting the coefficient of the JD_i term as ρ_t, which we interpret as the wage premium a J.D. enjoys t years after graduating from college, yields the regression specification:

$$\log w_{it} = \alpha^{nonJD} + \beta x_i + f^{nonJD}(t) + \rho_t JD_i + \varepsilon_{it}^{nonJD}. \tag{6}$$

Given a comprehensive longitudinal data set on lawyers' and nonlawyers' characteristics and earnings, we could directly estimate the J.D. premium ρ_t for each year t of a worker's career. Combining those estimates of the premiums with estimates of the other parameters in equation (6), we could estimate a given individual's earnings with and without a J.D. for each year, as is required for our computation of the difference in returns given in equation (3). However, because such a data set is not available, we take the following two-step approach.

First, we estimate ρ_t for a single period. We do this using data that have a very rich set of conditioning variables. Second, we estimate $f^{JD}(t)$ and $f^{nonJD}(t)$ to capture how individuals' wages evolve over time by using data that have sufficient time series observations. Because

$$E(\rho_t) = \alpha^{JD} - \alpha^{nonJD} + f^{JD}(t) - f^{nonJD}(t), \tag{7}$$

we can estimate ρ_t for all t by combining the estimates of $f^{JD}(t)$ and $f^{nonJD}(t)$ with the single estimate of ρ_t from the first step. Thus, the two-step procedure allows us to estimate all the parameters in equation (6) to determine an individual's wages with and without a J.D.

An important methodological point is that the estimate of ρ_t is not straight-forward, because it would be biased if the unobserved influences contained in the ε_{it} terms are correlated with the selection decision to attend law school. Namely, consider the specifications

$$\varepsilon_{it} = \phi_i + u_{it} \tag{8}$$

$$JD_i = \alpha_1 x_i + \alpha_2 z_i + \alpha_3 \phi_i + v_{it}, \tag{9}$$

where ϕ_i is an unobserved individual fixed effect, such as the desire to make a lot of money, which is relevant to both $\log w_{it}$ and JD_i, and u_{it} and v_i are mean-0 stochastic terms. If $\alpha_3 \neq 0$, then the ordinary least squares (OLS) parameter estimates of equation (6) would be biased.

We take the following approach to address the selection issue. First, we draw on a rich data set that potentially enables us to observe the critical variables that influence selection. Second, we consider a plausible instrumental variable based on parental characteristics that affect an individual's schooling choices but, holding other influences constant, do not affect an individual's income. Finally, we provide a robustness check based on propensity score matching (Black and Smith 2004), which compares individuals who have similar observed characteristics but differ in the "treatment" status of whether they have obtained a J.D. Given our rich data set and alternative estimation approaches, we do not find that the unobserved determinants of selectivity behavior are a potentially important source of bias to our estimate of the J.D. premium, and we proceed to investigate the heterogeneity in the returns to a J.D. for graduates of different quality tiers of law schools.

DATA TO ESTIMATE THE J.D. PREMIUM

Our analysis estimates the premium individuals have earned by graduating from law school in the year 2000 compared with what they would have earned if they pursued a different course of study and career. We estimate the premium for the years 2002 and 2007, before the Great Recession's economic effects took hold, and for the year 2011, after the Great Recession officially ended, although the market for lawyers was still feeling its ill-effects. We assess later how the J.D. premium has changed for individuals who graduated from law school after the Great Recession ended.

We represent earnings for prerecession law school graduates with data from the American Bar Foundation's "After the JD" survey (AJD), and we represent earnings for college graduates without a J.D. for the years 2002 and 2007 with data from the National Center for Education Statistics' Baccalaureate and Beyond (B&B) survey. Because the B&B survey is not available for the year 2011, we represent earnings for college graduates without a J.D. for that year with data from the Survey of Income and Program Participation (SIPP).

The AJD and B&B Samples

The AJD and B&B surveys follow a single cohort of graduates for several waves and contain detailed information about respondents' educational history, socioeconomic characteristics, and wages and employment for approximately ten years after college graduation. The AJD survey also contains information on respondents' legal education and the type of organization of their employer (for example, private law firm or federal government). Both surveys were conducted over roughly the same time frame. The B&B sample consists of a nationally representative cohort that graduated from college in 1993 and was surveyed in 1994, 1997, and 2003, while the first two waves of the AJD follow a group of lawyers who were admitted to the bar in 2000 and were surveyed in 2002 and 2007. To maintain comparability between the two samples, we restricted the AJD to include people who graduated from college after 1993.

The combined data set provides comprehensive information on an individual's undergraduate GPA, competitiveness of undergraduate institution (based on Barron's admissions categorization of "most competitive," "highly competitive," "very competitive," "competitive," "less competitive," or "noncompetitive"), and wages from approximately ten years after college graduation or seven years after law school graduation. Because the B&B data contain 2003 wages and the AJD data contain 2007 wages, we convert the B&B data to 2007 dollars using the CPI.

Our final sample consists of 793 observations from the AJD and 4,654 from the B&B, for a total of 5,447 observations used for estimation. Applying sample weights ensured that the data were representative of the population.[8] The summary statistics of both samples in table 2-1 show that the AJD is slightly more racially diverse and slightly less gender balanced and that J.D. respondents' fathers are more likely to be college graduates than are non-J.D. respondents' fathers. As expected, AJD respondents have, on average, higher undergraduate grades from more competitive undergraduate schools than B&B respondents have. The differences in the samples indicate that people who choose to go to law school (LS) do not represent a random sample of the population and that it is important to distinguish between the effects of those differences when estimating the effect of a law degree on earnings.

The table also shows that, on average, AJD respondents' salaries exceed B&B respondents' salaries. Figure 2-4 takes a closer look at lawyers' earnings and shows that the kernel density estimate of the wage distribution of lawyers from the top 20, middle, and lower-quality tiers of law schools suggests an overall distribution that is bimodal, with graduates from the top 20 law schools earning more than graduates from other law schools.[9] Hence, focusing on broad

TABLE 2-1. Summary Statistics, B&B/AJD Data

	B&B	AJD	Combined
Female	0.45	0.41	0.45
Black	0.06	0.08	0.06
Asian	0.05	0.10	0.05
Latino	0.04	0.10	0.04
Married	0.67	0.70	0.67
Dad college grad	0.46	0.58	0.46
Mom college grad	0.44	0.49	0.44
Hours/week	47.10 (9)	46.38 (7.7)	47.09 (8.9)
Salary (2007)	70,000 (46,000)	109,000 (55,000)	72,000 (45,000)
Undergrad: Top-Tier	0.03	0.23	0.03
Undergrad: Middle-Tier	0.31	0.55	0.31
Undergrad: Lower-Tier	0.66	0.22	0.66
GPA>3.5	0.13	0.48	0.13
GPA<2.5	0.30	0.03	0.29
Major: Business	0.26	0.13	0.26
Major: Engineering	0.08	0.02	0.08
Major: Science	0.11	0.07	0.11
Major: Social Science	0.15	0.36	0.15
LS: Top 10	–	0.11	<0.01
LS: 11–20	–	0.12	<0.01
LS: 21–100	–	0.49	<0.01
LS: 100+	–	0.28	<0.01
N	4,654	793	5,447

FIGURE 2-4. Lawyer Wage Distribution by Law School Tier, AJD Data

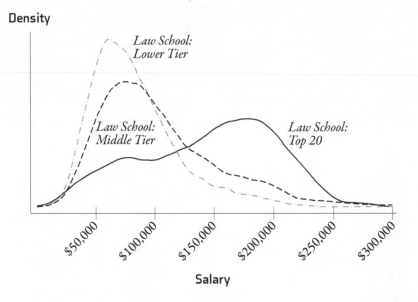

Density

Salary

averages across the population of lawyers without accounting for the heterogeneity of graduates from different-quality law schools may obscure important differences among lawyers.

The AJD and SIPP Samples

The third wave of the AJD (AJD3) was administered in 2012. It updates the previous waves by providing 2011 salary and job information. In 2011, the AJD respondents were in their eleventh year since passing the bar; thus, if their first jobs were as an associate at a private law firm, the decision by the firm to promote them to partner—which usually occurs in the associate's seventh year—had long been made. If an associate were not promoted to partner and took a job at another, less selective private firm, the temporal arc of AJD3 gave them enough time to be considered for partner by their new firm.

The data we use for non-J.D.s in 2011 are from the Survey of Income and Program Participation (SIPP), a survey designed to collect data related to income, labor force participation, social program participation, and general demographic characteristics. The major shortcoming of the SIPP is that, unlike the AJD and the B&B, it provides only general educational characteristics as indicated by a respondent's degree—high school, college, graduate, or professional—and no further educational information. We use the later waves of the 2008 panel, which provides data on respondents in 2011, the same year that the AJD Wave 3 covers. To ensure that the SIPP sample is comparable to the AJD Wave 3 sample, we restrict it to include respondents with at least a college degree, which was obtained in 1996.

Our final sample consists of 1,624 observations from the AJD3 and 1,069 from SIPP, for a total of 2,693 observations used for estimation. Again, we applied sample weights to ensure that the data were representative of the population. We summarize the means of the SIPP and AJD3 data in table 2-2. Consistent with the summary statistics presented for the AJD and B&B data, the average J.D. salary in the AJD3 data is substantially higher than the corresponding non-J.D. salary in the SIPP data; however, the variation is also much larger, which may reflect the effect of partnership decisions across heterogeneous law firms. As in the previous summary statistics, the ethnic makeup, marital status, and average hours per week appear comparable between the two samples.

TABLE 2-2. Summary Statistics, Sample
Means, SIPP/AJD3 Data

	SIPP	AJD3	Combined
Female	0.46	0.43	0.44
Black	0.09	0.08	0.08
Married	0.72	0.75	0.74
Hours/week	43.1	44.6	44.0
	(12.9)	(6.9)	(9.7)
Salary (2011)	72,000	144,000	116,000
	(61,000)	(184,000)	(152,000)
LS: Top 10	–	0.1	–
LS: 10–20	–	0.11	–
LS: 21–100	–	0.49	–
LS: 100+	–	0.28	–
N	1,069	1,624	2,693

Notes: Summary statistics for the B&B/AJD combined data set. Sample weights applied. Standard deviations are in parentheses. Salary rounded to the thousands. Other statistics rounded to the hundredths.

ESTIMATING THE J.D. PREMIUM

We begin by estimating some very simple earnings models to see how our estimate of the returns to a J.D. is affected by the inclusion of additional variables. We then explore various sources of heterogeneity in the returns to a J.D. before turning to the methodological issue of selection bias in the next section.

AJD and B&B Samples

We begin with OLS estimates of the average J.D. premium for a special case of the model in equation (6), where we exclude all the control variables x:

$$\log w_{10i} = \alpha' + \rho_{10}' JD_i + \varepsilon_i, \tag{10}$$

where w_{10i} is the respondent's salary ten years after graduating from college (expressed in 2007 dollars). The first column of results presented in table 2-3 includes just the J.D. indicator variable and reports an estimate of 0.449, which is statistically significant. We convert this estimate from a log scale to a percentage increase in the level of income and find that the average wage premium from obtaining a J.D. is 56 percent.[10] As shown in the second column of table 2-3, we obtained a very similar coefficient when we estimated the model using the well-known and widely-used CPS sample of earnings from 1996 to 2007, restricting it to individuals who were approximately ten years out of college.[11]

We expanded the specification in column 3 by including gender, race, marital status, father's education (mother's education tended to be statistically insignificant), and weekly hours of work.[12] Although those variables have their expected signs, are precisely estimated with the exception of race (which may reflect an insufficient number of Black workers in the sample), and increase the goodness of fit, they appear to bear little relationship to our estimate of the J.D. premium. Column 4 includes an individual's undergraduate major (humanities is the omitted base major) to control for other sources of an earnings premium and shows that the estimate of the J.D. premium is again not materially affected, possibly because individuals whose majors generate the highest earnings premiums, for example, business, math, and science, have tended to not become lawyers. Recently, many law schools have allowed applicants to take the GRE instead of the LSAT, in part to attract students from a wider variety of educational backgrounds. The final column includes variables to control for the quality of the undergraduate institution that an individual attended and their performance (a low-tier institution and a low GPA is the base). As expected,

TABLE 2-3. OLS Income Regressions with General J.D. Indicator Variable

SAMPLE:	(1) B&B/AJD	(2) CPS	(3) B&B/AJD	(4) B&B/AJD	(5) B&B/AJD
JD	0.449***	0.461***	0.431***	0.453***	0.342***
	(0.0184)	(0.050)	(0.0183)	(0.0187)	(0.0206)
Female			−0.124***	−0.0912***	−0.100***
			(0.0217)	(0.0217)	(0.0215)
Black			−0.0118	−0.0151	0.00173
			(0.0235)	(0.0233)	(0.0231)
Married			0.101***	0.0972***	0.103***
			(0.0192)	(0.0190)	(0.0188)
FemaleX Married			−0.127***	−0.123***	−0.123***
			(0.0260)	(0.0257)	(0.0254)
Dad College Grad.			0.0819***	0.0820***	0.0622***
			(0.0122)	(0.0122)	(0.0122)
Hours/Week			0.0602***	0.0573***	0.0584***
			(0.00631)	(0.00637)	(0.00651)
Hours Sq.			−0.0461***	−0.0435***	−0.0449***
			(0.00602)	(0.00610)	(0.00626)
Major: Business				0.0997***	0.107***
				(0.0181)	(0.0179)
Major: Engineering				0.239***	0.227***
				(0.0191)	(0.0191)
Major: Math or Science				0.0432**	0.0340*
				(0.0166)	(0.0164)
Major: Social Studies				0.117***	0.0962***
				(0.0201)	(0.0202)
Top-Tier UG: High GPA					0.337***
					(0.0445)
Top-Tier UG: Med. GPA					0.294***
					(0.0390)
Top-Tier UG: Low GPA					0.148*
					(0.0611)
2nd-Tier UG: High GPA					0.259***
					(0.0325)
2nd-Tier UG: Med. GPA					0.123***
					(0.0200)

TABLE 2-3. CONTINUED

SAMPLE:	(1) B&B/AJD	(2) CPS	(3) B&B/AJD	(4) B&B/AJD	(5) B&B/AJD
2nd-Tier UG: Low GPA					0.0741** (0.0242)
Low-Tier UG: High GPA					0.0993*** (0.0249)
Constant	11.03*** (0.00647)	10.17*** (0.0102)	9.252*** (0.162)	9.251*** (0.164)	9.163*** (0.167)
N	5,447	8,975	5,447	5,447	5,447
R-squared	0.10	0.13	0.23	0.25	0.26

Notes: Robust standard errors in parentheses. The dependent variable is log wage ten years after college graduation. Column (2), which uses CPS data, also includes controls for year dummies, and the sample is restricted to people who are ten years out of college, for comparability with the B&B/AJD sample. Top-Tier UG × High GPA is an indicator variable for whether the individual attended a top-tier undergraduate institution and attained a high GPA there. The other undergraduate quality × undergraduate GPA indicator variables are similarly defined, and the omitted category is low-tier undergraduate institution and low GPA. For the undergraduate major indicator variables, the omitted category is humanities.

* $p<0.05$, ** $p<0.01$, *** $p<0.001$.

individuals who attend top-tier colleges and have high GPAs receive the largest earnings premium. This measure of academic ability reduces the estimated J.D. premium by about one quarter to 0.34, which corresponds to a roughly 40 percent wage premium, indicating that higher-quality students from higher-quality institutions tend to become lawyers and that it is important to control for this source of selectivity.

As noted, J.D. earnings are likely to vary by law school tier, and the estimated J.D. premium may vary by those tiers as well. Table 2-4 documents that variation by including indicators of law school quality in the earnings specification, denoting schools ranked in the top 10, 11–20, 21–100, 101–200, and worse than 200. The first column replicates the original estimate of the premium in table 2-3 without any controls, column 2 presents estimates of the premium that vary by all possible tiers, and column 3 presents statistically significantly different estimates that vary by the top 20 schools, the second tier, and a lower tier composed of schools outside of the top 100. The individual coefficients are statistically significant and, as expected, indicate that higher-ranked schools are associated with higher earnings premiums and that the difference is large. For example, the coefficient for the premiums associated with the top 10 and first-tier schools exceeds 0.74, while the premium associated with schools outside of the top 100 is less than 0.24. When we included all of the controls that were previously included in table 2-3, we found that the premiums declined (see columns 2 and 3) but that the sharp and statistically significant variation in premiums across schools in different tiers remained.

TABLE 2-4. OLS Income Regressions with J.D. Indicator Variables by Quality Tier

Controls	(1) No	(2) No	(3) No	(1') Yes	(2') Yes	(3') Yes
J.D.	0.449*** (0.0188)			0.342*** (0.0206)		
LS: Top 10		0.792*** (0.0506)			0.659*** (0.0487)	
LS: 11–20		0.705*** (0.0454)			0.576*** (0.0432)	
LS: 21–100		0.414*** (0.0243)			0.324*** (0.0255)	
LS: 101–200		0.231*** (0.0428)			0.187*** (0.0423)	
LS: 200+		0.208*** (0.0395)			0.171*** (0.0444)	
LS: Top 20			0.745*** (0.0343)			0.612*** (0.0343)
LS: 2nd Tier (21–100)			0.414*** (0.0243)			0.323*** (0.0255)
LS: Lower Tier			0.220*** (0.0297)			0.179*** (0.0314)
Constant	11.03*** (0.00701)	11.03*** (0.00701)	11.03*** (0.00701)	9.163*** (0.167)	9.213*** (0.139)	9.211*** (0.139)
N	5,447	5,447	5,447	5,447	5,447	5,447
R-squared	0.0982	0.120	0.120	0.263	0.277	0.277

Notes: Robust standard errors in parentheses. The dependent variable is log wage ten years after college graduation. Regressions (1) through (3) do not include controls, and therefore show average differences in log wage between J.D.s of the specified type and non-J.D.s. Column (1) groups all J.D.s together; column (2) breaks J.D.s out into more specific categories, and column (3) uses the three categories that are used extensively in this paper. Columns (1'), (2'), and (3') use the full suite of controls that generally includes basic demographic and employment characteristics and undergraduate education characteristics as described in the body of the paper. The coefficient estimates for those explanatory variables are suppressed in this tablebut do not vary significantly between the separate regressions. Complete results for regression (1') are presented in table 2-3.

* p<0.05, ** p<0.01, *** p<0.001.

Of course, within each law school ranking category, substantial heterogeneity in individual lawyers' premiums is likely to exist. Some Yale, Stanford, and Harvard law school graduates go on to work as public defenders or other less remunerative positions, while some partners at top New York City law firms graduated from law schools that are not among the first-tier schools. Oyer and Schaefer (2016) found that most large law firms hired from local law schools, and Abrams and Engel (2015) found that the geographical proximity of a graduate's law school to a major legal market was a good predictor of that individual making partner at a big law firm.

Thus, we explored the variation in premiums by the types of employer organizations included in the AJD, namely, Private Law Firm, Industry (including in-house counsel), Federal Government, State or Local Government, General Practice (referring to lawyers who provide service to individuals in matters such as divorces, wills, personal real estate, and the like), and "Other" (including military, nonprofit, and other organizations that do not fit into the other categories). We present estimation results in table 2-5 interacting the employer organizations with the quality of law school attended, given that we have established the heterogeneity of returns by law school tier, and including the previous controls. Although many of the estimates are not very precise due to a low number of observations in some cells, it is clear that the highest premiums across schools of varying quality tend to be earned by lawyers who work in private law firms and industry.[13]

AJD3 and SIPP Samples

Using the combined AJD3 and SIPP samples, we estimated the J.D. premium at approximately fourteen years after college graduation. The results in table 2-6 indicate that the estimate of the unadjusted J.D. premium is about 0.77 log points (column 1). Controlling in column 2 for race, marital status, whether the respondent has a graduate degree, and hours worked reduces that premium to 0.44 log points.

The results in column 3 show the premiums associated with the three tiers of law school quality. Compared with the estimates in the last column of table 2-4, they indicate that the J.D. premia at fourteen years after college graduation have increased for all law school quality tiers relative to the premia at ten years after college graduation. The greater premia may reflect, as noted, the jump in earnings that lawyers tend to receive from becoming a partner in a law firm.

Alternatively, the greater premia may be biased upwards because we cannot

TABLE 2-5. OLS Regressions with Law School Quality and
Employer Organization Type Indicator Variables

	Log(wage)		Log(wage)
Other Controls	Yes	2nd-Tier LS:	0.309***
Top-Tier LS:	0.628***	Gen Practice	(0.0678)
Private	(0.0508)	2nd-Tier LS:	0.169*
Top-Tier LS:	0.725***	Other Law	(0.0768)
Industry	(0.0640)	Lower-Tier LS:	0.216***
Top-Tier LS:	0.733***	Private	(0.0509)
Fed Gov	(0.0847)	Lower-Tier LS:	0.340***
Top-Tier LS:	0.452***	Industry	(0.0790)
St/Lo Gov	(0.136)	Lower-Tier LS:	0.185
Top-Tier LS:	0.391***	Fed Gov	(0.143)
Gen Practice	(0.116)	Lower-Tier LS:	0.00567
Top-Tier LS:	0.440***	St/Lo Gov	(0.0848)
Other Law	(0.0849)	Lower-Tier LS:	0.101
2nd-Tier LS:	0.351***	Gen Practice	(0.0723)
Private	(0.0347)	Lower-Tier LS:	0.170*
2nd-Tier LS:	0.544***	Other Law	(0.0733)
Industry	(0.0548)	N	5,447
2nd-Tier LS:	0.223*	R-squared	0.286
Fed Gov	(0.0997)		
2nd-Tier LS:	0.0486		
St/Lo Gov	(0.0675)		

* $p<0.05$, *** $p<0.001$. See notes in table 2-4.

control, for example, for additional educational characteristics as we did previously. The 2007 AJD/B&B sample has a richer set of controls, variables capturing the quality of undergraduate education and undergraduate performance, for example, than the 2011 sample has. Including those richer controls reduced the estimated premium that we obtained without those controls by approximately 20 percent. If we assume that including the same controls in the 2011 sample would have also reduced the estimated premium by 20 percent, then we still obtain substantial returns. In addition, the gap between the premiums enjoyed by J.D.s from schools ranked 20 to 100 and from schools ranked 100+ seems to shrink.

TABLE 2-6. OLS Income Regressions with J.D. Indicator
Variables by Law School Quality Tier, AJD3/SIPP Sample

	(1)	(2)	(3)
J.D.	0.773***	0.443***	
	(0.03)	(0.04)	
Female		−0.263***	−0.262***
		(0.05)	(0.05)
Black		−0.298***	−0.298***
		(0.09)	(0.09)
Married		0.169***	0.169***
		(0.05)	(0.05)
Graduate Degree		0.259***	0.259***
		(0.05)	(0.05)
Hours/Week		0.085***	0.085***
		(0.01)	(0.01)
Hours Sq.		−0.01***	−0.01***
		(0.001)	(0.001)
LS: Top 20			0.755***
			(0.05)
LS: 21–100			0.399***
			(0.04)
LS: Lower Tier			0.348***
			(0.05)
Constant	10.877***	8.460***	8.460***
	(0.03)	(0.30)	(0.30)
N	2,693	2,693	2,693
R-squared	0.102	0.317	0.317

* $p<0.05$, ** $p<0.01$, *** $p<0.001$.

Other Possible Sources of Heterogeneity in J.D. Premiums

We have found that the premiums from attending law school vary by law school
tier and by the type of organization where a law school graduate works. Law
school premiums could also vary by the state of employment if certain states had
higher failure rates on their bar examinations, which would limit the supply of
lawyers and increase their earnings. For example, Pagliero (2010, 2011) finds
that the difficulty of a bar exam, based on the pass rate, has a strong positive
effect on lawyers' median entry-level salaries.

However, Pagliero overlooks the fact that people can, and, if necessary, do, take the bar examination multiple times until they pass it. Winston, Crandall, and Maheshri (2011) reported that 95 percent of law school graduates who take a bar examination eventually pass, and they argued that the main entry barrier to legal practice is being admitted to and graduating from an accredited law school. Data recently released by the ABA Section of Legal Education and Admissions to the Bar show that 89 percent of all 2016 law graduates who sat for a bar exam within two years of graduating passed it and that the passage rates of students graduating from first-tier and second-tier schools was 95 percent.[14] The bar passage rate generally increases over time, so students from lower-tier schools will be the source of the increase for 2016 graduates. However, when a large fraction of people who take the bar examination are repeat test-takers, the average exam score and pass rate can decline.[15]

The preceding facts suggest that it would be difficult to identify the effect of state bar examination difficulty on the earnings premium because there is little variation in the percentage of law school graduates who eventually pass. As an empirical check, we included a dummy variable in the earnings equation indicating the states with the hardest bar exams, based in part on the failure rate but also on the required preparation and length of the exam.[16] However, we found that the estimated coefficient for the dummy variable had a very small and statistically insignificant effect. We also attempted to interact the dummy variable for graduates from third-tier and fourth-tier law schools, but none of the graduates of those schools worked in the states with the hardest bar exams.

Premiums could also vary by postgraduation career paths. However, we limited our attention to this issue by showing premium variations in broad employer organizations because that is a plausible choice for a prospective lawyer, while more specific postgraduation career paths are uncertain. For example, students entering law school may expect that they would earn the largest premiums by taking a job at a major top 100 law firm following graduation and by making partner. But an individual's career path may not evolve in that way for at least three reasons. First, an individual may not have graduated from a law school among the limited range of schools that major law firms consider for recruiting and hiring associates. Second, if it were possible for a graduate from a lower-tier law school to secure a job at such a firm, the graduate may not feel comfortable in the firm's working environment and may not want to go through the demanding process of making partner. Recently, a large survey of law firm partners and associates indicated that, regardless of where they graduated from law school, roughly 60 percent of the associates who responded did not want to become partners at their current firm.[17] Third, certain law firms partly assess candidates on success-oriented behaviors that many law school graduates may simply not have: traits that are more associated with military service and success at competitive sports than with academic success.[18] In short, a law school graduate's career plans may not align with employers' idiosyncratic workplace cultures.

ACCOUNTING FOR SELECTIVITY

Our detailed data allow us to control for many important observed influences on earnings and to quantify the variation in J.D. premiums across law schools and, in the case of the AJD/B&B samples, across employer organizations, but they do not explicitly rule out the possibility that the estimates of the premiums may be biased by unobserved variables that influence individuals' choices to attend law school. We address selectivity bias by instrumental variables and, as a further check, by propensity score matching. We also discuss the qualitative conclusions of a test based on selection of unobservables. Our investigations do not suggest that selectivity bias is likely to be a factor in the lifetime earnings premium from earning a J.D. before the Great Recession.

Instrumental Variables

Our proposed instrument for the J.D. indicator variable is whether an individual in the sample has a parent who is a lawyer. Our logic is that a child's long-term exposure to a lawyer parent predisposes the child to wanting to become a lawyer.[19] Conditional on other control variables, an instrument is valid if it is a useful predictor of whether an individual obtains a J.D. (the relevancy condition) and does not affect earnings (the exogeneity condition). We verify the relevancy condition by presenting parameter estimates in appendix table A2-1 of a probit model based on the AJD/B&B sample that shows that an individual who has a lawyer parent has a higher probability of obtaining a J.D., holding the socioeconomic, employment, intellectual ability, and the quality of the undergraduate school controls constant, and the effect is statistically significant. The finding holds for all the law school tiers simultaneously and for each of the three tiers individually.

We raise and address several issues about whether having a lawyer parent is truly exogenous and does not affect the earnings of a child who attains a J.D. For example, the child may find better job opportunities and earn a higher salary through the parents' connections, but parental connections are likely to be less important in occupations such as the legal profession that have high skill requirements.

We provide supportive empirical evidence in appendix table A2-2, which shows in column 1 that the lawyer parent indicator variable has a positive, statistically significant effect on earnings when we include the previous controls except the J.D. indicator variable. But column 2 of the table shows that the parental indicator variable becomes statistically insignificant when we include the J.D. indicator variable as a control. That is, whether a parent was a lawyer is helpful in predicting one's wage to the extent that it helps to predict whether one obtains a J.D. In addition, column 3 of the table shows that among the sample of J.D.s, having a lawyer parent is not associated with higher earnings.

Law schools are likely to reduce the importance of parental connections because they have a strong incentive to help their students find jobs to increase their *U.S. News and World Report* rankings, which are affected by student placement. It is possible that lower-tier schools may find it more difficult to place their students than higher-tier schools do; thus, parental connections and assistance may benefit students who graduate from those schools. But we did not find that the effect of a lawyer parent on earnings was statistically significant even for lower-tier schools, possibly because of the legal profession's high skills requirements and a meritocratic culture that makes hiring and promotion decisions based on evidence of effort and performance, even for a first job where such evidence may be provided by, for example, the supervisor of an individual's summer internship.[20]

Instead of providing job connections, a lawyer parent may provide valuable career advice to a child that can contribute to higher earnings, such as the importance of networking with other lawyers at a workplace, especially the partners at a private law firm. However, Cleveland (2018) points out that law schools and law firms informally provide such advice to first-generation law students, and some have even taken specific actions with that purpose in mind. For example, the USC Gould School of Law instituted the First-Generation Professionals Program and the Latham Watkins law firm formed the First-Generation Professionals Group.

Our review of the literature that identifies the key determinants of whether an associate makes partner did not find that having a lawyer parent had any effect. As pointed out by Azmat and Ferrer (2017) and Polantz (2016), those determinants generally include meeting metric goals on annual hours billed and revenue collected, developing professional networks with marketing and sales skills, and having successful relationships with clients.

It is also possible that a high-achieving parent who went to law school will generally be more invested than a nonlawyer parent in their child's education and will motivate the child to work harder. However, we did not find any evidence that suggests that J.D.s with a lawyer parent worked harder and did better in law school and their subsequent careers than J.D.s without a lawyer parent. As noted, parents in general may have such influence in the early development of a child's life. By the time that a child reaches postgraduate education, it is quite likely that the child is self-motivated and that having a lawyer as a parent has little effect on the child's performance.

We acknowledge that there may be other channels through which a lawyer parent could influence a child's earnings, but we have identified the most important ones and provided plausible explanations for why they are unlikely to bias our instrument. We therefore maintain that whether an individual has a lawyer parent is a valid instrument for obtaining a J.D., and that it is appropriate to use it to re-estimate the earnings equation to explore endogeneity.

We present the estimated parameters for the J.D. indicator variable in table 2-7 for specifications that include the full set of controls. The first column presents the OLS estimates from table 2-3, and the second column presents the instrumental variable estimate of the average J.D. premium obtained by the Generalized Method of Moments (GMM). We find that the estimated premium from a J.D. actually increases, which suggests that selectivity may be causing us, if anything, to underestimate the premium. However, a Hausman exogeneity test does not reject the null hypothesis that the difference between the OLS and GMM coefficients is not statistically significant, which implies that unobserved variables affecting selection are not a potentially important source of bias.[21]

This finding is plausible if individuals choose to go to law school based on influences that are unrelated to unobserved characteristics that affect earnings. For example, although a researcher cannot observe whether an individual has a strong work ethic, it is not clear that this characteristic would push a student toward law school instead of graduate study in a different field or a highly remunerative career out of college, such as investment banking. Given that law schools do not have prerequisites other than an undergraduate degree in any major, the schools cannot even assume that their admittees have appropriate backgrounds or even an interest in law (Gibney 2019).

It may also be the case that the full set of control variables, in particular the undergraduate characteristics, effectively capture traits that are often treated as unobserved in earnings regressions that are estimated using, for example, the CPS. In our data set, work ethic may be captured by an individual's under-

TABLE 2-7. GMM Estimates

Estimation Method Sample: B&B +	OLS Any LS	GMM Any LS	OLS Top-Tier LS	GMM Top-Tier LS	OLS 2nd-Tier LS	GMM 2nd-Tier LS	OLS Low-Tier LS	GMM Low-Tier LS
J.D.	0.342***	0.465*	0.619***	0.748*	0.322***	0.604*	0.188***	0.816
	(0.0206)	(0.181)	(0.0379)	(0.352)	(0.0268)	(0.249)	(0.0300)	(0.706)
N	5,447	5,447	4,861	4861	5,030	5,030	4,864	4,864
R-squared	0.263	0.258	0.265	0.263	0.225	0.207	0.198	0.133

Notes: Robust standard errors in parentheses. The dependent variable is log wage ten years after college graduation. For the GMM estimations, the instrument is whether at least one parent was a lawyer. The full set of controls is used in each regression. The sample for each regression is a combination of the B&B sample of college graduates and subsamples of the AJD survey of J.D. holders, as specified in the column headers.

* p<0.05, ** p<0.01, *** p<0.001.

graduate GPA, and writing proficiency, which may make an individual more inclined to pursue a J.D., may be captured by the humanities major.

We note that table 2-7 also shows that the GMM estimates of each of three law school tiers are greater than the corresponding OLS estimates, although again, the differences are not statistically significant.[22] This finding provides additional support that individuals' self-selection to obtain a J.D. is not based to an important extent on unobserved variables that also influence postcollege earnings.

Finally, good examples of unobserved variables that may influence an individual's decision to obtain a J.D. degree as well as influence postcollege earnings are controversial changes in the nation's government and government policies. The Vietnam War during the 1960s and 1970s and the 2016 presidential election of Donald J. Trump (Ward 2018) have spurred many people to simultaneously pursue a law degree and seek a job that pays less than what a job with a private Big Law firm pays in return for opportunities to oppose certain individuals and their policies through the practice of law. However, those events did not occur during our sample period.

Propensity Score Matching

Because our data contain explanatory variables that appear to be sufficiently rich to account for the selection behavior of individuals of whether to attend law school, propensity score matching is an alternative appropriate method to estimate the J.D. premium. Like OLS, propensity score estimators are unbiased only if selection into the treatment group is accounted for by observable characteristics, but they do not impose a linear functional form on the (log) wage equation and are therefore a useful robustness check of our OLS estimates. We adapt the propensity score matching methodology that Black and Smith (2004) employ in their study of the effects of college quality on wages.

The basic idea of matching methods is to compare the outcomes of individuals who obtained a treatment—in our case, having a J.D.—to the outcomes of observably similar individuals who did not receive the treatment. The propensity score matching estimator is the average of the difference between those individuals' outcomes. The metric we use to decide that propensity scores from different individuals are "similar" is the nearest neighbor metric.[23] Thus, the wage of a person who chose to obtain a J.D. is compared with the wage of a person who had a similar likelihood of obtaining a J.D. but instead chose to immediately enter the labor force after graduating from college. The results from this method, presented in table 2-8, show that the average J.D. premium and the

TABLE 2-8. Propensity Score Matching Estimates

J.D.	J.D. (Top 20)	J.D. (2nd Tier)	J.D. (Low Tier)
0.348	0.616	0.312	0.150
(0.031)	(0.060)	(0.040)	(0.051)

top- and middle-tier law school premiums are very similar to the results from the OLS regression. The estimate for the premium of the low-tier J.D. is close, although it is significantly smaller than the OLS estimate (at the 0.05 level). In sum, the similarity of the propensity score results to the OLS estimates is reassuring and lends further credibility to those estimates.

Selection on Unobservables

Another possible approach to check whether unobservables are biasing the OLS estimates is to use a test by Altonji, Elder, and Taber (2005); Oster (2019) has a similar test. When we run the Altonji, Elder, and Taber test on our estimates, we find that the selection on unobservables would have to be about three times stronger than the selection on observables for the effect of a J.D. on earnings to be zero. Alternatively, we find that selection on unobservables would have to be twice as strong as the selection on observables for the estimated J.D. premium to be smaller than the premium required to make a J.D. worthwhile, after accounting for the costs.

ESTIMATING THE WAGE TRAJECTORIES

We now estimate how workers' wages evolve over the course of their nonlaw and counterfactual law career, and vice-versa, so we can determine the present value of the benefits of a law degree.[24] Consider the regression model

$$\log w_{it} = \alpha + \beta x_i + f(t) + \varepsilon_{it}, \tag{11}$$

where the individual characteristics x include a nonwhite indicator variable, a female indicator variable, a married indicator variable, a married female interaction indicator variable, a lawyer indicator variable, and $f(t)$ is specified as a cubic polynomial in t because higher order terms were not statistically significant.[25]

We estimated the model using data from the March supplement of the CPS for the years 1996 through 2007. Table 2-9 presents summary statistics of the CPS data, and table 2-10 presents OLS estimation results, with a particular focus on a lawyer's experience because of its importance for earnings in the legal profession. For example, the number of years of experience accrued at a major law firm can result in higher alternative wage offers even if an individual is not made a partner at the law firm (Sauer 1998). The coefficients in column 1 of table 2-10 show that the interaction of a lawyer and his or her experience has a statistically significant effect on wages over time; thus, lawyers have a different wage profile than the average wage profile of nonlawyer college graduates, and it is appropriate to estimate separate wage profiles for the two groups of workers. The estimates in columns (2) and (3), in particular the coefficients on the experience variables, indicate how wages evolve with experience. We use those to estimate the shape of the wage trajectories, $f^{JD}(t)$ and $f^{nonJD}(t)$.

We combine the trajectories and the estimate of the J.D. wage premium ten years out of college, ρ_{10}, to obtain estimates of ρ_t for $t=1,...,T$ and combine those with the previous estimates of the effects of the explanatory variables on wages, β, to estimate $\log w_t^{JD}(X)$ for $t=4,...,T$ (given $w_t^{JD}=0$ for the $t=1,2,3$ years a J.D. is in law school), and to estimate $\log w_t^{nonJD}(X)$ for $t=1,...,T$ (given w_t^{nonJD} for the $t=1,2,3$ years are the wages that a worker earns by going directly to work after graduating from college). Figure 2-5 presents those estimates, converted to annual wages. The circled points ten years after college graduation reflect the estimates of $w_{10}^{JD}(X) = \$91,000$ and $w_{10}^{nonJD}(X) = \$64,000$, which were estimated from the AJD/B&B data that provide wages for that period in lawyers' and nonlawyers' careers.[26] The difference between those points is the estimated

TABLE 2-9. Summary Statistics, CPS data, 2007

	Nonlawyers	Lawyers	All
Female	0.45	0.29	0.45
Nonwhite	0.18	0.08	0.18
Married	0.65	0.77	0.65
Experience	21.60	20.43	21.57
Salary (2007)	81,000	171,000	83,000
	(82,000)	(144,000)	(85,000)
Age	42.42	45.84	42.49
Lawyer	0.00	1.00	0.02
N	23,362	513	23,875

Notes: Sample is CPS, 2007. Sample weights applied. Standard deviations in parentheses. Salary rounded to thousands. Other statistics rounded to hundredths.

TABLE 2-10. Estimation of Wage Trajectory

	(1) All workers	(2) Nonlawyers	(3) Lawyers
Nonwhite	−0.0844*** (0.00474)	−0.0834*** (0.00474)	−0.151* (0.0609)
Female	−0.121*** (0.00604)	−0.121*** (0.00608)	−0.0799 (0.0494)
Married	0.276*** (0.00562)	0.277*** (0.00566)	0.192*** (0.0430)
FemaleX Married	−0.315*** (0.00733)	−0.319*** (0.00737)	−0.157** (0.0589)
Experience	0.0699*** (0.00124)	0.0723*** (0.00125)	0.0853*** (0.00778)
Exper. Sq.	−0.00204*** (0.0000573)	−0.00214*** (0.0000576)	−0.00276*** (0.000366)
Exper. Cubed	0.0197*** (0.000776)	0.0209*** (0.000780)	0.0294*** (0.00477)
LawyerX Exper.	0.103*** (0.00404)		
LawyerX Exper. Sq.	−0.00434*** (0.000274)		
LawyerX Exper. Cubed	0.0524*** (0.00440)		
Constant	10.18*** (0.0102)	10.17*** (0.0102)	10.71*** (0.0858)
N	209,997	205,245	4,752
R-squared	0.151	0.138	0.102

* $p<0.05$, ** $p<0.01$, *** $p<0.001$.

wage premium ρ_{10}, and the shapes of the wage trajectories are obtained from the estimates of $f^{JD}(t)$ and $f^{nonJD}(t)$.

RETURNS TO A J.D. FOR LAW STUDENTS WHO GRADUATED BEFORE THE GREAT RECESSION

We now pull the threads of our analysis together to estimate the returns to a J.D. for law students who graduated before the Great Recession began. We do so using the estimated earnings premia that are based on our various samples covering lawyer and nonlawyer earnings before and after the recession ended.

FIGURE 2-5. Expected Salary Profiles for Non-J.D.s. and J.D.s.

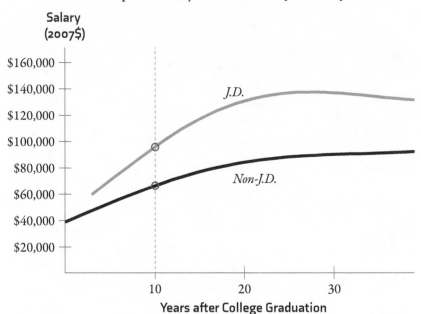

Returns before the Recession Ended

The expression for the returns to a J.D. given in equation (3) is:

$$-\textstyle\sum_{t=1}^{3}\frac{tuition_t+w_t^{nonJD}}{(1+r)^{t-1}} + \sum_{t=4}^{T}\frac{w_t^{JD}-w_t^{nonJD}}{(1+r)^{t-1}}.$$

The first term represents the total costs of attaining a J.D.; the second term is the benefits. The opportunity cost component of the first term, which we obtained in the previous section, is the estimate of the (non-J.D.) wages that one would have earned in the labor force.

Turning to the tuition costs, the AJD data do not specify precisely which law school an individual attended, but they do indicate the ranking, top 10, 11–20, and so on. Thus, we obtained tuition cost information from the *U.S. News and World Report*'s guide to graduate schools and computed the average tuition for students who attended a school in a given ranking category.[27] Based on those data, average law school prices for the 1998–2000 law school cohorts in 2007 dollars were $17,000 per year. The top 20 schools charged $23,000 per year, middle-tier schools charged $16,000, and lower-tier schools charged $15,000.[28]

We obtained estimates in the previous section of the benefits of law school given in the second term of the expression, so we proceed to compute the returns to a J.D. and use bootstrapping to obtain appropriate standard errors.[29] For our base case, we assume a discount rate r of 0.03, the rate of return for the average consumer, as recommended by the Office of Management and Budget. We assume a career length T of 39 years (36 for J.D.s), which corresponds to a retirement age of 61,[30] assuming workers graduate college at 22. We find that the difference between the net present value of obtaining a J.D. and not obtaining a J.D., on average, is about $600,000, with a standard error of approximately $40,000. Compared with the net present value of lifetime earnings of a non-J.D., the difference amounts to a 38 percent premium, which is equivalent to an 11.3 percent rate of return.[31] Given that the average rate of return to a college education appears to be roughly 10 percent,[32] the return from a legal education is substantial, especially because it is believed that there are diminishing returns to education after postsecondary schooling (see, for example, Heckman, Lochner, and Todd 2003). Simkovic and McIntyre (2013) also obtain large returns from a legal education, which imply that the net present value earnings differential between a J.D. and non-J.D. is closer to $800,000. The difference between our estimate and theirs may be because they do not adequately account for the fact that law school attracts individuals who would earn considerably more than their counterparts even if they did not obtain a J.D.

The average return to a legal education is informative; but as we showed earlier, there are considerable differences in the premia from attending law schools in different quality tiers. Accordingly, table 2-11 shows that the present value of the benefits of a law degree also varies significantly by the quality tier of the law school attended. Specifically, the returns from attending a top-tier law school are, on average, approximately six times larger than from attending a low-tier law school. Nonetheless, J.D.s from low-tier law schools earn a net present value of $200,000 more than they would have without a J.D., which generates more than a 15 percent increase in net lifetime earnings. The net value of a J.D. is still positive even if we assume a higher discount rate of 5 percent and a shorter career of thirty years (or twenty-seven years for J.D.s).

Returns after the Recession Ended

Our evidence indicates that attending law school before the Great Recession was clearly a sound investment, but was it still a sound investment after the recession? We address this question by using the 2011 earnings premia that we estimated from the AJD3/SIPP sample and combining it with the wage

TABLE 2-11. Net Present Value of Benefits of Law
School Attendance (millions of dollars)

r=.03	T=39			
	Average UG	**Top-Tier UG**	**2nd-Tier UG**	**Low-Tier UG**
Average LS	0.6			
Top-Tier LS	1.2	1.4	1.3	1.2
2nd-Tier LS	0.5	0.6	0.5	0.5
Low-Tier LS	0.2	0.2	0.2	0.2

r=.05	T=39			
	Average UG	**Top-Tier UG**	**2nd-Tier UG**	**Low-Tier UG**
Average LS	0.3			
Top-Tier LS	0.8	0.9	0.8	0.8
2nd-Tier LS	0.3	0.3	0.3	0.3
Low-Tier LS	0.1	0.1	0.1	0.1

r=.03	T=30			
	Average UG	**Top-Tier UG**	**2nd-Tier UG**	**Low-Tier UG**
Average LS	0.4			
Top-Tier LS	0.9	1.0	0.9	0.9
2nd-Tier LS	0.4	0.4	0.4	0.3
Low-Tier LS	0.1	0.1	0.1	0.1

r=.05	T=30			
	Average UG	**Top-Tier UG**	**2nd-Tier UG**	**Low-Tier UG**
Average LS	0.1			
Top-Tier LS	0.2	0.2	0.2	0.2
2nd-Tier LS	0.1	0.1	0.1	0.1
Low-Tier LS	0.1	0.1	0.1	0.1

Notes: Rather than displaying the (bootstrapped) standard errors, which are on the order of ten thousand, we rounded to the nearest hundred thousand. This more than accounts for the imprecision of the estimates.

trajectories that we previously estimated to simulate earnings premia over an individual's entire career. The estimated earnings, presented in table 2-12 as a difference in the net present value of career earnings as well as a rate of return, indicate that an education at a law school of any rank was still an attractive investment, and they provide a useful robustness check that the returns to a J.D.

TABLE 2-12. Premiums in Lifetime Earnings and Rates of
Return from a J.D. Based on Postrecession Data

	Any J.D.	JD (Top 20)	JD (2nd Tier)	JD (3rd Tier)
Premium in Lifetime Earnings (NPV, in 2007 dollars)	$500,000	$1,240,000	$400,000	$340,000
Rate of Return (%)	.091	.15	.08	.07

Source: Authors' calculations.

were not significantly affected for lawyers who had been working for several years before the recession began.

THE RETURNS TO A J.D. FOR POSTRECESSION LAW SCHOOL GRADUATES

We have found that lawyers who graduated from law school in the year 2000 have continued to earn sizable returns from their education both before and after the Great Recession. Of course, new and future lawyers, who entered law school after the recession, could have different labor market experiences than lawyers in previous decades have had because new job growth has been slow and may reflect structural changes in the way the law is practiced.[33] For example, law firms have diverted tasks once assigned to associates who just graduated from law school to paralegals or other less expensive forms of labor.

Norberg (2018) argues that job prospects have become a critical consideration to get a J.D. following the Great Recession. He points out that a group of twenty law schools have posted legal employment rates of 44 percent or lower during the past five years, and that all but two have average student debt loads of $100,000 or more. Norberg proposes that for accreditation, a law school must meet employment rates of at least 60 percent in at least two of the past five years. Many graduates from schools with weak employment rates are not able to repay their student loans, most of which are federally supported. Thus, the cost of law school for students who are unable to attain good jobs is passed on to taxpayers; that is, their loans effectively become federal taxpayer subsidies to the law schools.

We cannot use our previous methodology to determine whether the postrecession economic environment has affected the returns to a J.D. because AJD-type data on the earnings of lawyers who graduated from law school after the recession and who have been working as a lawyer for several years are not yet available. But we can draw on circumstantial evidence that indicates how prospective law students have adjusted—and how law school graduates have been forced to adjust—to changes in the market for lawyers following the recession to suggest how the returns to a J.D. may have been affected.

Prospective law students have become fearful of their job prospects following law school as indicated by the sharp decline in annual law school applications during this decade to some fifty thousand applicants, compared with as many as one hundred thousand applicants in certain years of the preceding decade. At the same time, law schools have generally kept class sizes stable. The top law schools have done so because they have historically turned down many qualified applicants, and they can continue to maintain high standards even if annual law school applications decline. Lower-tier law schools have done so because they need the tuition revenue; thus, the available evidence, as reflected in lower LSAT scores, lower bar passage rates, and the greater difficulty of obtaining employment in jobs that require a J.D., suggests that the quality of admitted law students has declined, especially among those students attending lower-tier law schools.

Prospective law students did not react immediately to the recession's effect on the market for lawyers because the sharp decline in applicants did not begin until 2011. Using that year as a benchmark compared with 2015, the median LSAT scores for the top 20 schools declined about 0.5 points, compared with declines of 4 points for both second-tier (ranked 21–100) and third-tier schools (ranked 101 or lower).[34] The declines are consistent with the growing share of students who are "at risk" of not passing a state bar examination (defined as having an LSAT score below 150). In 2010, thirty accredited law schools admitted classes consisting of at least 25 percent "at risk" students; in 2014, seventy-four schools did.[35]

Bar passage rates are a noisier reflection of student quality for comparisons across schools and over time because graduates take bar exams in different jurisdictions, some of which, as noted, have more difficult bar exams than others. In any case, the roughly 3 percentage points decline in passage rates for graduates of third-tier schools between 2011 and 2015 clearly exceeds the declines at second-tier and top 20 schools, which were less than 2 percentage points.[36] The more recent data that we reported from the ABA Section of Legal Education and Admissions to the Bar also indicated that law school graduates from first-tier and second-tier schools had extremely high pass rates, while that was not generally the case for law school graduates from lower-tier schools.

Finally, Winston, Crandall, and Maheshri (2011) point out that until the

Great Recession, a very large percentage of recent law school graduates—even from law schools that were not ranked in the nation's top 100—were employed as lawyers within nine months of graduation. The recession has made it more difficult for law school graduates to find jobs as lawyers; however, as shown in figure 2-6, since 2012, employment rates—the share of graduates with jobs requiring the passage of the bar—have recovered more quickly and from a higher starting point for graduates from higher-quality schools. By 2015, the employment rate for the top 20 schools exceeded 85 percent, compared with 62 percent for second-tier schools and 48 percent for third-tier schools. To be sure, the employment rates reflect both the demand for and supply of lawyers in various markets around the country, but the much lower employment rates among graduates of second-tier and third-tier schools surely reflect perceptions of the quality of their education and ability compared with the education and ability of graduates from top 20 law schools.

The changes in the quality of new law students suggest that the rate of return of a J.D. in the postrecession economy is likely to be markedly lower than in the past because (1) lower LSAT scores are associated with higher expected

FIGURE 2-6. Share of New J.D.s Employed in Jobs
That Require Bar Passage, 2012–2015

Source: Authors' calculations from Standard 509 Information Reports submitted by law schools to the American Bar Association.

law school debts;[37] (2) lower LSAT scores lead to lower bar passage rates, which clearly delays employment as a lawyer because students have to retake the exam a second or even a third time to pass; and (3) generally, employment as a lawyer is delayed in the current economic environment much more for graduates of law schools that are not among the top 20. Thus, even if the legal labor market eventually returns to its prerecession state, any delay that law school graduates experience in securing a job as a lawyer (or another job that provides the expected J.D. premium) could have a substantial impact on their returns from a J.D.

Table 2-13 shows that the rate of return to a J.D. becomes smaller as the delay between law school graduation and attaining a job that requires or rewards a J.D. increases. We assume that during the intervening years, workers are employed at their predicted non-J.D. wage, which we estimate with the AJD/B&B data.[38] Given the lower employment share and slower rate of recovery of new second-tier and third-tier law school graduates, it is plausible that a notable fraction of those graduates could take at least five years to acquire a job that requires a J.D. If so, that delay would virtually eliminate the positive returns to a J.D. for new graduates of third-tier law schools and would raise doubts about whether the modest returns for graduates of second-tier law schools are enough for them to risk the possibility that they may not acquire a job that requires a J.D. A further consideration is that because of their lower intellectual ability, as indicated by their lower LSAT scores, the earnings of new second-tier and third-tier law students who eventually acquire a job that requires a J.D. are likely to be depressed and their law school debt is likely to be greater.

Finally, recent evidence on the debt-to-earnings ratio for law school graduates compiled by the U.S. Department of Education also puts the returns to law schools in different tiers in perspective.[39] The department's information

TABLE 2-13. How the Rate of Return Changes with Delay in Acquiring a Job that Requires a J.D.

	Years Between LS Graduation and Obtaining a Legal Position				
	1	2	3	4	5
Average LS	0.097	0.084	0.073	0.064	0.057
Top-Tier LS	0.148	0.130	0.117	0.105	0.096
Middle-Tier LS	0.092	0.079	0.069	0.06	0.053
Low-Tier LS	0.054	0.043	0.035	0.027	0.020

Source: Authors' calculations.

reflects borrowing and earnings for 2015 and 2016 graduates and does not include any prior borrowing from undergraduate or other completed studies. The earnings data measure actual earnings in the first full calendar year after graduation. The debt-to-earnings ratio divides the median earnings into the median amount borrowed; thus, at a ratio of 1.00, debt matches earnings. Generally, ratios below 1.00 were obtained by graduates from first-tier law schools (for example, the ratio for Harvard graduates was 0.84 and the ratio for Stanford graduates was 0.77), while much higher ratios were obtained by graduates from second-tier and third-tier law schools (for example, the ratio for Whittier graduates was 5.31, and the ratio for Miami graduates was 2.90).

In sum, the findings in this chapter can be interpreted narrowly as simply indicating that prospective law students must weigh the costs and benefits of a legal education in the post–Great Recession era more carefully than in the past to avoid financial disappointment in their career choices. At the same time, there are social benefits from educating a sufficient cadre of lawyers who could provide a range of valued services. We briefly discuss in the next chapter various ways that the returns from a legal education could be increased efficiently so that individuals are not necessarily discouraged from providing legal services that could benefit the public, and we revisit that discussion in the conclusion when we consider how the novel coronavirus has further complicated the calculus underlying individuals' decisions about whether to attend law school.

TABLE A2-1. Probit Regressions with J.D. as Dependent Variable

Sample: B&B +	(1) All AJD	(2) Top-Tier AJD	(3) Mid-Tier AJD	(4) Low-Tier AJD
Female	−0.192* (0.0938)	−0.150 (0.156)	−0.206 (0.123)	−0.193 (0.128)
Black	0.442*** (0.110)	0.637*** (0.175)	0.492*** (0.138)	0.181 (0.167)
Married	0.217** (0.0793)	0.172 (0.135)	0.251* (0.103)	0.0969 (0.109)
FemaleX Married	−0.163 (0.112)	−0.213 (0.190)	−0.0780 (0.144)	−0.137 (0.154)
Dad College Grad.	0.0122 (0.0535)	0.114 (0.0958)	0.00288 (0.0679)	−0.0874 (0.0744)
Hours/Week	0.0517* (0.0242)	0.139* (0.0557)	0.0792* (0.0359)	−0.0100 (0.0305)
Hours Sq.	−0.0625** (0.0231)	−0.153** (0.0553)	−0.0914** (0.0352)	0.000650 (0.0286)
Top-Tier UG: High GPA	3.467*** (0.260)	7.355*** (1.375)	7.027*** (0.904)	1.955*** (0.313)
Top-Tier UG: Med. GPA	2.795*** (0.251)	6.632*** (1.382)	6.339*** (0.908)	1.476*** (0.290)
2nd-Tier UG: High GPA	3.322*** (0.245)	6.792*** (1.383)	6.976*** (0.906)	2.407*** (0.256)
2nd-Tier UG: Med. GPA	2.051*** (0.238)	5.371*** (1.385)	5.758*** (0.905)	1.431*** (0.240)
2nd-Tier UG: Low GPA	1.123*** (0.262)	4.269** (1.420)	4.725*** (0.918)	0.864** (0.272)
Low-Tier UG: High GPA	1.979*** (0.245)	5.499*** (1.388)	5.610*** (0.907)	1.377*** (0.254)
Low-Tier UG: Med. GPA	1.344*** (0.239)	4.683*** (1.387)	5.036*** (0.904)	0.931*** (0.240)
Major: Business	−0.0539 (0.0798)	0.0871 (0.147)	−0.0139 (0.0998)	−0.0980 (0.111)
Major: Engineering	−0.862*** (0.131)	−0.861*** (0.254)	−0.705*** (0.155)	−0.994*** (0.231)
Major: Math or Science	−0.568*** (0.0934)	−0.540** (0.167)	−0.553*** (0.121)	−0.452*** (0.132)
Major: Social Sciences	0.323*** (0.0608)	0.367*** (0.103)	0.255*** (0.0771)	0.248** (0.0848)
Lawyer Parent	0.865*** (0.130)	1.003*** (0.187)	0.855*** (0.158)	0.612** (0.200)
N	5417	4831	5000	4834
Pseudo-R-squared	0.328	0.437	0.308	0.178

* p<0.05, ** p<0.01, ***p<0.001.

TABLE A2-2. Wage Regressions and the Effect of Lawyer Parent

Sample	(1) B&B + AJD	(2) B&B + AJD	(3) AJD
Top-Tier UG: High GPA	0.561*** (0.0461)	0.336*** (0.0446)	0.0595 (0.0607)
Top-Tier UG: Med. GPA	0.438*** (0.0417)	0.294*** (0.0390)	0.107 (0.0625)
Top-Tier UG: Low GPA	0.148* (0.0611)	0.148* (0.0611)	
2nd-Tier UG: High GPA	0.469*** (0.0317)	0.259*** (0.0325)	−0.0577 (0.0482)
2nd-Tier UG: Med. GPA	0.184*** (0.0200)	0.122*** (0.0200)	−0.254*** (0.0484)
2nd-Tier UG: Low GPA	0.0877*** (0.0242)	0.0741** (0.0242)	−0.414*** (0.123)
Low-Tier UG: High GPA	0.155*** (0.0251)	0.0992*** (0.0249)	−0.307*** (0.0681)
Low-Tier UG: Med. GPA	0.0900*** (0.0183)	0.0695*** (0.0183)	−0.343*** (0.0561)
Major: Business	0.104*** (0.0181)	0.107*** (0.0179)	−0.00547 (0.0551)
Major: Engineering	0.190*** (0.0197)	0.227*** (0.0191)	0.324*** (0.0897)
Major: Math or Science	0.0675** (0.0206)	0.0962*** (0.0202)	−0.0178 (0.0715)
Major: Social Studies	0.0563*** (0.0169)	0.0341* (0.0164)	−0.0196 (0.0361)
Lawyer Parent	0.109* (0.0430)	0.0295 (0.0423)	−0.0225 (0.0582)
J.D.		0.340*** (0.0207)	
N	5,447	5,447	793
R-squared	0.224	0.263	0.180

Notes: Robust standard errors in parentheses. The dependent variable is log wage ten years after college graduation. The omitted category for the first two columns is low-tier undergraduate institution and low GPA. For the third column, the omitted category is top-tier undergraduate institution and low GPA (since there are insufficient observations in the low-tier undergraduate institution, low-GPA category). A constant term, black indicator variable, whether father is college graduate, and undergraduate major indicator variables were also included in the regression.

* $p < 0.05$, ** $p < 0.01$, *** $p < 0.001$.

THREE

A BRIEF ASSESSMENT OF THE MARKET FOR A LEGAL EDUCATION

We concluded that the Great Recession reduced the returns from investing in a law school education, but we found that the returns from law school still appear to be attractive for graduates of the top 20 schools while far less attractive for graduates of lower-ranked schools. Importantly, because the returns reflect the social value of certain skills that law school training provides, and because they also reflect significant rents that lawyers receive given the barriers to entry to the legal profession (Winston, Crandall, and Maheshri 2011), the long-term returns to a legal education may, in fact, be significantly inflated and could be threatened by entry deregulation that facilitates greater competition among lawyers.

In this chapter, we briefly raise some issues that if adequately addressed could make an investment in a law school education more attractive by increasing its benefits and reducing its costs. The discussion will provide useful context when we revisit the case for deregulating the legal profession in the final chapter.

REDUCING THE PRIVATE AND SOCIAL
COSTS OF A LEGAL EDUCATION

As discussed in Winston, Crandall, and Maheshri (2011), state legislatures were not interested in incorporating the American Bar Association's legal education accreditation standards into their occupational licensing of lawyers when they were introduced during the 1920s. States gradually started to adopt the ABA's standards only after more state legislators themselves graduated from approved schools; thus, it took decades for those standards to be broadly accepted.

Today, the ABA is involved in all aspects of legal education. For example, the ABA created a task force in response to declining law school enrollments and revenues. Their lead recommendation was to "help students take full advantage of the current federal loan programs."[1] Although that strategy could increase the private return to a law degree for some individuals, it could also reduce the returns to a law degree for other individuals because the federal government's student loan programs for graduate and professional studies provide students with subsidized loans regardless of the quality of the applicant and the school that the applicant seeks to attend, which enables law schools to raise their tuition in response to demand that otherwise would be unlikely to exist without the loan program (Tamanaha 2012).

Indeed, Merritt (2015) points out that at least one-quarter of newly licensed lawyers are not using their law licenses for which they invested time and their own or the public's money to obtain.[2] Since August 2016, the ABA has disciplined ten law schools—both for-profit and nonprofit schools—for enrolling students who were unlikely to graduate and pass the bar. In sum, law school loans should be provided to applicants such that they are much more closely aligned with the applicants' prospects for completing the J.D. degree, obtaining a job, and repaying the loans.

Generally, aspiring attorneys must graduate from an ABA-accredited law school if they want to take a state bar examination and obtain a license to practice law.[3] Accredited schools typically require three years of full-time study and cover a broad range of subjects.[4] ABA involvement in law school education may increase its costs and reduce its returns in at least two ways. First, it forces some individuals to accumulate large debts to pay for a three-year program that may not even be necessary for the rewarding but less intellectually demanding and less remunerative legal career they wish to pursue. For example, a person who wishes to specialize in family law could take an intensive sequence of courses that incorporates the relevant material in other areas of law such as contracts.

The second way it raises the costs of a legal education is that, as just noted, it encourages prospective students to participate in a federal loan program that inflates tuition.

Although they violate current ABA standards for an accredited course of legal study, alternative legal education programs that may be suitable for a modest, and possibly specialized, legal practice exist in principle, including:

- An undergraduate degree in law;

- Combined undergraduate and graduate programs in law, which could be completed more quickly than a conventional three-year law school degree but do not have the stigma of a substandard program that may have accounted for students' lack of interest in Northwestern University law school's two-year program;

- Online law courses that could provide specialized training in specific areas of practice. For example, Syracuse University in the fall of 2018 began to offer an online J.D. degree, which was the first to receive ABA accreditation. Online education has become more prevalent during the novel coronavirus and may be more widely used in a post-coronavirus world, subject to the ABA relaxing limits on the number of credits received for online courses; and

- Trade law schools that are designed to respond to the interests of law firms and corporations by graduating people who are prepared to practice immediately, rather than requiring an extensive amount of on-the-job training, as is currently the case in most law jobs.

Giving individuals greater flexibility to invest in the type of legal education that they feel is optimal for their abilities and legal career goals would enhance the returns from their legal education and, as discussed below, would provide social benefits by expanding the services that the legal profession provides to the nation.

INCREASING PRIVATE AND SOCIAL BENEFITS OF A LEGAL EDUCATION

As noted, the market for legal education fails to enable a broad range of prospective law students to pursue a course of study that is best aligned with their abilities and goals. Importantly, some of those people may choose to provide legal services that are currently not provided. For example, consider the nation's "justice gap," where people who are eligible for legal aid are often turned away because there are not enough attorneys available.[5] Clearly, some individuals could provide helpful legal assistance to those people if they were allowed to do so after completing a course of study that focused on the legal issues that were relevant to legal aid practice. Individuals could complete such a course online at minimal expense in both time and money.

There are many other areas of legal specialization that require only modest training, such as wills and trusts and simple divorces, which would attract capable individuals who do not want to make an investment in an expensive and time-consuming course of study at an ABA-accredited law school.[6] But those individuals are currently prevented from providing such services.[7] In contrast to the view that there appear to be too many lawyers, some of whom are struggling to pay off their student loans, social welfare could be increased by reducing barriers to entry that increase the cost of becoming a legal practitioner and restrict the supply of lawyers who could provide valuable services to the public.

Elite students with the ambition to present oral arguments in major cases before the U.S. Supreme Court or to represent corporations in high-pressure negotiations would continue to attend the best law schools in the country and would incur the cost. And certainly other students would continue to attend conventional law schools. But a notable fraction of individuals, including those who would not have pursued a legal career if they had to attend a three-year ABA-accredited law school, could develop a successful practice by investing in other forms of a legal education and training and would incur far lower out-of-pocket and time costs.[8] Importantly, the public's access to legal services would, in all likelihood, be expanded because of the lower cost and greater availability of practitioners in areas that tend to be underserved. In the final chapter of the book, we respond to the counterarguments to this proposal, which raise concerns about the competence of lawyers who have not completed a course of study from an ABA-accredited law school and who have not passed a state bar examination.

ABA-accredited law schools would compete to some extent with new entrants providing alternative legal education programs and may be forced to revise or expand certain parts of their curriculum (for example, to make it more practical) and reduce their tuition and other student fees. Such competition could also expedite coverage of new areas of law, which conventional law schools may be slow to cover. For example, the novel coronavirus is raising a host of new legal issues that merit academic attention. Given the array of new legal education alternatives, concomitant reforms in the federal loan program should also be made to reduce defaults and to encourage high-quality instruction that leads to employment in legal services.

Finally, law schools could enhance the benefits of a legal education by gaining a better understanding of how law school experiences vary for students of different races and genders and by taking steps to lessen undesirable differences that may reduce the private and social benefits of students' legal careers. For example, the results of a recent NALP Foundation (2020) survey of more than four thousand law students, including minority students, indicated that more than half of minority women, 52 percent, said that their academic performance was negatively impacted by adverse interactions with classmates or faculty, while just 21 percent of white men reported such interactions. And a mere 6 percent of minority women said they applied for clerkships, compared with 21 percent of white men who applied for those positions.

Part of the problem may be that there are very few tenured minority law professors at U.S. law schools who can mentor minority law students. Deo (2019) states that the racial and gender inequity that she experienced as a law student exists in parallel forms among the faculty. Deo concludes that the low number of Black tenured professors and other professors of color contributes to ongoing biases in legal academia.

In the next chapter, we discuss concerns about racial and gender biases at law firms. However, such biases appear to first emerge in law school and should prompt frank and constructive discussions among faculty and students to explore what could be done to prevent them from occurring.

LAW SCHOOL FACULTY AND COURSE QUALITY

Although law schools offer a postgraduate degree, the faculty educates law students to work primarily in the private sector or government; very few law school graduates become academics. However, law school faculty members are academics, and the standards that they are held to have long been questioned by academics in other disciplines because their most important and popular scholarly publication outlet, law reviews, is generally edited by law students. It would be unthinkable and unimaginable if, for example, the *American Economic Review* and *Econometrica* were edited by economics graduate students!

In addition, Chilton, Masur, and Rozema (2019) provide evidence that suggests that the standards for tenure at the top law schools are too low. At the country's top 14 law schools, 95 percent of professors hired on a tenure track receive it. The authors conduct simulations that show that increasing tenure denials by 10 percentage points would increase the academic impact of a law school's median professor by more than 50 percent based on citations, suggesting that scholars with low productivity are occupying faculty positions at the most prestigious U.S. law schools.

The market for law school professorships has recently raised concerns about law school faculty. In 2019, 411 people applied for such a position—a 50 percent decrease from 2010.[9] If the decline in applications reflects a combination of fewer available faculty positions and law schools' requiring additional qualifications, such as both an advanced nonlaw degree and a law degree, the quality of law school faculties may improve in the future. However, if the decline reflects potential scholars' growing concerns about working as a law school professor, it bodes poorly for the quality of law school faculties.

Law schools have also been criticized for simultaneously being too academic and too provincial. Law firms complain that law students are not ready to practice law and that they must provide considerable on-the-job training. Clients therefore resist paying high hourly wages to lawyers who they believe are not ready to provide high-quality legal services. Law schools are also slow to respond to the latest technological trends that have legal implications for private firms. For example, law schools have allowed a wall to exist between lawyers and technologists, and they are just starting to introduce courses in Big Data and Artificial Intelligence that could significantly reduce the time it takes students, and eventually legal practitioners, to find answers to legal questions.[10] We discuss the potential for greater innovation in the legal profession in the next chapter.

The effectiveness of law schools to educate an individual to become an effective policymaker can be questioned because law school graduates are trained to be adversarial, whereas several other alternative dispute resolution mechanisms exist in the policy area, including negotiated settlements and mediation. Thus, Schneider (2002) argues that by training lawyers in law school to take an adversarial approach and to wield power instead of knowledge, legal education may be contributing to polarization and limiting compromise to achieve better policy outcomes.

Finally, legal academics appear to be growing apart from the courts. Wasserman (2020) discusses the phenomenon of a select group of academic feeder judges, who historically "produced" a disproportionately large number of law professors from the ranks of their former clerks and made a judicial clerkship an important stepping stone to the legal academy. At the same time, law professors could be in touch with the judges for whom they worked and provide helpful academic perspective. However, Wasserman reports data indicating that a clerkship has become a less essential credential because fewer people are moving from chambers to a tenure-track law school faculty position and fewer faculty members are likely to have close relationships with judges.

In sum, law schools have faced challenges in attracting prospective students in the aftermath of the Great Recession due to the decline in the returns to a law school degree and the resulting decline in the quality and number of student applicants. We have also noted other concerns with the state of legal education, including the high costs, undesirable differences between the experiences of minority and white male students, limited curriculum, and faculty quality. In an effort to expand the pool of intellectually qualified applicants, law schools have recently let applicants take the GRE instead of the LSAT to attract students from a wider variety of educational backgrounds, such as science, technology, engineering, and mathematics. This appears to be a positive reform, but other reforms are clearly needed to improve legal education, practice, and public policymaking. We discuss those along with the additional challenges created by the novel coronavirus in the final chapter.

FOUR

LAW FIRMS

Lawyers in the private sector can affect public policy when they are appointed or elected to government positions. For example, Lovelace (2019) identifies law partners in a weekly report who were appointed to the federal judiciary and the U.S. Department of Justice who had announced their intention to run for higher office. In this chapter, we discuss law firms' economic features—profitability, competition, operations, and innovation—as well as their noneconomic features—gender and racial bias and quality of life—that affect the perspectives of lawyers in ways that may become particularly important if and when they serve in government.

Although causal empirical evidence on lawyers' experiences at a private law firm and their performance in the public sector is difficult to develop, we suggest that the "culture" of private law firms is a source of concern because it does not provide a strong foundation for formulating effective public policy, especially actions to remedy the public's limited access to justice. It could be argued that while our concerns may be applicable to lawyers from major (corporate) law firms and from major highly specialized plaintiffs' contingency law firms, they are less applicable to lawyers from other (smaller) law firms. However, private sector lawyers who take high-level positions in government departments and regulatory agencies and who are appointed to the judiciary often come from major private sector law firms.[1]

THE LEGAL INDUSTRY AND LAW FIRM PROFITABILITY

As reported in Gibney (2019), the U.S. Bureau of Economic Analysis estimates that the American legal industry's annual value added is roughly $260 billion. But because much legal work takes place within in-house law departments, the total is larger—perhaps as much as $400 billion. Corporations account for much of the spending, but individuals spend about $100 billion on legal services directly.

Based on profit margins, law firms appear to be highly profitable, but their margins are inflated because they do not account for the cost of equity partners. In any case, data from ALM Intelligence shows that since 2000, the top 25 law firms have greatly increased their profit per equity partner—from $1.2 million to nearly $3.5 million in 2018—far more than other law firms. Firms ranked 101–200, for example, increased their profits per equity partner during the same period from $400,000 to $700,000. On average, equity partners earn more than twice as much as chief legal officers and general counsels at corporations.

Despite their general profitability, law firms become insolvent and collapse at high rates. Kiser (2019) reported that nearly one-half of the firms listed in the Am Law 100 in 1987, a ranking based on gross revenues and profits per partner, have now dissolved, merged with stronger firms, or failed to maintain sufficient revenue or profitability to remain in the Am Law 100.

Successful plaintiffs' lawyers, who are usually affiliated with much smaller law firms, are also highly compensated. According to the U.S. Chamber of Commerce Institute of Legal Reform (2018), costs and compensation in the U.S. tort system totaled $429 billion in 2016, with plaintiffs only getting slightly more than half of the revenues, or 57 cents on the dollar. The rest primarily went to attorneys' fees.[2]

Generally, lawyers' earnings are inflated by premiums that are attributable to states' licensing requirements that constrain the supply of lawyers; ABA entry regulations that shield private law firms from additional sources of competition, including corporations and foreign law firms; and government policies that generate an ever-growing demand for legal services. Winston, Crandall, and Maheshri (2011) estimated that the earnings premiums for lawyers amounted to $64 billion in 2004, or $71,000 per practicing lawyer. The authors also found that although lawyers at all income levels received substantial premiums, the highest earners at the largest law firms received the greatest premiums. Top law firms tend to work not only on the most complex, valuable mergers and acquisitions deals but also on the riskiest litigation with the largest stakes. However, corporations that combine law, accounting, and financial services could potentially compete against top law firms, but they are prevented from doing so by ABA regulatory entry barriers.

In addition to the formal regulatory barriers to entry, there are other, more subtle barriers that make disruptive entry into the legal profession difficult. Alternative legal service providers have made only modest progress, at best, in reducing the cost of a limited amount of legal services. Similar to what has occurred in other industries, technological innovations could, in theory, lead to new law firms that could provide large consumer benefits and become industry leaders, but those firms have yet to appear in the legal industry.

The New York City market is a well-known example of the difficulty that new entrants have had in dislodging the leading firms. MacEwen and Stanton (2017) point out, for example, that the leading New York City law firms in 1957, as indicated by the number of lawyers, are still the leading firms today. It would be very hard to find another industry where the elite pecking order has remained so stable over the course of so many years. Given that the city is so intertwined with Wall Street, a financial corporation that provides legal services would be a formidable competitor; however, as noted, it would be prevented from competing because of ABA entry barriers.

In sum, lawyers who work at law firms comprise a heterogeneous sector in the legal profession, where partners at the largest law firms and certain plaintiffs' lawyers earn millions of dollars per year, associates at large law firms and lawyers in other law firms are well compensated, and some lawyers, generally solo practitioners, earn a modest income. A large fraction of lawyers' earnings reflects premiums that are attributable to entry barriers, which suggests that, as in the case of other industries where entry is regulated, the legal industry is not as competitive and efficient as it could be. We support this view with circumstantial evidence on law firms' operations, technological advance, and workplace environment.

OPERATIONS

Generally, ABA regulations prevent law firms from being managed by anyone other than a lawyer because a nonlawyer would not be bound by and share the same ethical rules as a lawyer. Setting aside whether this regulation is justified, it is useful to consider whether lawyers make good managers compared with managers with other educational backgrounds. Given the lack of variation in the educational background of people who manage law firms, Professor Todd

Henderson (2017) shed light on the matter by comparing the performance of CEOs with legal training (J.D.s) and CEOs with business training (MBAs). He argued that the benefit of legal training for a CEO was its focus on the downside of particular actions, whereas the benefit of business school training for a CEO was its focus on the upside of shareholder value from risk-taking. Henderson found that outside of firms that were involved in large amounts of litigation, a CEO's legal training had a negative effect on firm value because the benefits of that training in reducing litigation were offset by the CEO's overly cautious firm policies, which reduced cash flows and growth.

Professor William Henderson, a well-known expert on U.S. law firms, has opined that law firms' operations are very poorly run when compared with other businesses' operations (Henderson (2017)). At the same time, law firms are profitable and have little pressure to change inefficient practices. For example, law firms' primary focus on billable hours and revenues has been questioned because it neglects opportunities to become more profitable by reducing costs and becoming more innovative. Atrium, a legal software startup, shut down because it could not make a dent in law firms' operational efficiency (Ready 2020). Its CEO concluded that getting work done faster flew in the face of the traditional billable hours that sustain law firms. Hadfield (2020) argues that the high price of legal services is a consequence of an inefficient business model where lawyers spend a large fraction of their time on office administration, client acquisition, and satisfying licensing and continuing education requirements. Lower-paid workers and new technology could accomplish much of that work. Regulated industries have long been criticized for failing to know their customers' preferences and to adjust their operations and services accordingly (Winston 1998). Similarly, law firms and their clients have not had sustained discussions on how to achieve mutual benefits by aligning their long-term business interests (Henderson 2017).[3]

O'Flaherty and Siow (1995) characterize law firms' up-or-out model for associate lawyers as an important example of mismanagement because it causes law firm growth to be a slow and uncertain process—contributing a modest 5 to 7 percent of the present discounted value of a law firm's profits—given that performance as an associate lawyer is not a particularly informative signal about whether a lawyer would make a good partner and because the costs of mistaken promotion are relatively high. The authors point out that some workers are more productive in junior jobs and should stay there. At the same time, when senior associates leave large law firms before making partner, it costs approximately $2 million, on average, in training and recruitment costs to replace them (Ward 2019).

Still another example of law firm mismanagement is excess partner capacity. Altman Weil, a legal consultancy, conducts annual surveys of law firm leaders and offers circumstantial evidence on excess capacity by reporting that two-thirds of the leaders indicated that their equity partners were not sufficiently busy.[4] Industries, especially those that have been deregulated, have reduced excess capacity by restructuring. Similarly, Simons and Bruch (2017) concluded that five mergers between modest-sized law firms increased profitability, as measured by average compensation per partner, by enabling the merged firms to reposition their business to the most profitable services and by shedding both total and equity partners. However, like other industries, mergers are disruptive and often do not succeed. The majority of law firm mergers fail or run into difficulty because managers have not developed a coherent plan to capitalize on the combined client relationships and because they are not an efficient mechanism for reducing excess partner capacity.

Finally, occupational licensing requirements are increasingly contributing to law firms' inefficient operations because a greater percentage of law school graduates are flunking their state bar examination and having to retake it. According to the National Conference of Bar Examiners, 41 percent of people who sat for a bar examination in 2017 failed. In contrast, less than a third of bar takers failed in 2013. Lower first-time pass rates create problems for smaller law firms that hire from a wider pool of law schools beyond the elite schools whose students have a very high first-time pass rate. When a new hire fails the bar exam, a firm may allow the individual to study and retake the exam without pay. However, new hires are likely to be fired if they fail the bar exam again, which is costly to individuals and to the law firm because it delays training and mentorship that enables new hires to contribute to a firm's profitability. Alternatively, some firms are not hiring new law school graduates until they have passed the bar and have obtained a license to practice law.

INNOVATION

The legal industry has the potential to benefit significantly from innovations, which could greatly improve efficiency in contract review and in sorting through electronic discovery documents; improve the quality of legal research and written memorandums; and guide legal strategy by making profiles and predictions about judges and lawyers on the opposing side. In a recent illustrative study (LawGeex 2018), twenty experienced U.S. corporate lawyers were pitted against the LawGeex Artificial Intelligence (AI) system in a task to spot issues in five nondisclosure agreements. LawGeex AI achieved an average 94 percent accuracy rate, while the lawyers achieved an average 85 percent accuracy rate. In terms of efficiency, LawGeex AI completed its tasks, on average, in twenty-six seconds, compared with the lawyers taking an average of ninety-two minutes. Companies such as McKinsey and Deloitte predict that anywhere from 25 to 40 percent of legal jobs could eventually be automated.[5]

Innovation could also provide a way to overcome entry barriers to the legal profession. Simon et al. (2018) discuss the case of *Lola v. Skadden*, in which the Second Circuit stated that "tasks that could otherwise be performed entirely by a machine" could not be said to fall under the "practice of law." Accordingly, the court distinguished between mechanistic tasks and legal tasks and opened up a new source of entry that would not be subject to UPL statutes. Machines could evolve and eventually encroach on the practice of law, but their tasks would not, at this point, be regulated by professional rules governing the legal profession.

In 2012, the ABA updated its Model Rules of Professional Conduct to require lawyers to keep abreast of the benefits and risks associated with technology to provide competent representation. Although thirty-six states have thus far adopted the rule, it does not appear to be rigorously enforced.[6] In fact, the legal industry continues to be criticized for its lack of incentive to innovate, and practitioners have generally been slow to adopt new technology that potentially could be useful in their practice. Muro, Whiton, and Maxim (2019) find that despite the potential benefits of artificial intelligence (AI) applications, the legal industry is much less exposed to AI than are most other industries. According to the ABA's 2020 *Legal Technology Survey Report*, just 7 percent of respondents reported that their law firms used AI technology tools.

Altman Weil's *Law Firms in Transition Survey* concluded that change at law firms is "limited, tactical, and reactive," with little incentive for innovation because fellow law firms are also inclined toward the status quo.[7] For lawyers, the status quo means that the past is the master of both the present and the future; thus, the answer to why something is done a particular way is that it has always been done that way (Barton 2015).

Isaacson (2016) points out that in most industries, disruption is spurred by industry innovation, and clients follow. However, in the legal industry, law firms refuse to innovate unless clients force them to do so, and most law firm leaders believe their clients do not require innovation. Strom (2018) reports survey evidence that law firm partners are resistant to technological change. Finally, Flood and Robb (2018) argue that law firms have been slow to adopt new technologies because they lack a scientific base from which to analyze their needs with respect to technology and how their human capital could improve its practice. In contrast to medicine, for example, law has no institutions, such as a teaching hospital, that are heavily engaged in scientific research and development. A fundamental problem is that law firms are not structured to incentivize innovation by attracting strong data scientists because nonlawyers are second class citizens at a law firm, and they are typically seen as a cost, not a source, of revenue.

The failure of the legal industry to embrace new technology is reflected in two ways. First, as pointed out by Hadfield (2020), innovative new entrants, such as UpCounsel, LegalZoom, and AVVO, have been seen as threats to be eliminated and charged with the unauthorized practice of law. Second, entrepreneurs perceive that there are significant challenges to pitching new technology to the industry because they have provided only a small amount of venture funding to legal technology startups, less than $1 billion during the past several years, which pales in comparison with, for example, the growth of technology serving the finance industry (Hernandez 2016). Indeed, no legal tech company has been recently sold for billions of dollars.[8]

Recently, the chairman of Greenberg Traurig, Richard Rosenbaum, noted that traditional law firms cannot access the large amount of capital that public companies, private-equity funded companies, and large accounting firms can access to buy new technology.[9] Thus, Greenberg Traurig founded Recurve, a subsidiary that will partner with artificial intelligence providers and other startups to be innovation architects by identifying client needs but not engaging in the practice of law. While a start, this approach is inferior to a more direct approach whereby a law firm would become a public corporation and would raise capital to fund innovative technologies and to hire technical staff that would be integrated with the firm's legal and other operations. Unfortunately, ABA regulations generally prohibit the creation of this efficient entity.

WORKPLACE ENVIRONMENT

Beginning with law school, a career in the legal profession is stressful. For example, about 60 percent of Harvard Law School respondents to a mental health survey taken in 2017 reported some signs of depression (Sloan 2019). Many states have removed a question on their bar application asking if a law student has sought help to deal with a mental illness because the question might ostensibly discourage students from addressing mental health problems.

Many law school graduates who embark on a legal career also suffer from stress. Wilkins, Fong, and Dinovitzer (2015) estimate that nearly 30 percent of Harvard Law School graduates from four graduating classes are no longer practicing law in their jobs, and roughly seven in ten lawyers in California reported that they would change careers if the opportunity arose.[10] A survey of young Florida attorneys indicated that nearly one-third would not apply to law school knowing what they now know about the field, and nearly 60 percent feel that legal work is becoming "less desirable" and have considered changing careers or switching to a different firm.[11] Mental health issues have become so prominent among lawyers who work at major law firms that Hodkinson (2019) raised the issue in his article "Would Mandatory Psychologist Appointments Reduce Burnout in Big Law?" The stressful aspects of the workplace environment at private law firms that undoubtedly contribute to this state of affairs include factors such as promotion to partnership, racial and gender bias, and quality of life issues.

Promotion to Partner

The two alternative models of partnership at a law firm are a tournament model, based on *relative* performance where associates compete and the best ones are chosen for partnership, and an information model, based on an associate's *absolute* performance to meet a certain standard of quality. We are not aware of empirical evidence that indicates which model is most applicable to U.S. law firms and under what conditions. We thus report fragments of evidence that indicate the most important determinants of the partnership decision.

Polantz (2016) concludes from survey evidence that the key determinants for partnership include meeting metric goals on annual hours billed and revenue collected; developing professional networks with marketing and sales skills; and having successful relationships with clients. The importance of developing a professional network is consistent with the Abrams and Engel (2015) finding that the geographical proximity of a graduate's law school to a major legal market is a good predictor of that individual making partner at a big law firm. For example, Catholic University's Columbus School of Law in Washington, D.C., is ranked 108 among accredited law schools but ranked 32 in the number of alumni who become partners at the largest law firms. Regardless of the law school attended, law school grades do not predict who makes partner (Wilkins, Fong, and Dinovitzer 2015).

Finally, law firms distinguish between equity partners, who derive at least half of their income from law firm profits, and nonequity partners, who typically do not receive income from corporate profits. To advance to equity partner, a partner is generally expected to hit certain profit margins and to bill a certain number of hours. ALM Intelligence reports that among the top 100 law firms, the percentage of equity partners has been steadily declining since 2000, from nearly 80 percent to less than 60 percent in 2018.[12] During the same period, the share of nonequity partners has roughly doubled.

Evidence indicates that women are less successful than men in obtaining and keeping a partnership. Liebenberg and Scharf (2019) report that while women account for between 45 percent and 50 percent of law school graduating classes, they accounted for only 20 percent of law firm equity partners in 2018, indicating a high attrition rate for women attorneys, especially at large law firms. Brodherson, McGee, and dos Reis (2017) add that women are 29 percent less likely than men to reach the first level of partnership. Women also have higher attrition rates than men as they move up in seniority—according to the ABA, women over forty represent 41 percent of lawyers at law firms, but that share falls to only 27 percent for women over fifty.

Even when women become equity partners, their growth rate of compensation is much slower than male equity partners' growth rate of compensation. Major, Lindsey & Africa, a legal recruiting firm, found that male equity partners in major law firms saw an increase of 42 percent in their overall compensation over the past decade, while female equity partners' increase over the same period was roughly half as much.

Azmat and Ferrer (2017) argue that gender gaps in lawyers' earnings and promotion appear to be explained largely by differences in career goals and productivity instead of by discrimination. They find that male lawyers bill 10 percent more hours and bring in more than double the new client revenue to their law firm as female lawyers do, and, given the presence of preschool children, male lawyers have greater aspirations to become a partner. Women's greater intensity of household production, including home care, childcare, and shopping, and a law firm business model that stresses long hours and that may penalize women for taking time off are also likely to contribute to the gender gap (Bertrand, Goldin, and Katz 2010; Goldin 2014).

Those explanations, while undoubtedly valid, raise a different but relevant issue of why female lawyers originate much less new client revenue than male lawyers. A troubling possibility is that the legal profession is still mired in "good old boys" networks and women, in general, are able to engage in only lower-rate work.

Racial and Gender Bias

Considerable survey evidence indicates that racial and gender bias at law firms is a serious problem. Liebenberg and Scharf (2019) conclude that women leave Big Law because of a systematic culture of bias. Their study found that only 50 percent of women are satisfied with the recognition of their work, as opposed to 70 percent of men being satisfied with their recognition. About 45 percent of women surveyed said they were satisfied with their opportunities for advancement, while 69 percent of men reported such satisfaction. Women also reported high levels of overt gender discrimination. For example, 82 percent of women reported they have been mistaken for a low-level employee based on their gender.

A study by Women Lawyers on Guard (2020) collected survey evidence from more than two thousand respondents indicating that sexual harassment by law firm partners and supervising partners does not appear to have lessened in the last thirty years. Because more than half of the survey respondents said that when they reported harassment, the harasser suffered no consequences, the study concluded that the system for addressing sexual harassment in the legal profession is still broken.

In an extensive survey and analysis conducted for the ABA, Williams et al. (2018) concluded that women and people of color continue to face barriers in hiring, promotions, assignments, and compensation. Of the top 100 American law firms, twelve have 1 percent or fewer Black partners.[13] Scheindlin et al. (2017) and Alvare (2018) discuss the lack of women as lead counsel. The ABA has acknowledged part of the problem by resolving to address women partners' objections to demeaning communications, unwanted sexual advances, and denial of salary increases and bonuses.[14]

External pressures may also help to reduce racial and gender bias in three ways. First, in the wake of the #MeToo Movement, providers of employment practices liability insurance are shying away from covering law firms because they are characterized as a high-risk industry (Antillia 2019). Second, 170 general counsel and corporate legal officers signed an open letter to big law firms saying that they need to improve their diversity or they will lose business. The letter indicated that the corporations they represent will prioritize their spending on law firms that are clearly committed to diversity and inclusion in their hiring and partnership decisions.[15]

In addition, companies, including Microsoft, Intel, and U.S. Bancorp, are asking the law firms they hire to indicate the diversity of their lawyers and assignments. Law firms may lose business if they do not provide satisfactory responses.

Finally, the recent deaths of Black men at the hands of white police officers have spurred a renewed conversation about racism in all aspects of American lives. Black lawyers are beginning to speak candidly about working in a law firm without fear of being "blackballed" (for example, Skerrett 2020), which may help the legal community, including partners and white male associates, to realize their blind spots and to provide Black lawyers with better career guidance, inclusion in more cases, and greater opportunities to participate in other activities that would help to advance their careers. In a study for the American Bar Association titled *Left Out and Left Behind*, Peery, Brown, and Letts (2020) report that 70 percent of female minority lawyers have left or considered leaving the legal profession because they "continue to face firm cultures where their efforts and contributions are neither sufficiently recognized nor rewarded." The authors make recommendations to law firms that essentially ask them to be more introspective about whether they have been as fair and as unbiased as they could be in their decisions. In some situations, however, it can be difficult to address bias and inappropriate behavior. For example, anecdotal evidence indicates that law firm partners who bring in money and clients but who have been alleged to sexually harass female colleagues have simply moved laterally to another law firm. In fact, some partners have moved more than once for this reason (Randazzo and Hong 2018).[16]

Quality of Life

The quality of life that lawyers achieve by working at a law firm appears to involve significant tradeoffs. On the one hand, equity partners who make a lot of money appear to be happier than other lawyers and are unwilling, according to survey evidence, to trade compensation for nonmonetary benefits (Chen 2019). Yet McLellan (2020), reporting on ALM's Mental Health and Substance Abuse Survey, which was sent to lawyers in private law firms in the United States and abroad, suggests that something is seriously wrong with lawyers' quality of life because 31.2 percent of the more than 3,800 respondents say they are depressed, 64 percent say they have anxiety, 10.1 percent say they have an alcohol problem, and 2.8 percent say they have a drug problem. Overall, 73 percent said that their work environment contributed to those mental health issues, and 74 percent said the legal profession had a negative effect on their mental health over time.[17]

Artz, Green, and Heywood (2020) provide empirical evidence on the relationship between the introduction of performance pay and a greater incidence of alcohol and drug use for a cross-section of young workers in various occupations. The authors conjecture that the relationship reflects a coping mechanism for dealing with greater stress and work effort associated with performance pay.

The ABA has recognized that steps should be taken to address substance abuse and mental health problems in the legal profession, and it has unveiled an initiative to address those problems with a seven-point framework that it has asked law firms to adopt.[18] Law firms are adding on-site counseling as they grow more concerned about the mental health of some of their employees. Millennial lawyers may accelerate workplace reforms because they care less about money and power than previous generations have and care more about work-life balance (Blakely 2018).

IMPLICATIONS OF THE DISCUSSION

Kiser (2019) argues that, in theory, an important part of a law firm's culture is instilling in its attorneys a social purpose and sense of responsibility to society, but that, in reality, many attorneys do not find a larger purpose—or even a minor sense of purpose—in their practices. And most do not believe that their firm supports such a purpose.

This characterization of law firms is especially troubling because they can be a breeding ground for important government policymakers. For example, Fallon and King (2019) argue that prior work at a major law firm representing corporate clients is a significant qualification for an appointment to the federal judiciary, given that nearly 60 percent of all 175 circuit-court judges, who serve at the level just below the Supreme Court, were once corporate law partners. Fallon and King also point out that lawyers from such firms are also far more likely than other lawyers to get their cases heard by the Supreme Court.

Following Kiser (2019), lawyers who are either appointed or elected to important policymaking positions are not instilled by their law firm experience with the value of efficient and compassionate public policy because they have benefited significantly from inefficient policies that protected them from potentially important sources of competition; had little exposure to using other intellectual disciplines to solve policy problems; and had little opportunity to develop much empathy for those in less advantageous economic circumstances with significantly different life experiences. However, lawyers from private law firms have been instilled with a desire to experience at least a modicum of (political) power and to enrich their long-run earnings premiums through various "revolving doors."[19]

FIVE

SELF-SELECTION OF GOVERNMENT LAWYERS AND THE EARNINGS PENALTY

The vast majority of practicing lawyers choose to work in the private sector. But, as noted in the introduction, somewhat more than one hundred thousand lawyers (7.5 percent of the profession) choose to work in various levels of government. In this chapter, we consider the factors that influence the self-selection of lawyers to work in government, paying particular attention to the earnings penalty from doing so because a large earnings penalty could allocate legal talent away from the government and adversely affect the quality of its legal representation and policy performance.[1]

In general, private and public sector organizations compete to attract and retain skilled and experienced workers. Competition for lawyers is especially important because of their critical role in the formulation and implementation of nearly all government policies and because they represent firms and other organizations in many important legal matters. When legal disputes arise between government and private entities, public sector lawyers compete directly against their private sector counterparts.

Beginning with Boskin (1974), research has shown that compensation—including wages and benefits—is an important factor in occupational and sector choices. Thus, it is important to know whether the compensation that lawyers receive if they work for the government compares favorably with the compensation they would receive if they work in the private sector. Must lawyers accept a significant earnings penalty if they work for the government and, if so, what are the characteristics of lawyers who are willing to accept such a penalty?

Falk (2012) confirmed a widely held belief that the federal government offers attractive compensation relative to the private sector by reporting that for comparable jobs during the 2005 to 2010 period, the federal government paid total compensation that, on average, was 16 percent higher than the private sector paid.[2] But the subset of government workers who held jobs that required a Ph.D. or a professional degree were paid 18 percent *less* per hour worked compared with workers in the private sector who had that level of education. Note that this estimate is purely descriptive and does not account for differences in the unobserved characteristics of individuals who self-select to work in the federal government and the private sector.

We are not aware of previous estimates of the earnings penalty from working specifically as a lawyer in government. *A priori*, its magnitude is not clear because the penalty measures the percentage reduction in a lawyer's earnings from working in the government *after* controlling for differences in the job characteristics and in the observed and unobserved skills, abilities, and personal goals of the lawyers who work in the public and private sectors. As we discuss later in more detail, private sector attorneys' annual earnings, on average, exceed government lawyers' annual earnings. But that simple comparison does not necessarily indicate that government lawyers incur a significant earnings penalty because the aforementioned factors may largely explain the observed difference in earnings.

Lawyers in government may incur an earnings penalty because of a tension between regulation of the legal profession and the relative inflexibility of the government to set wages that are competitive with wages that lawyers earn in the private sector. As we have discussed, states' requirements that lawyers obtain a license to practice law, as well as American Bar Association regulations of legal practice, constitute barriers to entry, which have been found to generate rents that raise lawyers' earnings at all income levels. At the same time, government pay schedules limit government lawyers' earnings and may restrict government lawyers' ability to claim a large share of those rents.[3]

We use the American Bar Foundation's "After the JD" survey (AJD, described in chapter 2) to estimate the government earnings penalty and to determine whether it significantly contributes to the observed difference between government and private sector lawyers' earnings. We find that the earnings penalty is large—roughly 60 percent—and that it increases with the quality of the lawyer, as measured by the ranking of the law school from which the lawyer graduated. It could be argued that some lawyers begin their careers in government with the long-run objective of raising their earnings when they switch to the private sector, but such a strategy to build human capital still incurs an earnings penalty that is not offset by later earnings.

The large penalty is consistent with evidence that the government is not able to attract and retain lawyers of the same intellectual quality as the private sector can. For example, deHaan et al. (2015) found that roughly one-third of the Securities and Exchange Commission lawyers in their sample left the commission to join private law firms and that those lawyers tended to graduate from leading law schools and to have had the best enforcement records at the agency. We discuss in later chapters that this allocation of legal talent may affect government performance, especially when it engages in legal disputes with the private sector, and we offer some circumstantial evidence consistent with that view.

A FRAMEWORK FOR ESTIMATING
THE GOVERNMENT EARNINGS PENALTY

We confine our analyses of sector choices and earnings to lawyers who work in either the government (federal, state, and local) or in private law firms. Federal, state, and local governments and private law firms hire licensed lawyers to perform similar legal work that places a premium on providing effective advice on legal issues, completing negotiations, and winning disputes that are litigated. Generally, both sectors look for strong academic credentials and hire from a broad range of law schools, although the leading large law firms tend to hire predominantly from elite law schools. Given that some lawyers over the course of their careers switch between working in the government and working in a private law firm, it is reasonable to consider the sectors as alternative places of employment.

Government lawyers include those who work in agencies and departments implementing and interpreting bills and laws and participating in litigation. Unfortunately, the AJD identifies only whether a lawyer works in the federal government or in state and local government, but does not identify the specific type of work that a lawyer performs or their position.

Because we are interested in the earnings and sector choices of lawyers who shape the resolution of public policy disputes, we did not include "in-house counsel" or other lawyers who work for business firms (classified as the business sector) in our analysis.[4] Such private business firms whose primary focus is not law, but who nonetheless employ lawyers, offer a heterogeneous work environment and a wide range of responsibilities for lawyers that is not always comparable to employment in government or a private law firm. In fact, roughly 50 percent of the lawyers in the AJD who were employed in the business sector do not practice law.[5]

We estimate an earnings model that controls for the difference in the job characteristics (for example, hours worked per week) in each sector; the observed characteristics, abilities, and reported personal goals of the lawyers who work in each sector; and the choice of whether to work in the government or private sector. However, the sector choice is endogenous because the unobserved characteristics of lawyers are correlated with their choice to work for the government or the private sector. Hence, we estimate a selection model to control for the lawyers' unobserved characteristics in the earnings equation and to obtain a causal estimate of the effect of sector choice on earnings and a consistent estimate of the government earnings penalty.

Our identification strategy is to use lawyers' personal goals and parental characteristics as exogenous influences on sector choice, which, given the other controls in the earnings equation, do not affect earnings. We conduct a number of tests to support this strategy. In what follows, we derive the formal econometric model, specify the earnings and sector-choice equations, summarize the sample, provide evidence to support the identification strategy, and present the findings and robustness tests. The nontechnical reader can skip the derivation of the model and turn directly to the section that describes the variables that we use to explain lawyers' sector choice of work and their earnings.

Formally, the earnings model for a given lawyer is:

$$Y = X'\beta + \gamma G + \varepsilon$$

$$E(X'\varepsilon \mid G) = 0 \tag{1}$$

$$E(G'\varepsilon) \neq 0,$$

where Y is the log of annual earnings, X represents other, exogenous explanatory variables, G is a dummy variable indicating whether a lawyer works in government, ε represents unobserved variables that affect a lawyer's earnings, and β and γ denote parameters.[6]

We address the endogeneity bias that arises because G is correlated with ε by using the threshold-crossing, sector-choice model:

$$G = I(\mathbf{Z}\alpha + v > 0)$$

$$E(v|X,Z) = E(\varepsilon|X,Z) = 0$$

$$cov(\varepsilon, v) = \rho \tag{2}$$

$$v \sim N(0,1),$$

where Z and v are, respectively, observed and unobserved variables that influence a lawyer's choice to work in government; α is a vector of parameters; ε and v are jointly distributed with mean 0 and covariance ρ; and the marginal distribution of v is standard normal. We assume that Z is exogenous with respect to both the sector-choice model and the earnings equation and thus independent of both v and ε. We discuss the specific variables in Z and the support for our assumption that they are exogenous in the section on identification.

Given those assumptions, we can derive the control function (Heckman 1976):

$$E[\varepsilon|G] = \rho[G\lambda(\mathbf{Z}'\alpha) - (1 - G)\lambda(-\mathbf{Z}'\alpha)], \tag{3}$$

where $\lambda(\cdot)$ represents the inverse Mills ratio, given by the ratio of the normal probability density function to the normal cumulative distribution function. Accordingly, this model implies that the conditional mean of Y is:

$$E[Y|X, G] = \mathbf{X}'\boldsymbol{\beta} + \gamma G + E[\varepsilon|G]$$

$$= \mathbf{X}'\boldsymbol{\beta} + \gamma G + \rho[G\lambda(\mathbf{Z}'\alpha) - (1 - G)\lambda(-\mathbf{Z}'\alpha)] \tag{4}$$

where the control function captures the unobserved differences between workers who choose to work in government and those who do not.

We obtain consistent parameter estimates of the earnings equation by using the parameters α that we obtained from our binary probit model of sector choice to construct an estimate of the control function. We include the control function in the earnings equation and estimate that augmented earnings equation using OLS with robust standard errors.[7] We show the robustness of our estimates of the government earnings penalty by: (1) estimating the augmented earnings equations using alternative exclusion restrictions and thus instruments for the sector choice, (2) estimating the full model by the Generalized Method of Moments (GMM), as outlined in the appendix, to avoid making the assumption that the error terms of the sector-choice model are normally distributed, and (3) estimating the full model on a detailed data set of lawyers who graduated from the University of Michigan Law School.

SPECIFICATION OF THE VARIABLES IN THE
EARNINGS AND SECTOR-CHOICE MODELS

Earnings equations that specify individuals' earnings as a function of their supply characteristics and demand factors have a long history in economics, although we are not aware of previous estimates of earnings equations for lawyers.[8] Similarly, we are not aware of any previous research that has estimated lawyers' choices to work for the government or a private law firm. Goddeeris (1998) estimated the choice to work for a public interest or a private law firm and found that preferences for public-interest work were based on nonpecuniary aspects of the job that were related to personal goals, political activism, and beliefs. Blank (1985) estimated a model of the choice to work in the public or private sector for many occupations and found that the choice was influenced by demographic and educational variables. We outline the variables in our base case specifications here and provide additional discussion when we turn to the exclusion restrictions and robustness tests.

Earnings Equation

Our dependent variable for earnings is a lawyer's logged annual salary, including bonuses.[9] We use a lawyer's annual instead of hourly salary because lawyers who work in government and the private sector also receive nonwage considerations. It is important to assess any potential biases that those considerations may introduce using available empirical evidence, and it is easier to do so using annual adjustments. That said, we did conduct robustness tests using a lawyer's logged hourly wages as the dependent variable, and we found that our estimates of the government earnings penalty were only marginally smaller and that they remained highly statistically significant.

The earnings variable does not include fringe benefits, but the potential bias from excluding those benefits should be small in our analysis for two reasons. First, the three AJD samples discussed below measure the earnings and sector choice of lawyers for eleven years after they passed the bar examination. Those lawyers are likely to place a lower value on health coverage and pensions than do older lawyers. Second, although benefits are more generous, on average, in the government, Falk (2012) found that for workers with a professional degree or doctorate, the average cost of benefits was comparable for workers in the government and the private sector. This is not surprising because postgraduates are the most educated workers in society, and private sector employers must compete for them by offering attractive wage and nonwage benefits.[10]

Job security could be interpreted as a relevant control variable in an earnings equation. For example, Biggs and Richwine (2011) characterize job security as a source of compensation from working in government because security is provided from the outset. They estimate the value of job security for a broad cross-section of workers—both in and out of the government—to be 17 percent of annual compensation; a specific estimate for government lawyers is not available. Private lawyers, however, have the opportunity to eventually make partner at a private law firm, although perhaps not at the firm where they began their career. This partnership possibility could provide a comparable form of job security for all lawyers who work for private law firms.[11] And while partners' and senior partners' earnings are undoubtedly subject to larger annual fluctuations than are senior government lawyers' earnings, their mean earnings are also much higher.

An alternative view is that job security as an outcome of the labor market would be a "bad control" in our model. Because we do not have an explicit measure for job security, we conduct a sensitivity analysis using the Biggs and Richwine (2017) estimate, and we conclude that our findings are not significantly affected if we account for a measure of job or income security.[12]

The influences we included in the earnings equation are: (1) a dummy variable indicating whether a lawyer works in government; (2) employment characteristics, including regional dummies indicating where a lawyer is employed, a dummy variable indicating whether employment is full time, and weekly hours of work, which is an important measure of productivity;[13] (3) demographic variables, including age, race, and gender; and (4) educational variables that measure intellectual ability, including the ranking of the law school granting the lawyer's degree and the lawyer's law school GPA. In chapter 2, we interacted law school rank with GPA, but those interactions did not have sufficient explanatory power here and were statistically insignificant.[14]

Sector Choice

We specify the probability of a law school graduate selecting to work in the government as a function of: (1) demographic variables, including age, race, and gender; (2) educational variables, including the ranking of the law school granting the lawyer's degree, the lawyer's law school GPA, and educational debt; (3)

a lawyer's personal goals toward helping society and accumulating wealth; (4) parental characteristics, including whether the lawyer's parent is a citizen and whether the parent is a lawyer; and (5) regional dummies to capture unmeasured characteristics of alternative workplace locations throughout the country.[15]

Because the personal goals were measured when a lawyer was already working for the government or for a private law firm, they may be endogenous to sector choice. We therefore test this potential source of endogeneity below in several ways after we discuss our sample.

AJD SAMPLE

Our analysis is based on nationally representative data from the AJD survey of lawyers who were admitted to the bar in 2000. As noted in chapter 2, the "After the JD" project tracks the professional lives of more than five thousand lawyers over time and has been administered by the American Bar Foundation in three waves. Wave 1 of the questionnaires was administered two to three years into the new lawyers' careers.[16] Wave 2 was administered in 2007, which marked a crucial period[17]: In the seventh year of an attorney's career, lawyers working in private law firms must decide whether to pursue promotion to partnership within their firm or elsewhere; whether to seek a different job in the private sector, such as in business, solo practice, or in a small firm; whether to shift from the legal sector into government; or even whether to leave the legal profession entirely. Those in government positions face similarly important decisions about their long-term career paths.[18]

Finally, Wave 3 was administered in 2012 and provides 2011 earnings and job information.[19] By 2011, the AJD respondents were in their eleventh year since passing the bar; thus, their promotion to partnership and sector shift had long been made. In addition, Wave 3 enables our analysis to capture how a lawyer's career has evolved both before and after the Great Recession, which officially began in 2007 and ended in 2009.

The AJD survey contains detailed information on lawyers' annual earnings and employment, demographics, education, personal goals, and parental characteristics. Sampling weights are included in all waves of the survey so that each sample is representative of the national population of lawyers who were admitted to the bar in 2000 and who therefore have roughly the same amount of legal work experience.

As noted, we did not include "in-house counsel" or other lawyers who work for business firms (classified as the business sector) in our analysis. To this point, data from AJD Wave 1 indicate that roughly 50 percent of AJD respondents in the business sector worked in positions in which they did not practice law. In contrast to lawyers who work in business firms, this share was about 20 percent for respondents in the federal government, 15 percent for respondents in state or local governments, and 5 percent for respondents in private law firms.[20]

Sample size limitations prevented us from performing separate analyses for federal, state, and local government lawyers. In addition, those lawyers are very similar in terms of their desire to help society and achieve financial security, which are important determinants of a lawyer's decision to work for the public or private sector. As discussed later, our identification strategy depends on variation in those personal goals; thus, we could not expand our choice set to distinguish nonfederal from federal government legal work. However, based on data on other characteristics of government lawyers, we can assess how the earnings penalty varies between federal and state or local government lawyers.

We summarize the first wave of the AJD sample in table 5-1. The majority of the 1,332 lawyers in the sample work for private law firms, which is consistent with national population estimates of the share of lawyers in different sectors (Winston, Crandall, and Maheshri 2011).[21] As expected, lawyers who are employed at private law firms earn higher annual salaries and work more hours per week than do lawyers who work for the government. Private and public sector lawyers also appear to differ systematically across a variety of demographic and background characteristics. Minority and female lawyers, for example, compose a greater fraction of the government attorney labor force. Although roughly 10 percent of both types of lawyers have a lawyer parent, private law firm attorneys are more likely to have a parent who is not a U.S. citizen. We capture lawyers' personal goals and values using a 5-point scale that measures the importance of a lawyer's desire to help society versus a desire to obtain financial security and accumulate wealth in their decision to attend law school. Those goals and values vary by sector choice, with government lawyers reporting a greater desire to help society and private law firm attorneys indicating a greater desire to obtain financial security and wealth. Later, we report the findings of various tests that suggest that respondents' goals and values were established before they obtained employment in a particular sector.

Perhaps most striking, however, are the differences in intellectual ability, as measured by law school rankings and GPA. In particular, table 5-1 indicates that private law firm attorneys are nearly two-thirds more likely than their government counterparts to have graduated from law school with a GPA greater than 3.5, while the share of lawyers earning degrees from a top 10 law school is

TABLE 5-1. Summary Statistics for AJD Wave 1 Lawyers

	Government	Private Firm
Labor and Earnings		
Average Annual Salary (2002 dollars)	$49,960	$87,861
Employed Full-Time	98.8%	97.9%
Hours Worked per Week	45.0	49.9
Demographics		
Age	31.7	31.6
Nonwhite	18.4%	13.4%
Female	48.8%	47.7%
Education		
Law School GPA Greater than 3.5	18.5%	30.4%
Attended a Top 10 Law School	3.0%	9.1%
Attended a Top 11–20 Law School	6.2%	10.2%
Educational Debt	$60,853	$60,197
Preferences[1]		
Desire to Help Society	3.7	3.1
Desire for Financial Security/Wealth	3.8	4.2
Parental Characteristics		
Has Noncitizen Parent	11.1%	17.8%
Has Lawyer Parent	10.9%	10.3%
Sample Size	281	1,051

[1] In Wave 1, law graduates were asked: "How important was each of the following goals in your decision to attend law school?" Answers are given based on a five-point scale, with 1 meaning "not important" to their decision and 5 meaning "very important" to their decision. In Wave 2, law graduates were asked a parallel set of questions, namely: "How important are each of the following long-term goals to you?" Again, answers are given based on a five-point scale, with 1 meaning "not important " and 5 meaning "very important."

three times higher in the private sector than in government.[22] However, average educational debt at the time of law school graduation for lawyers in each sector is virtually identical.[23] The median and 90 percentile differences in the AJD sample were also small, while lawyers in each sector reduced their debt at similar rates seven years after leaving law school.

In appendix table A5-1, we present the characteristics of lawyers in federal and state or local government. Of the 281 government lawyers in our sample, approximately 25 percent work in the federal government, while the remaining 75 percent work in state and local government. Federal and nonfederal government lawyers are very similar in terms of their goals and the number of hours that they work per week. Compared with state and local government lawyers, federal government attorneys are paid more and have better academic credentials.

Table 5-2 shows that the work and education-related differences between lawyers who work for private law firms and lawyers employed by the government are more pronounced for attorneys in the top decile of each sector's earnings distribution. In this subsample, private sector lawyers' annual earnings

TABLE 5-2. Characteristics of Lawyers in the Top Decile of Each Sector's Earnings Distribution (AJD Wave 1 and AJD Wave 3)

	Government	Private Firm
Labor and Earnings[1]		
Annual Salary, average (2 years of experience) (2002 dollars)	$77,840	$169,436
Annual Salary, median (2 years of experience) (2002 dollars)	$80,000	$170,000
Annual Salary, average (11 years of experience) (2002 dollars)	$131,171	$422,338
Annual Salary, median (11 years of experience) (2002 dollars)	$126,400	$308,000
Hours Worked per Week	45.2	53.2
Education		
Law School GPA Greater than 3.5	38.2%	44.7%
Attended a Top-10 Law School	18.7%	38.0%
Attended a Top 11–20 Law School	9.1%	17.2%
Preferences[2]		
Desire to Help Society (5-pt. scale: 1 = not important; 5 = very important)	3.7	3.0
Desire for Financial Security/Wealth[1] (5-pt. scale: 1 = not important; 5 = very important)	3.6	4.1

[1] These salary measures at eleven years of experience are from AJD Wave 3. All other statistics in this table are from AJD Wave 1.

[2] In Wave 1, law graduates were asked: "How important was each of the following goals in your decision to attend law school?" Answers are given based on a five-point scale, with 1 meaning "not important" to their decision and 5 meaning "very important" to their decision.

after two years of experience are about $170,000, on average, roughly $90,000, or 120 percent more than government lawyers' average annual earnings. In 2011, when the respondents had about eleven years of experience as J.D.s, the average earnings for the top decile of private sector lawyers was $422,000 (in 2002 dollars), nearly $300,000, or 230 percent, more than the average earnings for the top decile of government lawyers. The 95th percentile of earnings was roughly $300,000 in the private sector, compared with roughly $125,000 in the government. Those private sector lawyers also work eight hours more per week than government lawyers. Representation of graduates from top 20 law schools is roughly two times greater in the private sector than in government. In addition to graduating from better law schools, private sector lawyers were more likely to achieve a GPA above 3.5.

In contrast, the self-reported personal goals and values of the most financially successful private sector and government lawyers do not differ much from those of private sector and government attorneys in the entire sample, suggesting that lawyers' goals and values are *not* strongly correlated with their earnings. Of course, we could simply be observing the convergence over time between a lawyer's goals and values; hence, we probe the matter in more detail below.

The sharp increase from two years to eleven years of experience in the earnings differential between private and government lawyers at the top decile reflects the significant increase in earnings that a lawyer obtains from making partner at a private law firm. Note also that the average and median earnings of lawyers with two years of experience at private law firms are nearly identical but that the median earnings are much less than the average earnings for lawyers with eleven years of experience, indicating that the gains from making partner vary significantly among the top tier of private sector lawyers. At the same time, only a small share of private sector lawyers with eleven years of experience has annual earnings that exceed $300,000.

To construct Wave 2 of the survey, the American Bar Foundation recontacted the lawyers surveyed in Wave 1. There was some attrition from Wave 1, and some new individuals were surveyed in Wave 2; thus, the Wave 2 sample has 904 lawyers and is primarily composed of lawyers who were also part of Wave 1.[24] As in the case of Wave 1, we applied appropriate sample weights to Wave 2 to ensure it was representative of the population of lawyers who were admitted to the bar in 2000 and were therefore seven years into their legal career. Summary statistics of Wave 2 were consistent with those of Wave 1 in identifying differences between the characteristics of government and private sector lawyers.

Finally, the American Bar Foundation recontacted lawyers who were surveyed in previous waves to construct Wave 3. There was considerable attrition from the previous waves, with 585 lawyers in our final Wave 3 sample, composed of 491 lawyers who were in all three waves and 94 new individuals who were surveyed. In what follows, we present detailed findings based on AJD Waves 1 and 2, and we present findings using appropriate sample weights based on AJD Wave 3 as robustness checks.

IDENTIFICATION

We discuss two sets of assumptions we make that enable our sector-choice-earnings model to be identified. First, we assume that lawyers' personal goals are exogenous in the sector choice model. In other words, although we observe career goals after the choice to be a lawyer has been made, we assume career goals are stable and are not influenced by the sector choice. Second, given the other controls in the earnings equation, lawyers' personal goals and parental characteristics do not affect earnings.

Exogeneity of Lawyers' Personal Goals

We provide support for our assumption that lawyers' personal goals are exogenous to their sector choice in three different ways. First, we used the first two waves of the AJD to compare changes in the personal goals of lawyers in the sample who switched sectors with changes in the personal goals of lawyers in the sample who did not switch sectors (as we'll discuss later, very few lawyers switched sectors between AJD2 and AJD3). If those goals are endogenous to the selection of private or public sector work, we would expect them to change as lawyers moved into or out of government. As we show in appendix table A5-2, however, changes in sector choice tend to have a small and statistically insignificant effect at conventional levels on preferences for helping society and accumulating wealth, regardless of whether a lawyer selected into or out of government. Those findings, which are largely confirmed by more expansive models that control for basic demographic and family background characteristics, provide some support for our assumption that lawyers' personal goals are exogenous.

Second, in addition to being asked about their desires to help society and for financial security, respondents in the first wave of the AJD were asked a series of questions regarding the factors that were important in determining the sector in which they began their professional career. Importantly, "medium to long-term earnings potential" and the "opportunity to do socially responsible work" were included in this list of sector-choice factors. If lawyers' self-reported desires to help society and for financial security actually reflect underlying personal goals and values, then we would expect the two sector-choice measures to mediate the influence of the original personal goals variables on the choice of sector. We tested this hypothesis by estimating a sector-choice model that included both lawyers' responses to the sector-choice-factor questions about "medium to long-term earnings potential" and "the opportunity to do socially responsible work," and the original personal goals variables. We found that those self-reported sector-choice factors had large and statistically significant effects on the probability of working for the government, and that the signs of the effects were as expected; however, their inclusion caused the coefficients for the original personal goals variables to become small and statistically insignificant. Those findings provide additional support that the self-reported personal goals variables in our sample are primarily capturing lawyers' stable preferences and goals.

Finally, we analyzed a set of variables in the first wave of the AJD survey that asked respondents whether they participated in certain activities during law school to determine whether those activities were correlated with their personal goals. Specifically, the AJD asked respondents whether they participated during law school in law review, moot court, school government, political advocacy, a college alumni association, the American Bar Association student division, a public interest law group, pro bono work with clients, and a gender-, race-, or ethnicity-based organization. We ran a regression of the effects of those activities on the desire to help society and found that the activities that are most directly related to helping society (a public interest law group, pro bono work, political advocacy) were statistically significant and had the expected positive sign. Participation in a gender-, race-, or ethnicity-based organization also had a statistically significant effect, perhaps because those groups tend to have a strong social justice focus. In contrast, when we ran a regression of the effects of those activities on the desire for financial security and wealth, we found that both the public interest law group and pro bono work with clients were statistically significant and negatively associated with the financial security goals. Given that none of the activities deal directly with enhancing financial security, it is not surprising that we did not find that any of them had a positive and statistically significant association with that goal.

Together, the preceding tests provide credible empirical evidence that lawyers in our sample established their personal goals prior to working in government or the private sector and that their goals have not been influenced by their earnings during employment since they passed the bar. In addition, we performed a robustness test to determine whether using the desire to make money as an instrument affected our findings. We found for both waves of the AJD sample that our estimates of the earnings penalty and their precision changed very little when we did not include the desire for wealth variable as an instrument. We also found that the inverse Mills ratio was not estimated as precisely but was still statistically significant at the 10 percent level for AJD1 and at the 5 percent level for AJD2.

Exclusion Restrictions

We exclude both the personal-goals variables and the parental-characteristics measures from the earnings equation. We have provided multiple sources of evidence that lawyers' personal goals reflect desires to help society and to acquire financial wealth that were established prior to selecting a job and are unrelated to their productivity. In addition, recall that the descriptive statistics reported in tables 5-1 and 5-2 implied that lawyers' goals are not strongly correlated with their earnings. Thus, it is reasonable to exclude those variables from the earnings equation. Although the desire for financial wealth and security could impact earnings through its association with ambition and the willingness to work, we capture those correlations by controlling for the number of hours worked per week and law school GPA in the earnings equation. Similarly, the number of hours worked per week will capture a lawyer's desire to help society. (It is unlikely that a lawyer who has a strong desire to help society will choose to work for a private law firm and substitute a large share of hours worked per week for more pro bono work.)

It is also justifiable to exclude parental characteristics from the earnings equation. A parent's citizenship bears no direct relationship to an individual's earnings. To the extent that children of immigrants are pushed harder to succeed than are children whose parents were born in America, this difference in upbringing should be captured in law school GPA and number of hours worked per week in the earnings equation. It may be argued that having a lawyer parent could help an individual find better job opportunities and earn a higher salary through the parent's connections. But those connections are likely to be less important for advancement in the legal profession because the profession places a premium on analytical and expository skills; has a meritocratic culture based on work effort and performance; and its practitioners often make initial hiring decisions based on the recommendations of the supervisors of an individual's summer internship. For example, Rivera (2015) argued that parents do not directly connect their children with elite jobs; rather, it is through the intergenerational transmission of elite education that parents help their offspring land elite employment. Thus, any genetic component of having a lawyer parent is largely captured by the individual's educational variables.[25]

Finally, we excluded educational debt from the earnings equation because, although lawyers who are saddled with large amounts of debt may feel compelled to work harder than lawyers with less debt to pay off, we likely capture that effect by controlling for hours worked in the earnings equation. As noted, we performed various robustness checks by estimating the augmented earnings equations using alternative exclusion restrictions and thus instruments for the sector choice. It was particularly striking that we found that our estimates of the earnings penalty and the inverse Mills ratio were robust when we included the parental characteristics in the earnings equation instead of including them in the sector-choice equation. In all likelihood, law school GPA and law school quality capture the information relevant for earnings that parental characteristics capture.

ESTIMATION RESULTS FOR THE SECTOR-CHOICE EARNINGS MODELS (AJD1)

We estimated our model of a lawyer's preferences for working in government or the private sector along with a lawyer's earnings to control for unobserved characteristics of lawyers that may affect earnings when we estimate the earnings penalty from working in government. We first present estimation results for sector-choice preferences and earnings based on the Wave 1 (AJD1) survey.

The parameter estimates of the probit sector-choice model presented in the first column of table 5-3 indicate that lawyers with different observed characteristics have distinct sector preferences. Lawyers who are not white are more likely to work for the government, but the other demographic variables (age and gender) have small and statistically imprecise effects.[26] Lawyers graduating from a top 10 law school and with a law school GPA greater than 3.5 are less likely to work for the government. On the other hand, lawyers who graduated from a law school outside of the top 20 and who graduated with a GPA below 3.0 are more likely to work for the government. Given the conventional view that the high cost of law school is causing many law graduates to seek private sector jobs, it is interesting that whether lawyers had accumulated large educational debt (greater than $50,000) upon graduation did not bear a statistically significant relationship to their sector choice.[27] Lawyers who indicated a desire to help society are more likely to work for the government, and lawyers who indicated a desire for financial security and wealth are less likely to work for the government. Finally, lawyers who have a parent who is not a U.S. citizen are less likely to work for the government, possibly because: (1) they may not meet national security requirements; (2) they feel less of an obligation to work for the U.S. government; or (3) they may come from less-affluent economic backgrounds and are more attracted to the high paying jobs in the private sector. But—importantly for our identification strategy—a lawyer's sector choice is not influenced by having a lawyer parent.[28]

We also present OLS estimates of the earnings equation in table 5-3. The specification in the second column of estimates does not include the correction for selectivity bias. The dummy variable indicating whether a lawyer works in government is central to our analysis, and it indicates that government lawyers' earnings are roughly 40 percent lower than what they could earn at a private law firm. Our finding is qualitatively consistent with Falk's (2012) finding that federal workers with a professional degree or doctorate suffer a nontrivial earnings penalty, but our estimate of the specific earnings penalty for government lawyers is roughly twice as large as the earnings penalty that Falk reports for all federal workers with a professional degree or doctorate.

We noted concerns that our estimate of the earnings penalty could be biased because the measure of lawyer earnings does not include some nonwage considerations. We explored the contention that lawyers in the private sector work much harder and have less downtime than do government lawyers by multiplying government lawyers' hours per week by two-thirds and re-estimating the earnings equation. We found that the government earnings penalty declined modestly from 40 to 35 percent.

To account for the "quality" instead of only the number of work hours, we explored whether government lawyers are more satisfied with their jobs than are private lawyers. According to evidence from the AJD survey, the answer for lawyers who remain in their sector is no. The AJD survey included questions related to job satisfaction that were measured on a 7-point scale, with 1 corresponding to "highly dissatisfied" and 7 corresponding to "highly satisfied." We created a "satisfaction index" by computing the average response across all job satisfaction variables (except for questions relating to work travel and pro bono work, which may not be pertinent to all lawyers in the private and public sectors) for each lawyer in our sample.[29] We found that the difference in the index for private and public sector lawyers who were in the first two survey waves and

TABLE 5-3. Sector Selection and Earnings Equations for AJD Wave 1, 2002

	Probit Selection Model (1 = government lawyer; 0 = private firm lawyer)	Earnings Equation[3] without Correction for Selection	Earnings Equation[3] with Correction for Selection
	Coefficient (Robust SE)	Coefficient (Robust SE)	Coefficient (Robust SE)
Works in Government (1 = government; 0 = private firm)	X	−0.401 (0.0217)	−0.592 (0.0866)
Employed Full-Time (1 = yes; 0 = otherwise)	X	0.464 (0.102)	0.462 (0.103)
Hours Worked per Week	X	0.00294 (0.00083)	0.00296 (0.00082)
Age (years)	0.0365 (0.0465)	0.0679 (0.00974)	0.0684 (0.0098)
Age Squared (years)	−0.000498 (0.000577)	−0.000894 (0.00012)	−0.000901 (0.00012)
Nonwhite (1 = nonwhite; 0 = white)	0.362 (0.144)	0.0773 (0.0278)	0.0858 (0.0277)
Female (1 = female; 0 = male)	−0.0333 (0.100)	−0.0596 (0.0202)	−0.0568 (0.0201)
Law School GPA>3.5 (1 = yes; 0 = otherwise)	−0.244 (0.124)	0.204 (0.0239)	0.193 (0.0249)
Law School GPA<3.0 (1 = yes; 0 = otherwise)	0.339 (0.126)	−0.165 (0.0263)	−0.146 (0.0277)
Law School Did Not Give GPA (1 = yes; 0 = otherwise)	0.514 (0.408)	0.00789 (0.0594)	0.0471 (0.0604)
Attended a Top 10 Law School (1 = yes; 0 = otherwise)	−0.777 (0.244)	0.385 (0.0402)	0.360 (0.0424)
Attended a Top 11–20 Law School (1 = yes; 0 = otherwise)	−0.318 (0.192)	0.253 (0.0335)	0.239 (0.0339)
Attended a Top 21–100 Law School (1 = yes; 0 = otherwise)	0.174 (0.120)	0.0866 (0.0241)	0.0970 (0.0245)
Graduated with Over $50k of Educational Debt (1 = yes; 0 = otherwise)	0.0661 (0.103)	X	X

	Probit Selection Model (1 = government lawyer; 0 = private firm lawyer)	Earnings Equation[3] without Correction for Selection	Earnings Equation[3] with Correction for Selection
	Coefficient (Robust SE)	Coefficient (Robust SE)	Coefficient (Robust SE)
Desire to Help Society[1]	0.210 (0.0438)	X	X
Desire for Financial Security/ Wealth[1]	−0.212 (0.0448)	X	X
Has Noncitizen Parent (1 = yes; 0 = otherwise)	−0.526 (0.184)	X	X
Has Lawyer Parent (1 = yes; 0 = otherwise)	0.0619 (0.155)	X	X
Regional Dummies[2]	Yes	Yes	Yes
Inverse Mills Ratio	X	X	0.120 (0.0531)
Constant	−1.004 (0.977)	9.615	9.655
R^2	0.124	0.592	0.594
Sample Size	1,332	1,332	1,332

[1] In Wave 1, law graduates were asked: "How important was each of the following goals in your decision to attend law school?" Answers are given based on a five-point scale, with 1 meaning "not important" to their decision and 5 meaning "very important" to their decision.

[2] Wave 1 regions, which indicate where an individual currently lives, include: New York City, District of Columbia, Chicago, Los Angeles, Atlanta, Houston, Minneapolis, San Francisco, Connecticut, New Jersey, Florida, Tennessee, Oklahoma, Indiana, St. Louis, Utah, Oregon, and Boston. New York City was used as the reference case in the above regression.

[3] Dependent variable is ln (Annual Salary), in 2002 dollars.

who did not switch sectors between waves 1 and 2 became statistically insignificant by wave 2. If we included switchers, however, the difference in satisfaction between public and private sector lawyers persists through wave 2 and favors working in the private sector.[30]

Finally, we questioned whether government lawyers got a premium from greater job security because private sector lawyers could become partners, which could also provide job security. In any case, if we used Biggs and Richwine's (2011) 17 percent figure as an upper-bound estimate of the premium to all government workers from greater job security, the earnings penalty would still be a sizable 29 percent.

The remaining variables in the earnings equation have plausible signs and are precisely estimated. Lawyers' earnings are positively related to working full time and more hours per week. The latter variable may be endogenous for private sector lawyers, but, in alternative specifications, we found that its inclusion barely affected the estimate of the works in government dummy.[31] A lawyer's age is positively related to earnings, although at a declining rate, as is being a member of a minority race or ethnicity, which may reflect public and private sector efforts to promote diversity in the workplace.[32] However, female lawyers' earnings continue to lag behind male lawyers' earnings. Greater intellectual ability, as indicated by a higher law school GPA and graduating from a higher-ranked school, has a positive effect on earnings.

When we include the inverse Mills ratio in the specification to control for selectivity (see the third column), its effect is statistically significant, the earnings penalty from working for the government becomes larger and approaches roughly 60 percent, and the coefficients of the remaining variables are virtually unaffected. The change in the estimated penalty suggests that any bias from omitted nonwage benefits from working as a lawyer in government is likely to be small, because if less-productive people self-select to work in government to seek, among other benefits, less risk of losing their job because of poor performance and less-stressful work, benefits that are not available in the private sector, then the penalty from working in government should have decreased, not increased, when we included the inverse Mills ratio.

Finally, because we were not able to conduct various empirical tests to support our exclusion restriction on the parent characteristics in the earnings equation, as we did for personal goals, we conducted a robustness test of our findings by including the parent characteristics in the earnings equation and re-estimating the model; thus, lawyers' personal goals and educational debt were the instruments for the endogenous sector choice. We found that the estimate of the government earnings penalty was virtually unaffected and that neither of the parent characteristics was statistically significant. This is consistent with our argument that their effects should be captured in the observed ability measures and hours worked per week that we include in the earnings equation.

What unobserved influences may be responsible for the increase in the government earnings penalty? Because only lawyers can share ownership of a private law firm, law firms do not generally hire highly paid professionals from nonlaw backgrounds. In contrast, government lawyers must work with a broad range of people at their workplace because formulating and implementing public policy requires regular interactions with civil service employees, elected and appointed government officials, and even members of the public. For example, compared with private sector lawyers, government lawyers in our AJD sample reported greater responsibilities for keeping their clients updated on relevant legal matters.

Another important consideration is that a government lawyer may be the only lawyer or part of a small group of lawyers in an agency or government office. Thus, government lawyers often have to mainly mediate issues between nonlawyers, which can require considerable patience, understanding, and other noncognitive skills because nonlawyers do not know certain laws and do not understand their rationale. Lawyers who work at private law firms, on the other hand, are likely to find it easier to speak with colleagues, because they know the law, and with clients who seek legal services, because they expect a lawyer to know the relevant laws. We therefore conjecture that our selectivity correction increases the earnings penalty because lawyers who choose to work in government have certain interpersonal skills and noncognitive attributes that are not being fully compensated.

The simple two-step estimation procedure employed above makes potentially restrictive distributional assumptions (that is, normality) on the form of the selectivity correction. We therefore re-estimated the earnings equation by the generalized method of moments (GMM), using, as before, lawyers' personal goals, parental characteristics, and educational debt as instruments for the endogenous choice of whether to work for government or a private law firm (see the appendix for our procedure). We found that the magnitude of the dummy for working in government increased modestly to -0.709 (with a standard error of 0.111) and that we could not reject the validity of the instruments according to Hansen's Test of Overidentifying Restrictions (p-value $= 0.489$).

ESTIMATION RESULTS FOR THE SECTOR-CHOICE
EARNINGS MODELS (AJD2, AJD3)

Based on the AJD2 sample, the parameter estimates of the probit sector-choice model presented in the first column of table 5-4 can be distilled into the same basic findings that we obtained for the AJD1 sample: lawyers with high intellectual ability, based on academic performance, are less likely to work for the government; lawyers who have a strong desire to help society are more likely to work for the government; and lawyers who have a strong desire to accumulate wealth are less likely to work for the government.

The main finding from our OLS estimates of the earnings equation in the second and third columns of table 5-4 is that lawyers who work for the government suffer an earnings penalty that is again greater when we correct for selectivity, and its magnitude of slightly more than 60 percent is comparable to the penalty we estimated for lawyers in AJD1. When we re-estimated the model by GMM, we found that the estimated earnings penalty was about 60 percent (−0.603, with a standard error of 0.0882), and that we could not reject the validity of our instruments by Hansen's Test of Overidentifying Restrictions (p-value = 0.979).

Finally, we estimated the sector-choice-earnings model using the 585 lawyers included in the AJD3 sample, which covers the aftermath of the Great Recession. The estimates of the full model indicated that our preceding estimates based on AJD1 and AJD2 are robust to the dramatic change in the macroeconomy, as the earnings penalty was slightly more than 60 percent (the estimated coefficient was −0.602, with a standard error of 0.0939).[33] At the same time, this estimate of the earnings penalty suggests that job security does not have an important effect on our findings. That is, any differences in public and private sector job security should be small for lawyers in their eleventh year because private sector lawyers would have had more than enough time to become a partner or obtain greater security at their place of work. Hence, it is unlikely that our estimate of the government earnings penalty is significantly biased upward.[34]

In sum, we have found that government lawyers have suffered a large earnings penalty that has persisted during the eleven years since they have passed the bar and launched their careers. It could be argued that some lawyers begin their careers in government with the long-run objective of raising their earnings when they switch to the private sector, but we could not find any evidence to support that strategy.[35] Thus, it is appropriate to characterize our estimate as an earnings penalty from working in government.

VARIATION IN THE GOVERNMENT EARNINGS
PENALTY BY LAW SCHOOL RANKING

The government earnings penalty could vary for different types of lawyers, especially in accordance with their intellectual abilities as indicated by where they graduated from law school. To explore this issue, we re-estimated our model of lawyers' sector choice and earnings for sub-samples of the AJD1 sample that included 299 lawyers who attended the top 20 law schools in the country and 632 lawyers who attended law schools ranked 21–100.

We found that the earnings penalty from working as a lawyer in government is positively related to school quality: the penalty for lawyers who graduated from a top-20-ranked law school is −0.975 (with a standard error of 0.233), and the penalty for lawyers who graduated from a law school ranked 21–100 is −0.547 (with a standard error of 0.107). Furthermore, this finding, combined with the summary statistics in appendix table A5-1 that show that federal government attorneys have better academic credentials than state and local government attorneys, suggests that federal government lawyers likely suffer a larger earnings penalty than state or local government lawyers do.

As a robustness check for our estimate of the government earnings penalty for a lawyer who graduates from a top law school, as well as a robustness check for our overall approach, including our model and sample based on the AJD survey, we estimated a sector-choice-earnings model using a dataset from the University of Michigan Law School. The Michigan survey, which started in 1967, is administered to alumni fifteen years after graduation, and it was later expanded in 1972 to include alumni five years after graduation.[36] Although the survey does not collect data on career goals, respondents were asked whether they were more or less concerned than other lawyers their age about "making a lot of money" and about "the impact of [their] work on society." Similar to the personal goals variables used in the analyses of the AJD data, those two measures serve as proxies for lawyers' underlying preferences that affect sector choice, and they are assumed to be exogenous to earnings. The Michigan survey, however, did not have data on the respondents' parental characteristics.

To facilitate initial comparisons between the AJD and Michigan datasets, we limited our analyses to the 2,517 lawyers who (1) were five years out of law school, and (2) took a job in the government or with a private law firm. We summarize the means of the key variables in appendix table A5-3. Consistent with the AJD survey, lawyers who are employed at private law firms earn higher annual salaries and work more hours per week than do lawyers who work for

TABLE 5-4. Sector Selection and Earnings Equations for AJD Wave 2 Lawyers, 2007

	Probit Selection Model (1 = government; 0 = private firm)	Earnings Equation[3] without Correction for Selection	Earnings Equation[3] with Correction for Selection
	Coefficient (Robust SE)	Coefficient (Robust SE)	Coefficient (Robust SE)
Works in Government (1 = government; 0 = private firm)	X	−0.391 (0.0295)	−0.614 (0.0699)
Employed Full–Time (1 = yes; 0 = otherwise)	X	0.433 (0.108)	0.409 (0.108)
Hours Worked per Week	X	0.00425 (0.00184)	0.00427 (0.00184)
Age (years)	0.0116 (0.105)	0.0608 (0.0312)	0.0567 (0.0308)
Age Squared (years)	0.000146 (0.00126)	−0.000778 (0.000383)	−0.000701 (0.000378)
Nonwhite (1 = nonwhite; 0 = white)	0.320 (0.165)	0.0497 (0.0394)	0.0686 (0.0393)
Female (1 = female; 0 = male)	0.113 (0.112)	−0.133 (0.0317)	−0.121 (0.0319)
Law School GPA Greater than 3.5 (1 = yes; 0 = otherwise)	−0.332 (0.142)	0.0769 (0.0403)	0.0583 (0.0413)
Law School GPA Less than 3.0 (1 = yes; 0 = otherwise)	0.0694 (0.146)	−0.168 (0.0363)	−0.165 (0.0361)
Law School Did Not Give GPA (1 = yes; 0 = otherwise)	−0.238 (0.366)	−0.0504 (0.113)	−0.0583 (0.116)
Attended a Top 10 Law School (1 = yes; 0 = otherwise)	−0.433 (0.245)	0.424 (0.0572)	0.393 (0.0572)
Attended a Top 11–20 Law School (1 = yes; 0 = otherwise)	−0.303 (0.189)	0.153 (0.0721)	0.134 (0.0721)
Attended a Top 21–100 Law School (1 = yes; 0 = otherwise)	−0.196 (0.129)	0.0531 (0.0371)	0.0387 (0.0365)

	Probit Selection Model (1 = government; 0 = private firm)	Earnings Equation[3] without Correction for Selection	Earnings Equation[3] with Correction for Selection
	Coefficient (Robust SE)	Coefficient (Robust SE)	Coefficient (Robust SE)
Graduated with Over $50k of Educational Debt (1 = yes; 0 = otherwise)	−0.000611 (0.115)	X	X
Desire to Help Society[1]	0.396 (0.0598)	X	X
Desire to Accumulate Wealth[1]	−0.475 (0.0595)	X	X
Has Noncitizen Parent (1 = yes; 0 = otherwise)	−0.213 (0.169)	X	X
Has Lawyer Parent (1 = yes; 0 = otherwise)	−0.0961 (0.191)	X	X
Regional Dummies[2]	Yes	Yes	Yes
Inverse Mills Ratio	X	X	0.163 (0.0480)
Constant	−0.596 (2.142)	9.618 (0.633)	9.769 (0.625)
Sample Size	904	904	904
R^2	0.196	0.384	0.393

[1] In Wave 2, law graduates were asked: "How important are each of the following long-term goals to you?" Answers were given based on a five-point scale, with 1 indicating "not important" and 5 meaning "very important."

[2] Wave 2 provides information on the state in which a respondent is currently employed. Due to sample size limitations, we only included dummy indicators for whether the respondent lived in the Northeast, the District of Columbia, the South, or the West.

[3] Dependent variable is ln (Annual Salary), in 2002 dollars.

the government. A greater share of minority and female lawyers work for the government. Lawyers at private law firms have law school GPAs that are higher than government lawyers' GPAs, while their debt from attending law school is similar to that of government lawyers' debt. Finally, compared with lawyers at private firms, government lawyers state they have greater concern about the social impact of their work relative to other lawyers their age, but less concern about making money.

The Michigan survey enabled us to specify sector-choice and earnings equations that were very similar to our previous specifications. We estimate that the earnings penalty for Michigan law school graduates who worked in government five years after graduation was roughly 78 percent (see appendix table A5-4). This estimate is consistent with our AJD-based findings that the government earnings penalty increases with law school quality. Specifically, *U.S. News and World Report* consistently ranks the University of Michigan Law School among the top 20 law schools in the country. Furthermore, note that the earnings penalty for Michigan alumni exceeds the roughly 55 percent earnings penalty for lawyers in the AJD survey who graduated from a law school ranked 21–100.

IMPLICATIONS FOR GOVERNMENT ATTRACTION
AND RETENTION OF LAWYERS

The large earnings penalty that we have estimated for government lawyers is of potential concern because it is consistent with and could largely explain our descriptive evidence that the top law school graduates are more likely to sort into private law firms than to work for the government. We acknowledge that we do not have an estimate of the supply elasticity of lawyer quality to the government sector. But, as noted in the introduction, it has been empirically well established that sector choice is strongly influenced by relative compensation.

The government may have attracted lawyers who have unobserved or unmeasured (by us) noncognitive skills that are well suited for working in the public sector, which may explain why some lawyers—at least initially in their career—prefer to work for the government despite its lower salaries. Such behavior is consistent with a matching story whereby certain extroverted job-seekers are willing to sacrifice considerable income in order to work in environments that involve frequent interactions with a broad range of coworkers (see, for example, Krueger and Schkade 2008).

We also suggest that the government earnings penalty may constrain the government's ability to retain its most talented lawyers. Roughly 26 percent of the lawyers who worked in the government in AJD1 switched to working in a private law firm in AJD2, usually as an associate attorney. The exit rates for federal and state and local government lawyers do not appear to vary much; however, it is notable that, in general, the government lawyers who switched to the private sector had greater intellectual ability than the lawyers who stayed in government based on law school rankings and GPAs. We confirmed this point econometrically by using the first two waves of the AJD to estimate a probit model of the factors that influence lawyers to stay in government, including demographic characteristics and measures of academic performance.[37] The sample consisted of lawyers who worked in government in Wave 1 whom we also observed in Wave 2; lawyers who left the survey after Wave 1 and lawyers who are new to the survey in Wave 2 were not included in the sample. In the appendix, we explain that we can justify excluding those lawyers from our analysis sample by using Wave 2 sample weights to estimate this model; thus, the parameter estimates are not biased.

The estimates shown in table 5-5 indicate that lawyers who are older and not white are more likely than other lawyers to stay in government, while lawyers whose law school GPA exceeded 3.5 and who graduated from a top 10 law

TABLE 5-5. Probit Model of a Lawyer's
Decision to Stay in Government

	Coefficient (Robust SE)
Age (years)	0.0820 (0.0333)
Nonwhite (1 = nonwhite; 0 = white)	0.588 (0.332)
Law School GPA>3.5 (1 = yes; 0 = otherwise)	−0.564 (0.385)
Law School GPA<3.0 (1 = yes; 0 = otherwise)	−1.366 (0.380)
Attended a Top 10 Law School (1 = yes; 0 = otherwise)	−1.980 (0.612)
Constant	−1.202 (1.009)
Sample Size	130
Pseudo R^2	0.226

Note: 1 = stay in government; 0 = switch to private.

school are less likely than other lawyers to stay in government. Attorneys with GPAs less than 3.0 are also less inclined to stay in government, which may raise the average GPAs of government lawyers. In any case, the government appears to be unable to retain its most intellectually able lawyers.[38] Recall the De Haan et al. (2015) detailed study of lawyers who leave the Securities and Exchange Commission that we refer to in the introduction to this chapter. Their findings provide corroborating evidence, given that roughly one-third of their sample of SEC lawyers left during the period from 1990 to 2007 to join private law firms, and that those lawyers tended to have graduated from leading law schools and to have had the best enforcement records at the agency.[39]

In the final two chapters, we discuss how government performance may be affected by the quality of its lawyers and how reforming public policy toward the legal profession may help to address that issue.

Appendix

This appendix outlines GMM estimation of the earnings equation accounting for lawyers' endogenous choice of whether to work in the government and explains why the probit model that estimates the influences on lawyers to stay in government is not subject to attrition bias.

GMM Estimation

The earnings model in the text is given by:

$$Y = X'\beta + G\gamma + \varepsilon,$$

where all variables are defined as before, β and γ are the unobserved parameters to be estimated, and the following conditions are met:

$$E(\varepsilon) = 0, Var(\varepsilon) = \Sigma$$

$$E(X\varepsilon) = 0$$

$$E(G\varepsilon) \neq 0$$

$$E(Z\varepsilon) = 0.$$

Note X is a k-element vector of exogenous explanatory variables, Z is a vector of exogenous instruments that may include some subset of X but include at least one variable not in X, and G is an endogenous dummy variable capturing sector choice. The disturbance term ε, with mean 0 and variance Σ is potentially correlated with G but not with X or Z. All the variables are measured at the individual level; we have suppressed the indexes for simplicity.

$E[X\varepsilon] = E[X(Y - X'\beta - G\gamma] = 0$ and $E[Z\varepsilon] = E[Z(Y - X'\beta - G\gamma] = 0$ constitute $k + m$ distinct theoretical moment conditions. The sample counterparts of those conditions can be used to estimate the $k + 1$ parameters of the model (β and γ). If $m = 1$, there are as many moment conditions as parameters and the model is exactly identified. If $m > 1$, there are more moment conditions than parameters, and the model is overidentified. In the overidentified case, estimation proceeds by choosing the parameters that minimize the criterion function

$$m(\hat{\beta}, \hat{\gamma})' W m(\hat{\beta}, \hat{\gamma}),$$

where m represents the vector of sample moments and W is a positive definite weighting matrix. The optimal weighting matrix is the inverse of the covariance matrix of the moment conditions (Hansen 1982), which we denote V^{-1}.

Although V^{-1} is unobserved, it can be estimated consistently by an iterative procedure whereby the moment conditions are initially weighted with an identity matrix to obtain consistent estimates of β and γ. Those estimates are then used to estimate V^{-1}, which is used as the weighting matrix in the next iteration to obtain more precise estimates of β and γ. The process continues until the improved precision of the parameter estimates is sufficiently small such that convergence is achieved.

PROBIT MODEL OF A LAWYER'S DECISION
TO STAY IN GOVERNMENT

This model requires data from the first two waves of the AJD survey, so we assess the potential bias caused by not including lawyers in the estimation who dropped out after participating in Wave 1. Such attrition is fundamentally a problem of sample selection. As is well known, the probit model may be motivated as a latent variable threshold-crossing model:

$$S^* = XB + u$$

$S = 1$ if $S^* > 0$, where S^* is the latent variable such that if $S^* > 0$, then the lawyer stays in government, X denotes exogenous explanatory variables, and u is an unobserved component that affects the decision to stay in or exit from the government sector. In a probit model, u is assumed to conform to a standard normal distribution.

If individuals were dropped from the sample at random, then the distribution of u would be unchanged, and the probit estimation would maintain consistency. It is possible, however, that individuals who attrit from Wave 1 may vary systematically in u from those who do not attrit. Suppose, for example, that those who attrit are more likely to stay in government; thus, the distribution of u would change, specifically, $E[u|in \ sample] < 0$, and probit estimation would no longer be consistent.

We therefore apply the Wave 2 sample weights to our estimation sample. The idea here is that instead of dropping the lawyers who attrit from the Wave 1 sample, we are dropping the newly added lawyers from the Wave 2 sample. The newly added lawyers were presumably exogenously selected for the survey, thus their inclusion in, or removal from, the sample should have no effect on the distribution of u. In contrast, the lawyers who attrit from Wave 1 may, by their choice to attrit, be revealing information about their unobserved component u.

Although those processes of exclusion are conceptually different, in either case, the remaining sample involves the same individuals. By applying the Wave 2 sample weights, the data from the newly added observations that are dropped can be assumed to be missing at random, thus probit estimation maintains consistency.

APPENDIX TABLE A5-1: CHARACTERISTICS OF LAWYERS IN FEDERAL
GOVERNMENT AND IN STATE/LOCAL GOVERNMENT

	Federal Government	State/Local Government
Annual Salary (2002 dollars)	$61,085	$46,383
Hours Worked per Week	45.4	44.9
Law School GPA Greater than 3.5	27.2%	15.7%
Attended a Top 10 Law School	9.4%	0.9%
Attended a Top 11–20 Law School	8.7%	5.4%
Desire to Help Society[1] (5-pt. scale: 1 = not important, 5 = very important)	3.6	3.7
Desire for Financial Security/Wealth[1] (5-pt. scale: 1 = not important, 5 = very important)	3.6	3.9

[1] In Wave 1, law graduates were asked: "How important was each of the following goals in your decision to attend law school?" Answers are given based on a five-point scale, with 1 meaning "not important" to their decision and 5 meaning "very important" to their decision.

APPENDIX TABLE A5-2. Probit Model of Changes in Personal Goals

	Altruism		Wealth	
	(1 = helping society was more important in Wave 2 than in Wave 1; 0 = otherwise)		(1 = financial security/wealth was more important in Wave 2 than in Wave 1; 0 = otherwise)	
	Without Controls	With Controls	Without Controls	With Controls
	Coefficient (Robust SE)	Coefficient (Robust SE)	Coefficient (Robust SE)	Coefficient (Robust SE)
Age (years)	X	0.00488 (.00843)	X	0.00692 (0.00978)
Nonwhite (1 = nonwhite; 0 = white)	X	−0.160 (0.109)	X	−0.128 (0.126)
Female (1 = yes; 0 = otherwise)	X	−0.0294 (0.0841)	X	0.140 (0.0967)
Attended a Top 10 Law School (1 = yes; 0 = otherwise)	X	−0.166 (0.135)	X	−0.162 (0.181)
Has Noncitizen Parent (1 = yes; 0 = otherwise)	X	0.562 (0.125)	X	0.468 (0.145)
Has Lawyer Parent (1 = yes; 0 = otherwise)	X	0.0464 (0.126)	X	0.143 (0.147)
Switched from Government to Private Law Firm (1 = yes; 0 = otherwise)	−0.0505 (0.175)	−0.0626 (0.181)	0.254 (0.186)	0.273 (0.188)
Switched from Private Law Firm to Government (1 = yes; 0 = otherwise)	0.00921 (0.137)	0.0246 (0.137)	−0.278 (0.181)	−0.265 (0.183)
Constant	−0.722 (0.0432)	−0.893 (0.272)	−1.266 (0.0506)	−1.589 (0.324)
Sample Size	1,625	1,585	1,625	1,585
Pseudo R^2	0.0001	0.016	0.0049	0.023

APPENDIX TABLE A5-3. Summary Statistics for Michigan Law Graduates

	Government	Private Firm
Labor and Earnings		
Annual Income (2002 dollars)	$67,054	$105,390
Employed Full-Time	97.9%	95.9%
Hours Worked per Year	2,419	2,599
Demographics		
Age	32	32
Nonwhite	19.5%	11.3%
Female	44.7%	32.6%
Education		
Law School GPA (standardized by graduation year)	0.052	0.199
Attended University of Michigan as Undergraduate	18.2%	21.9%
Attended Ivy League School as Undergraduate	14.6%	14.3%
Educational Debt	$40,385	$43,184
Preferences[1]		
Concerned about Societal Impact of Work (7-pt. scale: 1 = much less than most lawyers, 7 = much more than most lawyers)	5.49	4.35
Concerned about Making a Lot of Money (7-pt. scale: 1 = much less than most lawyers, 7 = much more than most lawyers)	2.73	3.65
Year of Law School Graduation	1991	1990
Sample Size	329	2,188

[1] Respondents were asked: "In comparison to most lawyers your age, how would you rate yourself with regard to the following traits or qualities?" Answers were recorded on a seven-point scale, with 1 indicating "much less than most" and 7 indicating "much more than most."

APPENDIX TABLE A5-4. Sector Selection and Earnings Equations for Michigan Law Graduates

	Probit Selection Model (1 = government lawyer; 0 = private firm lawyer)	Earnings Equation[2] without Correction for Selection	Earnings Equation[2] with Correction for Selection
	Coefficient (Robust SE)	Coefficient (Robust SE)	Coefficient (Robust SE)
Works in Government (1 = government; 0 = private firm)	X	−0.388 (0.0210)	−0.785 (0.0682)
Employed Full–Time (1 = yes; 0 = otherwise)	X	0.336 (0.0613)	0.328 (0.0599)
Hours Worked per Year	X	0.000180 (0.0000224)	0.000182 (0.0000222)
Age (years)	0.246 (0.131)	0.0176 (0.0343)	0.0460 (0.0344)
Age Sq. (years)	−0.00328 (0.00182)	−0.000321 (0.000480)	−0.000698 (0.000481)
Nonwhite (1 = nonwhite; 0 = white)	0.317 (0.109)	0.113 (0.0270)	0.135 (0.0269)
Female (1 = female; 0 = male)	0.122 (0.0761)	−0.0182 (0.0171)	0.00338 (0.0177)
Law School GPA (standardized by graduation year)	−0.0976 (0.0457)	0.135 (0.0110)	0.129 (0.0110)
Attended University of Michigan as Undergraduate (1 = yes; 0 = otherwise)	−0.107 (0.0932)	0.0127 (0.0176)	0.00742 (0.0175)
Attended Ivy League School as Undergraduate (1 = yes; 0 = otherwise)	−0.169 (0.106)	−0.0105 (0.0281)	−0.0130 (0.0278)

	(1)	(2)	(3)
Graduated with Over $50k of Educational Debt (1 = yes; 0 = otherwise)	X	X	−0.255 (0.0894)
Concerned about Impacting Society[1]	X	X	0.304 (0.0331)
Concerned about Making a Lot of Money[1]	X	X	−0.248 (0.0331)
State and Cohort Dummies[3]	Yes	Yes	Yes
Inverse Mills Ratio	0.251 (0.0426)	X	X
Constant	10.121 (0.626)	10.627 (0.624)	−6.995 (2.347)
R2	0.371	0.358	0.225
Sample Size	2,517	2,517	2,517

[1] Respondents were asked: "In comparison to most lawyers your age, how would you rate yourself with regard to the following traits or qualities?" Answers were recorded on a seven-point scale, with 1 indicating "much less than most" and 7 indicating "much more than most."

[2] Dependent variable is ln (Annual Salary), in 2002 dollars.

[3] In addition to including dummies for state of current residence, analyses include cohort dummies indicating the year in which the lawyer graduated from law school.

SIX

RESOURCE CONSTRAINTS FOR LAWYERS IN GOVERNMENT

The Case of the U.S. Office of the Solicitor General

In recent years, the U.S. legal system has operated under substantial resource constraints. As pointed out by Yang (2016), prosecutors' and public defenders' offices and courts nationwide have faced severe budget cuts. At the same time, judicial vacancies increased prosecution and trial costs. Prosecutors have responded to the resource constraints by screening out cases with more contestable evidence and by trying to negotiate plea deals to avoid going to trial.

In this chapter, we explore the possibility that resource constraints on time and material support are affecting the performance of lawyers at the highest level of government by evaluating the U.S. Department of Justice's Office of the Solicitor General in its role of supervising and conducting government litigation before the Supreme Court of the United States (SCOTUS). The United States government is involved in approximately two-thirds of all cases that SCOTUS decides on the merits each year.[1] The solicitor general leads the office in deciding which government cases to petition to the Supreme Court and in crafting the government's position in its SCOTUS arguments. Supporting the solicitor general's work are the office's attorneys, deputy solicitors general, and assistants to the solicitor general, who participate in preparing the petitions, briefs, and other papers filed by the government in the Supreme Court and in making oral arguments before the court.

The Office of the Solicitor General, although employing only fifty-five people, including attorneys, has the advantage of attracting probably the best lawyers in government, including top litigators who spend part of their careers in private practice. Covert and Wang (2020) argue that the office is the most influential litigant that appears before the Supreme Court, and it initiates many cases that it expects to win in part because it has earned a reputation as the "tenth justice." In our sample, the solicitor general's office wins the majority, 62 percent, of its cases.

The office also provides an opportunity to explore whether it faces resource constraints because its performance can be evaluated on a relatively clear and unambiguous metric: does the federal government win or lose a case before the U.S. Supreme Court. The fact that the same top litigators represent the government and the private sector before the Supreme Court during their careers offers a unique strategy to identify the interactive effect of the litigators' bounded rationality, the quality of their subordinates, and the work environment on the office's performance. More specifically, we identify a set of top advocate lawyers who have argued cases before the Supreme Court both as attorneys for the solicitor general's office and as private sector lawyers. *Ceteris paribus*, we contend that public sector–private sector differences in a top advocate's probability of winning a case reflect sector-based differences in organizational and personnel-based resource constraints, which affect their performance.

Several selectivity differences may arise when top advocates represent the public and the private sector at different times during their careers before the Supreme Court, including the relative difficulty of the cases, strength of the opposing counsel, ability to cherry-pick the easiest cases to win, and litigation experience before the court. We address those issues and show that they do not affect our identification strategy. Ultimately, we find that, holding observable case characteristics fixed, the same set of top Supreme Court advocate lawyers contribute significantly to winning a case when they are working for the private sector, but they have no effect on winning a case when they are working for the public sector.

We attempt to explain our finding quantitatively by first estimating enriched models that control for differences in the quality of the public top advocate's legal support, the quality of the opposing private sector lead attorney and the law firm, and the difficulty of the case, but our findings are robust to those controls. We then estimate additional models that provide evidence of resource constraints by assessing the performance of the top advocate in government for the most important government cases, which we characterize as cases where the private sector is either represented by a top advocate or by an attorney from an elite law school. In those cases, we find that the top advocates contribute significantly to the government winning—in fact, they perform just as well as the top advocates perform when representing the private sector entity.

Of course, it may not be socially desirable for the U.S. government to win all its cases before the Supreme Court. However, it is reasonable to assume that the government's litigation before the court attempts to enhance the public welfare; thus, the ineffectiveness of top advocates who represent the government— even if this occurs in less important cases—constitutes government failure that should be of concern.

We suggest that failure in the solicitor general's office occurs because of constraints attributable to organizational design, which limit the time that a top government advocate can spend on a case, and constraints attributable to the workplace personnel and environment, which limit the support that a top advocate can receive. Those constraints, which do not arise when a top advocate works in the private sector and can focus on a single Supreme Court case, force top advocates representing the government to concentrate their efforts on and to receive additional resources for a few (important) cases where they perform well. Given the various jurisdictions, competing demands on their time and attention, and difficulty in regulating their workload, these top advocates have no effect on the outcome of other (albeit less important) cases where they face lower-quality private lawyers who are not top advocates.

FRAMEWORK AND SAMPLE

The effects of case characteristics and justice ideology on Supreme Court decision-making have been well documented by legal scholars and political scientists (George and Epstein 1992; Law and Zaring 2010). Less academic attention has been paid to the litigators themselves, although there is some evidence suggesting that the quality of legal representation can shape SCOTUS outcomes (Lazarus 2008). Thus, to assess the effects of top advocates on the outcomes of Supreme Court cases that involve the government, we employ the following simple specification:

$$Pr(W) = f(C, I, L), \tag{1}$$

where $Pr(W)$ is the probability that a SCOTUS case ruling favors the government instead of a private entity; C encapsulates the legal issues and ambiguities that underlie the case in question; I represents the preferences and ideologies of the justices hearing the legal dispute; and L captures differences in the quality of government and nongovernment legal representation, which we specify in terms of whether the government or the private entity is represented by a top Supreme Court advocate. We defined such advocates as: (1) presenting the oral arguments in the case, (2) arguing at least one case on behalf of the federal government and at least one case on behalf of a private entity in our sample of disputes, and (3) arguing at least twenty cases before the Supreme Court by 2010.[2]

We stress that the same top advocates in our sample represent the government and a private entity before the Supreme Court at different times, but not at systematically different times in their careers, as we show below. If the same top advocates represented the government and a private entity at systematically different stages of their career paths (for example, they represented the government earlier in their career), that could explain why the same top advocates perform less effectively when they represent the government than when they represent the private sector.

By focusing on lawyers who have represented both government and nongovernment clients, we are able to observe how the same top Supreme Court advocates perform in public and private sector workplace environments. Holding case and justice characteristics constant, any systematic differences in those advocates' influences on Supreme Court case outcomes suggest that there are critical differences in the quality of government and private sector lawyers who provide support to the top advocates; institutional differences in the private and government sector organizations that either hamper or enhance the performance of high quality lawyers; and/or institutional differences in the private and government workplace environments that either hamper or enhance the performance of high-quality lawyers. The second and third explanations are related to the first because the government and the private sector may have to attract lawyers of higher quality to offset any competitive disadvantages that are attributable to unfavorable aspects of their organization and work environments.

We estimate the specification in equation (1) as a binary probit using a sample of cases drawn from the well-known Supreme Court Database. Originally created by Harold Spaeth and a team of political scientists and lawyers in the 1980s, this unique dataset (hereafter referred to as the Spaeth Database) provides detailed information on the legal characteristics and outcomes of each Supreme Court case decided between 1946 and 2012 (Spaeth et al. 2013).

Our sample consists of all modern (1980 to 2012) split-decision Supreme Court cases that pitted the federal government against private entities.[3] In our base case analysis, we exclude unanimously decided cases because we expected

lawyer performance to matter little in disputes that are judged to be legally unambiguous, and evidence exists that unanimous decisions serve as markers for
cases with strong legal precedent (Epstein, Landes, and Posner 2012). (We do
find in a robustness check that our findings are not affected when we include all
of the unanimously decided cases.) Our definition of the "federal government"
relied upon Spaeth's classification of different types of petitioners and respondents and included a broad array of federal agencies, departments, bureaus, and
commissions.[4] We considered any party that is not affiliated with the federal
government or a state to be a "private entity."[5] Finally, we limited our sample to
cases in which the Supreme Court heard an oral argument, because the links between lawyer performance and case outcomes are likely to be strongest in those
types of disputes (Black et al. 2011; Johnson, Wahlbeck, and Spriggs 2006).[6]

To control for the legal characteristics of a case, we included twelve issue-area
dummy variables, which have been used extensively by political scientists and
legal scholars (see, for instance, Lauderdale and Clark 2012). The indicators,
which are derived from preconstructed variables in the Spaeth Database, group
disputes into mutually exclusive categories based on the Supreme Court's own
statements regarding the main substantive legal questions and matters of a case.
The twelve substantive issue areas observed in our dataset are: criminal procedure, civil rights, First Amendment, due process, privacy, attorneys, unions,
economic activity, judicial power, federalism, federal taxation, and miscella-
neous. Thus, the issue-area dummies control for the possibility that certain of
those legal arenas are more likely to favor progovernment outcomes than others.

We also included an indicator for whether the federal government is the
petitioner in a case. The side that brings the case to the Supreme Court is identified as the petitioner, and while the petitioner considers the facts of the case
and the rulings of a lower court, the petitioner is also more likely to bring a case
that it expects to win. Thus, the petitioner dummy variable controls for the fact
that, within a legal issue area (for example, criminal law), the government may
appropriately expect that certain cases are harder to win than others.

We account for the ideological makeup of justices by controlling for a full set
of "natural court" dummies that indicated periods of time during which there
were no changes to the Supreme Court bench.[7] We were therefore able to account for both the ideological composition of the court and any changes in overall court attitudes toward government that might arise from justice turnover.[8]

Finally, we constructed our top Supreme Court advocate dummy variables
using two datasets. First, we identified Supreme Court lawyers who argued at
least twenty times before the Supreme Court using data published by Bhatia

(2012). Specifically, Bhatia ranked recent SCOTUS lawyers according to the number of cases they had argued between 2000 and 2010, as well as provided lifetime numbers of Supreme Court appearances for each of those lawyers. We then used data published by the Oyez Project—a multimedia archive of all Supreme Court cases heard since 1946—to identify which petitioners and which respondents in our sample of split-decision cases were represented by one of the top Supreme Court advocates.

Note that the construction of the top advocate dummy variables is based only on cases between the government and the private sector that the top attorneys argued before the Supreme Court throughout their careers, not on all of the cases that they have argued. However, the designation of top advocate does not depend on the outcome of a particular Supreme Court case or even cases; instead, it ultimately depends on the myriad of factors that enable a lawyer to acquire the reputation as a distinguished attorney who has earned a partnership in the appellate practice of a leading law firm that represents clients' wishes before the court and who has received an offer to head the Office of the Solicitor General.

Identification

It is useful to raise and address some immediate concerns that may prevent us from identifying the effect of a top advocate in government and in the private sector on Supreme Court case outcomes. First, it is known that lawyers often gain Supreme Court exposure as government litigators (Bhatia 2012); thus, it is possible that top advocates' career paths may show advancement from the solicitor general's office, where they gain experience, to working in private law firms that engage in high-stakes litigation before the Supreme Court. If so, our measures of top advocates representing the government and the private sector could largely capture career advancement as a litigator. However, table 6-1 reports the years that top attorneys represented the federal government in our sample of cases, and it does not show a clear pattern of government work preceding private-firm litigation. Moreover, many of the top advocates spent a number of years working in the private sector before assuming prominent litigant roles in the federal government.[9] Accordingly, the top advocates do not have systematically different levels and types of experience when they represent the government in cases before the Supreme Court compared with when they represent the private sector in cases before the court. Finally, we conducted statistical robustness tests that assessed whether top advocates who began their career in government gained an advantage in the probability of winning a case, as well as whether previous experience representing the other side helped top advocates gain an advantage in the probability of winning a case. The tests indicated that our main findings were robust to those considerations.

Second, it is possible that there are unobserved variables that may affect the case outcome and whether a top advocate works on a case in the private or public sector. For example, it could be argued that elite attorneys at private law

TABLE 6-1. Career Trajectories of Top Supreme Court Advocates

Top Advocate[a]	Years in Federal Government	Years out of Federal Government
Andrew J. Pincus	1985, 1986, 1987	2008
Carter G. Phillips	1981, 1983	1992, 1995, 1999, 2008, 2011
Charles A. Rothfeld	1984, 1985, 1986, 1987	2007, 2009
Donald B. Verrilli	2011, 2012	2002
Gregory G. Garre	2002, 2003, 2007, 2008	2011
John G. Roberts Jr.	1989, 1990	1989
Maureen E. Mahoney	1991, 1992	1993, 1998, 2006, 2008
Patricia A. Millet	2002, 2004, 2005	2009
Paul D. Clement	2001, 2002, 2003, 2004, 2005, 2006, 2007	2011
Stephen M. Shapiro	1980	2004
Theodore B. Olson	2001, 2002, 2003	1995, 2008, 2009

Note: Table shows the years in which a top advocate argued at least one of the Supreme Court cases in our analysis sample. Thus, the table does not list an advocate's total number of years of government and nongovernment service but rather lists the years in our sample of cases in which the lawyer argued on behalf of the government or a nongovernment entity.

[a] The government positions held by these top advocates are as follows: Andrew J. Pincus (Assistant to the Solicitor General); Carter G. Phillips (Assistant to the Solicitor General); Charles A. Rothfeld (Assistant to the Solicitor General); Donald B. Verrilli (Associate Deputy Attorney General, Solicitor General); Gregory G. Garre (Assistant to the Solicitor General, Principal Deputy Solicitor General, Solicitor General); John G. Roberts, Jr. (Special Assistant to the Attorney General and Principal Deputy Solicitor General); Maureen E. Mahoney (Deputy Solicitor General); Patricia A. Millet (Assistant to the Solicitor General); Paul D. Clement (Principal Deputy Solicitor General, Acting Solicitor General, Solicitor General); Stephen M. Shapiro (Assistant to the Solicitor General); Theodore B. Olson (Assistant Attorney General, Solicitor General).

firms intentionally avoid hard cases in order to improve their win-loss record. However, attorneys representing the private sector will appeal a case to the Supreme Court if their client is willing to pay for the service, and they will try to get the best outcome for the case.

The government is more careful than the private sector about the cases that it brings before the Supreme Court because it plans to bring many cases and does not want to lose credibility by setting a precedent of bringing weak cases. Thus top advocates may have more flexibility in their case selection when they represent the government than when they represent the private sector, but their balancing of precedent and the pressure to defend certain statues makes it hard for them to avoid difficult cases.

Finally, it is important to bear in mind that the Supreme Court agrees to hear less than 1 percent of case petitions that are brought before it. Given those odds, it is difficult to envision a scenario in which the court's selection of petitions enables top advocates in either the public or the private sector to consistently "cherry pick" the easiest cases to win.

Description of the Sample

Table 6-2 presents a descriptive overview of the 527 split-decision cases that constitute our sample. Criminal procedure cases account for more than one-third of the court's cases, while cases involving civil rights and economic activities combine to account for another 25 percent of the cases; thus, those three issue areas account for more than 60 percent of the court's split-decision cases. The nine remaining issue areas each account for less than 10 percent of the total cases. Win margins for most cases cluster around one, three, five, and seven votes. The outcomes of nearly a third of those cases hinge on the vote of a single justice.[10]

Turning to case outcomes, the government is represented before the Supreme Court by the solicitor general's office, with the solicitor general, deputy solicitors general, and assistants to the solicitor general involved in preparing and arguing cases.[11] Our sample indicates that the government wins more than 60 percent of its cases. Taking a closer look at the data, the federal government is the petitioner in about half of the cases in the sample and wins 67 percent of those cases, which is consistent with the advantage that we claimed that the government has when it is the petitioner. It is interesting that in 10 percent of the cases, the lead government attorney is a top advocate yet the government wins slightly fewer of those cases, 60 percent, than it wins over all of its cases,

TABLE 6-2. Characteristics of Split-Decision Government versus Private Cases

Case Issue Area	
Criminal Procedure	37%
Civil Rights	14%
First Amendment	9%
Due Process	3%
Privacy	2%
Attorneys	1%
Unions	5%
Economic Activity	10%
Judicial Power	9%
Federalism	1%
Federal Taxation	8%
Miscellaneous	1%

Case Outcomes	
Win Margin	
1 Vote	31%
2 Votes	4%
3 Votes	25%
4 Votes	4%
5 Votes	20%
6 Votes	2%
7 Votes	14%
Government Wins	62%
Government is the Petitioner	52%
Government Wins when it is the Petitioner	67%
Federal Government Attorney is a Top Advocate	10%
Government Wins when its Attorney is a Top Advocate	60%
Private Sector Wins when it is the Petitioner	45%
Private Sector Attorney is a Top Advocate	4%
Private Sector Wins when its Attorney is a Top Advocate	80%
Number of Cases	527

62 percent. This suggests that the Office of the Solicitor General gives the most difficult cases to its best lawyers; we explore that interpretation empirically after we present our initial findings.

In contrast to the government, the private sector wins a much smaller share of its cases when it is the petitioner, 45 percent; however, although it is represented by a top advocate in fewer of its cases, 4 percent, it wins 80 percent of them, more than double its overall win rate. Thus, our sample indicates that the advantage of being a petitioner in a case before the Supreme Court is much greater for the government than it is for the private sector, which is at variance with the well-known Priest and Klein (1984) finding that plaintiffs have roughly a 50 percent success rate,[12] and that top advocates are more likely to be on the winning side when they represent the private sector than when they represent the government.[13] We now explore top advocates' causal effects on the case outcome depending on the side they represent.

FINDINGS

Table 6-3 presents estimates of the Supreme Court case outcome probit model.[14] The top advocate dummies for the same set of attorneys have striking effects.[15] Specifically, we find that the chances of a government win are substantially reduced when its private rivals are represented by a top Supreme Court advocate.[16] In fact, our findings indicate that, on average, private respondents who hire a top advocate can completely offset any advantages that the federal government gains by virtue of being a petitioner in a case.[17] In contrast, when those same lawyers bring their skills to represent the federal government, their effects on the probability of a government win are quantitatively negligible and statistically insignificant.[18] Thus, although the public sector wins more than half the time, primarily because it is the petitioner in more than half of its cases and because it has advantages in certain issue areas,[19] top Supreme Court advocates are more effective as private attorneys than as government litigators. Given the relative sample sizes of the top advocate lawyers representing the government and the private sector, the credibility of our finding is strengthened further.[20]

Basic Robustness Tests

We conducted some basic tests to explore the robustness of our main findings about the effectiveness of top advocates when they represent the government and the private sector. First, we controlled for a top advocate's career path by

TABLE 6-3. Probit Model of a Government Win in
a Split-Decision U.S. Supreme Court Case

	Coefficient (Robust SE)
Case Topic Dummies	Yes
Natural Court Dummies	Yes
Petitioner Is Federal Government (1 = yes; 0 = no)	0.327 (0.1218)
Federal Government Attorney Is Top Advocate (1 = yes; 0 = no)	0.0220 (0.200)
Private Attorney Is Top Advocate (1 = yes; 0 = no)	−0.676 (0.299)
Constant	−1.561 (0.784)
Sample Size	527
Pseudo R-squared	0.082

Note: 1= Government wins case; 0 = Government loses case.

including dummy variables in the baseline model that indicated whether a top advocate began his or her career in the government. However, the dummy variables were statistically insignificant, and their inclusion had little effect on the original estimates of the top advocate dummy variables and their precision. Thus, beginning one's career in government did not appear to help top advocates win cases whether they represented the government or the private sector. Second, we controlled for experience representing the other side by including dummy variables in the baseline model that indicated whether a case was the first case the top advocate argued for the government (or private sector) after having spent the earlier part of his or her career representing the private sector (or government). Those dummy variables were also statistically insignificant, and their inclusion had little effect on the original estimates of the top advocate dummy variables and their precision. Finally, we constructed a variable for experience as the year the case was argued minus the year a top advocate obtained a J.D. However, the experience variables for top advocates representing the private sector and the federal government were apparently highly collinear and could not be used to enrich the specification.

As an additional robustness test, we re-estimated our baseline specification and included the 380 unanimously decided cases. Recall, we excluded such cases because we expected lawyers' performance to matter little in disputes that are judged to be legally unambiguous. In any case, our initial conclusions were not affected by the larger sample, because the magnitude of the private attorney top advocate coefficient slightly increased and the magnitude of the federal government top advocate coefficient slightly decreased.

Assessing Some Natural Explanations

What explains the relatively lower effectiveness of the top Supreme Court lawyers when they work for the government? Certainly, top advocates have very similar incentives to win regardless of which sector they represent because they want to enhance their reputation as successful advocates in cases that are highly visible and have large stakes. Moreover, it does not appear that a private party in a Supreme Court case is likely to significantly outspend the federal government because the relatively shorter duration of Supreme Court cases generally requires fewer lawyers and less research than other cases require, and because law firms typically charge far less to handle an entire Supreme Court case than they charge to handle other cases.[21] In some instances, law firms provide pro bono Supreme Court service for state and local governments.[22]

We would also argue that the findings do not reflect unobserved differences in the difficulty of cases being argued by top attorneys in the private and public sectors. Drew S. Days III (1994–1995), for example, points out that a long-standing tradition of respect has developed for the solicitor general's independence within the entire executive branch, meaning that the president does not pressure top attorneys in the solicitor general's office to select and argue cases for political and other reasons that would be especially difficult to win.[23] As an empirical test, we operationalized "harder" SCOTUS cases as those with a smaller win margin (that is, the number of majority votes minus the number of dissenting votes) and we found that case difficulty was only weakly correlated with whether the case was argued by a top attorney in either sector. This finding suggests that sector-based differences in case difficulty are not driving our results. We perform an additional test of the potential importance of case difficulty in explaining our findings below.

The Relative Quality of Opposing Attorneys and Case Difficulty

Top advocates may perform worse in government than they do in the private sector because they face stronger legal competitors in the private sector. Thus, we perform estimations where we control for the quality of the attorneys in the private sector that top advocates in the public sector face and for the quality of the attorneys in the public sector that the top advocates in the private sector face.

We present the estimation results of four different models in table 6-4. Model (1) expands our original specification to include the following five variables that measure attorney quality: (a) whether the private attorney who argued the case is or was employed by a top 200 law firm, as measured by gross annual revenue;[24] (b) whether the private attorney who argued the case graduated from a top 5 law school,[25] as ranked by the 2016 *U.S. News and World Report* survey;[26] (c) whether the federal government attorney graduated from a top 5 law school; (d) the total number of SCOTUS cases argued by the federal government attorney; and (e) the total number of SCOTUS cases argued by the private attorney.[27]

To provide additional supportive evidence to our previous discussion about the difficulty or legal ambiguity of a case, we also control for the case's win margin.[28] In particular, large win margins—for example, 8-1 decisions or 7-2 decisions—may signal relatively clear-cut cases, while small win margins—for example, 5-4 decisions—may indicate cases that both sides find challenging to argue. Of course, the win margin may be endogenous because it likely reflects both the innate ambiguity of the case and the legal efforts and resources of the opposing parties; thus, we did not include this control in our main specification.

We find that the additional controls do not affect our basic findings about the performance of the top advocates in government and in the private sector, as the effect of the former remains small and statistically insignificant and the effect of the latter is even larger and remains statistically significant. Two of the additional controls are statistically significant in Model (1): government attorneys who have argued more SCOTUS cases are *less likely* to win,[29] while larger win margins are associated with greater likelihoods of a federal government victory. The sign of win margins indicates that the government is more likely to win easier cases and less likely to win more difficult (closely decided) cases. We argue below that the government is resource constrained; thus, this finding is plausible given that more difficult cases are likely to require more resources. The sign on the government SCOTUS variable is unexpected—and it may re-

TABLE 6-4. Robustness Checks

	(1)	(2)	(3)	(4)
Case Topic Dummies	Yes	Yes[a]	Yes[a]	Yes[a]
Natural Court Dummies	Yes	Yes[a]	Yes[a]	Yes[a]
Petitioner Is Federal Government (1 = yes; 0 = no)	0.358 (0.124)	0.729 (0.321)	0.373 (0.235)	0.196 (0.221)
Federal Government Attorney Is Top Advocate (1 = yes; 0 = no)	0.0384 (0.198)	0.428 (0.471)	0.356 (0.395)	0.262 (0.439)
Private Attorney Is Top Advocate (1 = yes; 0 = no)	-1.112 (0.441)	-0.943 (0.408)	-1.463 (0.5185)	-0.680 (0.312)
Private law firm Is a Top 200 Law Firm (1 = yes; 0 = no)	-0.0422 (0.177)			
Federal Government Attorney Graduated from Top 5 Law School (1 = yes; 0 = no)	-0.121 (0.135)			
Private Attorney Graduated from Top 5 Law School (1 = yes; 0 = no)	0.0786 (0.139)			
Number of SCOTUS Cases Argued by Federal Government Attorney	-0.00323 (0.00161)			
Number of SCOTUS Cases Argued by Private Attorney	0.00952 (0.00680)			
Win Margin	0.0614 (0.0281)			
Constant	-1.862 (0.831)	-0.138 (0.573)	0.243 (0.750)	-0.510 (0.578)
Sample Type	Full Sample	Cases argued by top-200 law firms	Cases argued by private attorneys who graduated from a top 5 law school	Cases argued by private attorneys who have argued at least three cases before SCOTUS
Sample Size	527	95	142	150
Pseudo R^2	0.0974	0.227	0.127	0.0989

Notes: Parameter estimates are from probit regressions. Dependent variable is 1 if the government wins the case and 0 otherwise. Robust standard errors are in parentheses.

[a] Some case topic and natural court dummies were collapsed due to small sample sizes.

flect the allocation of more difficult cases to more senior government attorneys. That is, tougher cases get assigned to more experienced government lawyers, but this significant effect may be driven by outliers. Indeed, when we log both government and private SCOTUS variables, the government SCOTUS variable becomes statistically insignificant.

An interesting feature of the additional controls is that they indicate that in our sample of cases, lawyers with less experience arguing before the Supreme Court and who graduated from lower-ranked law schools represent the private sector more often than they represent the government. For example, the share of attorneys in each sector arguing before the Supreme Court who graduated from a top 5 law school was 65 percent for federal government attorneys but only 25 percent for private attorneys. If the caliber of non-top attorneys who present SCOTUS oral arguments were higher in the solicitor general's office than in private law firms, then the value-added of having a top attorney argue a SCOTUS case would be smaller in government than in the private sector.

Thus, models (2) to (4) in table 6-4 attempt to raise the quality of the average private sector lawyer and show that our results are not the product of the private sector having lower-quality lawyers, on average, than the public sector. Specifically, model (2) shows parameter estimates of our initial specification for the ninety-five cases in which the private attorney came from a top 200 law firm; model (3) shows parameter estimates of that specification for a subsample of cases in which the private attorney arguing the case graduated from a top 5 law school; and model (4) shows parameter estimates of that specification for a subsample of cases in which the private attorney argued at least three cases before the Supreme Court. Note that in roughly 72 percent of our full sample of cases, the private sector attorney had argued two or fewer SCOTUS cases; thus, the model (4) sample is limited to the top quarter of private sector attorneys, as measured by total number of SCOTUS arguments. Thus, in all of those models, the quality of the average private sector lawyer has greatly improved. Yet, we continue to find that when top Supreme Court advocates represent the government, they do not have a statistically significant effect on the probability of the government winning a case, but when the same top advocates represent the private sector, they have a large and statistically significant effect on the probability of the government losing a case.

ORGANIZATIONAL AND PERSONNEL CONSTRAINTS
ON GOVERNMENT PERFORMANCE

The solicitor general's office is chartered by law to conduct virtually all litigation in the Supreme Court on behalf of the United States and federal agencies. As noted, the office is not pressured by the executive branch to select and argue cases for political and other reasons that would be especially difficult to win. And it has been able to attract staff lawyers with strong law school records, clerkships with noted judges, and often some experience at an elite law firm (Schwartz 1988).[30] But from an organizational and personnel economics perspective, the solicitor general's office is shaped by rules that constrain its resources and potentially compromise the performance of top advocates when they work for the office.

Organizational Constraints

The top Supreme Court advocates in our sample worked in the solicitor general's office as a solicitor general, deputy solicitors general, or assistants to the solicitor general (table 6-1). Compared to their work in the private sector when they can focus on a single Supreme Court case, the top advocates in government have multiple jurisdictions, face competing demands on their time and attention, and are likely to find it more difficult to regulate their workload.

   Springer (1984) reports that Supreme Court justices say that briefs matter a great deal more than oral arguments in influencing the outcome of a case. He further argues that good briefs are written by experienced and knowledgeable individuals, not by committees or assembly lines. Thus, top advocates in the solicitor general's office must take primary responsibility for their briefs; at the same time, however, the organizational design—the office is small and its attorneys currently include the solicitor general, four deputies, and seventeen other attorneys—prevents the top advocates from working only on cases in their specialty.[31] Consequently, top advocates in government may not have deep knowledge of the issues in a particular Supreme Court case, whereas when they are in the private sector, they can work in their area of specialization and, if necessary, they can get assistance from an experienced partner at their law firm who is also likely to have deep knowledge about the particular issue at hand.

Workplace Constraints

The top advocates in government are supported by (generally high-quality) staff attorneys in the solicitor general's office. But those lawyers also have to work in a variety of issue areas and they may not have had the opportunity to develop deep knowledge of the issues in any particular Supreme Court case. Moreover, civil service hiring regulations prevent the office from quickly hiring more lawyers when a top advocate's workload significantly expands, or from quickly terminating a government lawyer whose performance is not adequate and finding a suitable replacement in a timely fashion.[32] Top advocates in government can rely on lawyers from other government agencies, but the quality of those lawyers may vary.

An important factor that militates against specialization is the relatively rapid turnover of staff lawyers within the solicitor general's office, primarily due to low salaries relative to those offered in the private sector (McGinnis 1992).[33] Although a handful of lawyers are committed to a career in the office, the majority stay roughly three years before moving on (Schwarz 1988). Such turnover may also undermine cohesion and overall performance, as well as result in a long-term mismatch between organizational demands and employee skillsets—a mismatch that is likely to persist because civil service rules make it difficult to terminate an employee.

In sum, top advocates in government face organizational and workplace resource constraints on aligning their caseload with their area of specialization and on the assistance that they can receive from their staff. We hypothesize that as a rational response to those constraints, the top advocates attempt to enhance the public interest by focusing their attention on the most important Supreme Court cases involving the government at the expense of their performance on less important cases.

Empirical Evidence of Resource Constraints

It is difficult for us to measure notable changes in the solicitor general's office when it is litigating a case before the Supreme Court that it believes involves large stakes and is potentially of great importance to the nation. However, it is likely that the private sector would be represented in such a case by either a top advocate, as defined here, or by an attorney who graduated from an elite law school. We therefore identified the most important cases in our sample as those for which the private attorney arguing before the court is (the number of cases where this occurs and the government is represented by a top advocate is given in brackets): (1) a top Supreme Court advocate {3}, or (2) is not a top Supreme Court advocate but graduated from a top 5 {19} or top 3 {17} law school.[34] This procedure captures high profile cases such as the Affordable Care Act suit[35] and the litigation over the Federal Communications Commission's ban on the use of obscene language on television broadcasts.[36]

Our empirical test of resource constraints in the solicitor general's office is whether the contribution by top government advocates to winning important Supreme Court cases is comparable to the contribution by top private advocates to winning those cases. If so, that would constitute empirical evidence that top government advocates allocate their and their staff's scarce resources to put the government in the best position to win the most important cases before the court. As a side effect, however, the top government advocates do not influence the outcome of the government's less important cases because they spend less time and resources on them.

Table 6-5 presents three models that capture the results of our empirical tests. Model (1) interacts the private and public top advocate dummies and shows that while the top government advocate dummy remains small and statistically insignificant, the interaction term is large and positive, although the large standard error indicates that the true parameter value could be considerably higher or lower. In any case, the model suggests that while top advocates do not increase the chances of a government win in cases that *do not* involve top private sector advocates, they do increase the chances of a government win in cases that involve top private sector advocates, which may indicate a case of great national importance. The estimate of the interaction effect, however, raises questions about the sign of the effect of the private top advocate, so it is useful to explore our other indicators of an important case.[37]

Models (2) and (3) interact the top government advocate dummy with: (a) a dummy for whether the private attorney graduated from a top 5 law school, and (b) a dummy for whether the private attorney graduated from a top 3 law school.[38] In both models, the interaction term is positive and large, and the statistical significance of the estimate improves as the criterion for being a top private attorney, thereby signaling an important case, becomes more stringent. Taken together, the models confirm that the value added of a top government advocate is greater for cases involving higher-quality private attorneys. In particular, estimates of model (3) indicate that when a top advocate in government competes against a private attorney from a top 3 law school, he or she has a positive impact of helping the government win the case (measured by combining

TABLE 6-5. Evidence of Resource Constraints

	(1)	(2)	(3)
Case Topic Dummies	Yes	Yes	Yes
Natural Court Dummies	Yes	Yes	Yes
Petitioner Is Federal Government[a]	0.325	0.344	0.335
	(0.122)	(0.122)	(0.122)
Federal Government Attorney Is Top Advocate[a]	−0.0536	−0.210	−0.220
	(0.200)	(0.237)	(0.233)
Private Attorney Is Top Advocate[a]	−0.944	−0.721	−0.727
	(0.330)	(0.304)	(0.303)
Top Government Advocate and Top Private Advocate[a]	1.519		
	(0.984)		
Private Attorney Graduated from Top 5 Law School[a]		0.0220	
		(0.145)	
Government Attorney Top Advocate AND Private Attorney from Top 5 School[a]		0.7074	
		(0.440)	
Private Attorney Graduated from Top 3 Law School[a]			−0.0236
			(0.163)
Government Attorney Top Advocate AND Private Attorney from Top 3 School[a]			0.897
			(0.459)
Constant	−1.549	−1.608	−1.605
	(.795)	(0.793)	(0.788)
Sample Size	527	527	527
Pseudo R2	0.0864	0.0867	0.0880

Notes: Parameter estimates are from probit regressions. Dependent variable is 1 if the government wins the case and 0 otherwise. Robust standard errors are in parentheses. The government and the private party were represented by a top advocate in three cases. Of the cases where the government was represented by a top advocate, the private party was represented by a graduate of a top 3 school in seventeen cases and by a graduate of a top 5 school in nineteen cases.

a. 1 = yes; 0 = no.

coefficients 0.897–0.220 = 0.677). But that positive impact is offset if the private attorney is also a top advocate (coefficient of –0.727).[39] At the same time, top government advocates do not appear to perform any better than non-top advocate government attorneys on cases involving non-top advocate private sector lawyers. The findings therefore suggest that top government advocates concentrate their own and the office's resources on a subset of the most important cases.

Importantly, the results do not appear to be driven by differences in the quality of non-top government attorneys who go up against top and non-top private sector attorneys. That is, the presence of a positive top government advocate effect for cases involving high-quality private attorneys and a negligible top government advocate effect for cases involving lower-caliber private attorneys is not because the average quality of non-top government attorneys is less in cases involving higher-quality private attorneys.[40] Similarly, there is no reason to expect that the quality of lawyering matters less for cases involving higher-quality private sector lawyers.[41]

POTENTIAL IMPLICATIONS OF THE FINDINGS

The U.S. Office of the Solicitor General can attract one of the best workforces in the federal government, which is comprised of a large fraction of attorneys who graduated from the best law schools in the country. In its representation of the federal government, the office was in our sample the petitioner in more than half of the cases before the Supreme Court, and the government won more than 60 percent of its cases. Nonetheless, we have provided evidence that the office's organizational and personnel resource constraints have caused top Supreme Court advocates who were working for the government to focus their energies on the most important cases, which has negated their effect compared with non-top government attorneys on the outcomes of less important cases.[42] Because any case before the Supreme Court is of some importance, the ineffectiveness of top advocates who represent the government in a large number of cases constitutes government failure that should be of some concern.

If important resource constraints exist at the Office of the Solicitor General, resource constraints are also likely to be a source for significant failures across the whole of government. For example, Frakes and Wasserman (2017) followed patent examiners throughout their careers and noted that as they are promoted, they are given other responsibilities that diminish the time that they can devote to patent examinations. The authors then found that as patent examiners are given less time to review patent applications, the average quality of the patents that they approved declined. Poor quality patents create a hostile climate for innovation because they are more likely to be challenged in court and because high levels of litigation depress venture capital investment (Tucker 2014).

In fact, departments and agencies are likely to be more compromised by resource constraints than the solicitor general's office because they are often led by individuals who were appointed for political reasons instead of for their knowledge and substantive accomplishments in a particular area of policy, whereas the office carries unique prestige within the legal profession and is able to attract more relatively qualified leaders than other parts of government are able to attract. In addition, other departments and agencies may be more affected by the constraints of the civil service system, especially the difficulty of firing an unsatisfactory employee, because they do not attract the (higher) quality of employees that the office attracts.

SUMMARY

Because of the significant role that lawyers play in the functioning and performance of the U.S. government, we have explored how government lawyers may be adversely affecting that performance. In the preceding chapter, we argued that the large government earnings penalty appears to have made it difficult for the government to attract the highest-quality lawyers. In this chapter, we have argued that even when the government is able to attract highly capable lawyers, the effectiveness of those lawyers may be reduced by the government's organizational and workplace constraints. In this case, the government is the source of the problem, but the outcome still reflects poorly on the legal profession's contribution to government performance. We turn in the next chapter to still another way that government lawyers may be adversely affecting government performance, which is partly attributable to the training and values of the legal profession—the increasing importance of ideology in Supreme Court decisions.

SEVEN

JUSTICE IDEOLOGY AND SUPREME COURT DECISIONS

The Supreme Court of the United States (SCOTUS) plays a central role in determining the nation's economic and social policies. In contrast to Congress and the Executive Office of the President, the Supreme Court is generally thought to be an independent and apolitical body because justices are appointed for life, are not ambitious for higher office, decide which cases they wish to hear, and are not subject to reversal by a higher court (Segal and Spaeth 2002). This perceived aloofness from politics has bolstered public trust in the court, and public opinion polls have repeatedly shown that of the three branches of government, Americans hold the judicial branch in the highest regard.

But perceptions of the Supreme Court are changing. Chemerinsky (2014), for instance, has characterized the justices in the two most recent courts—the Roberts court, named after Chief Justice John G. Roberts, and the Rehnquist court, named after Chief Justice William H. Rehnquist—as politicians in fine robes, who simply reflect the views of the president who appointed them. Although provocative, such claims are not without evidence. Legal scholars, for example, have pointed to the recent and precipitous rise in split-decision rulings as an indicator of the court's growing polarization and politicization.[1] Speculation that political ideology is increasingly influencing court rulings finds further support in the fact that the Roberts court has made more major decisions along partisan lines than have previous courts.[2]

The partisan politics that surrounded the confirmation of Justice Neil Gorsuch, following the passing of Justice Antonin Scalia, and the confirmation of Justice Brett Kavanaugh, following the retirement of Justice Anthony Kennedy, reflected the blurred line between law and politics. Then Senate Judiciary Committee Chairman Charles E. Grassley (R-Iowa) reinforced this view by claiming that the "confirmation process has gotten political precisely because the court has drifted from the constitutional text and rendered decisions based on policy preferences."[3] Senator Sheldon Whitehouse (D-Rhode Island) expressed dismay that such preferences had created a "crisis of credibility" at the U.S. Supreme Court, with the Roberts court showing an "undeniable pattern of political allegiance" by siding with the Republican political interest in seventy-three 5-4 decisions.[4]

After losing the 2018 midterm elections, President Trump said that the Republican Party "must always hold the Supreme Court," as if it were another branch of the legislature.[5] The passing of Justice Ruth Bader Ginsburg in September 2020 launched a bitter political battle over the timing of the confirmation hearings for her ultimate replacement, Amy Coney Barrett, on the court. Following Justice Barrett's rushed confirmation, the possibility was raised that the Democrats might attempt to "pack the court" to redress the imbalance if they had the opportunity to do so.

Finally, legal scholars have provided considerable circumstantial evidence indicating that ideology is increasingly shaping judicial behavior. Jacobi and Sag (2019) analyzed transcripts of SCOTUS oral arguments and concluded that since the late 1990s, justices were using those arguments more frequently to form ideological camps to comment on and question the side with whom they ultimately disagree. Rishikof, Messenger, and Jo (2009) showed that the justices' recent hiring of law clerks is occurring much more along party lines than in the past. Because those clerks play critical roles in selecting the petitions that the justices agree to hear and in drafting their opinions, the authors argued that such partisan hiring practices have contributed to the court's polarized environment. Bonica et al. (2019) find that law clerks exert modest influence on justices' voting overall but that they have substantial influence in cases that are high-profile, legally significant, or decided on close decisions.[6] And when former clerks argue as attorneys before the Supreme Court, Black and Owens (2020) find that they are 16 percent more likely to capture the vote of the justice they clerked for than an otherwise identical attorney who never clerked.

The theoretical explanation for why the justices' ideology is likely to be a potentially important influence on SCOTUS outcomes is that SCOTUS justices are appointed for life and their decisions are not subject to reversal by a higher court. As a result, those policymakers enjoy greater freedom than elected officials to allow their ideological preferences to influence their decisions. Posner (2008) also argues that because justices do not share a commitment to a logical premise for making a decision (for example, cost-benefit analysis), they are ideological because they cannot be anything else. Posner reinforces the point that the justices' ideological instincts are derived from the fact that they have been trained and gained work experience as lawyers, which, in all likelihood, intensifies instead of reduces the effect of other factors on their ideological instincts, such as the growing politicization of the appointment process.

Newly appointed Justice Barrett claimed that by adhering to the text of the U.S. Constitution and statutes enacted by Congress, she is following the "original meaning" of that text and not the meaning that she wishes it were. However, Sunstein (2020) argues that it is a myth to say that judges can always "apply the law as written" because when cases get to the Supreme Court, the original sources often leave gaps and ambiguities. If one examines the highlights of the voting record of the "originalist" Justice Scalia, they fit consistently with the views, if not, ideologies, of the Republican Party.

To be sure, if justices based their decisions solely on their ideologies, they could damage their reputations as fair justices, discredit the president who appointed them, and possibly undermine the court in the eyes of the public, which could lead to certain actions such as term limits or even retention elections (Rosen 2013). It seems likely, then, that ideology is an important but not the only factor shaping SCOTUS decision-making.

While the view that ideology influences SCOTUS outcomes is compelling, it is still an empirical question as to whether stronger ideological preferences are making the Roberts court more polarized than previous courts. Chief Justice Roberts has, himself, acknowledged the policy importance of this question, claiming that, if the court were to adopt the extreme partisanship that currently characterizes the other branches of the federal government, it would seriously damage SCOTUS's reputation among the public, as well as jeopardize the judicial nomination and confirmation process. Accordingly, Roberts has sought to assuage concerns that the court is functioning as a political entity by publicly pledging to embrace Chief Justice John Marshall's conception of the judicial branch as a nonpartisan steward in a polarized democracy.[7]

Kaplan (2018) points out that Roberts has become the swing vote with Justices Gorsuch and Kavanaugh joining the court, and that he has joined the liberal wing to defuse certain issues such as abortion and healthcare. However, concern still exists that partisan entrenchment on the court could lead to partisan entrenchment in other branches of government because of the court's ability to influence the electoral process (Bazelon 2018). Moreover, the recent appointment of Justice Barrett, a conservative, will significantly limit the ability of Justice Roberts to be a swing vote that attempts to curtail the court's partisanship.

Legal scholars who have attempted to determine systematically whether the Supreme Court is becoming more polarized under Chief Justice Roberts are divided. For example, Chemerinsky's (2008) assessment of the Roberts court after three years bemoans the new justices who have forged a "solid conservative voting majority" and concludes that the court is exceedingly probusiness, while Adler (2008) disagrees and says the court is only "moderately more conservative than it had been immediately before" and is not notably probusiness. Adler points out that the smaller number of case petitions that the Roberts court accepted during the period suggests caution should be exercised about making sweeping judgments about its ideological trajectory. Lee Epstein, Landes, and Posner (2013a) performed a statistical analysis of business cases and concluded that the conservatives on the Roberts court are extremely probusiness and that the liberals are only moderately liberal. Richard Epstein (2013) challenged their finding, stressing that the authors do not control for potential selectivity bias in the case petitions that the Roberts court accepts.

In this chapter, we explore the influences of justice ideology in the Roberts court by analyzing the determinants of its rulings and the Rehnquist court's rulings on business cases, controlling for the cases that those courts selected to hear. This issue is important because compared with rulings based on careful cost-benefit analysis, ideologically based rulings may be more influenced by experienced and effective legal advocates who represent business firms. In contrast, consumers are often not in a position to hire their own advocates but must depend on the government to represent them.

Business cases are useful to analyze because justices tend to have well-defined preferences toward business and the policies favored by most business interests, and their political ideology (liberal or conservative) can serve as a good proxy for those preferences, with conservative justices' doctrinal commitments making it more likely that they will make decisions that favor business firms and liberal justices' doctrinal commitments making it less likely that they will make decisions that favor business firms (Epstein, Landes, and Posner 2013a; Adler 2016). We isolate the effects of political ideology on judicial rulings by developing a joint mixed-logit model that accounts for both justice preference heterogeneity and the selection of petitions by SCOTUS.

Although it has long been argued that failure to control for case selectivity can bias analyses of court outcomes (Priest and Klein 1984), previous empirical studies of SCOTUS rulings have not formally incorporated case-selection decisions into an econometric analysis.[8] As a result, this chapter contributes to the broader study of SCOTUS decisionmaking by addressing a potentially critical, but largely ignored, source of estimation bias. In particular, a court with strong ideological preferences may mask or exacerbate those preferences by agreeing to hear more or fewer cases of a certain type (for example, politically divisive cases).

Epstein, Landes, and Posner (2013a) estimate a binary probit model of case outcomes and specify dummy variables for each justice to account for their ideology. We extend their model to account for potential selectivity bias by also estimating the justices' choices of cases to hear. Doing so turns out to require a complex econometric model because binary choice models are used to characterize both the selectivity behavior (petition selection) and the case outcome of interest (justices' individual rulings for or against a business entity), and because the selection error is correlated with the random coefficients in the case-outcomes model.[9] We argue that we are able to identify this joint model because variables, including monthly calendar dummies and docket size, capture the effects of exogenous resource constraints and idiosyncrasies in the court's schedule on the justices' petition-selection decisions but they do not affect the justices' voting tendencies on specific business cases, and they are unlikely to be correlated with unobserved influences on case-outcome votes.

We find that justices' ideologies have a statistically and quantitatively important influence on their rulings on business cases. Moreover, when we compare justices' ideological preferences in the Rehnquist court with those in the Roberts court and implement our methodology to control for case selection, we find strong evidence of growing politicization and polarity on the Supreme Court. This finding holds even when we confine our analyses to those justices who have served on both courts. In contrast, we obtain much weaker evidence on growing politicization and polarity if we do not control for case selection, indicating that the Roberts court's justices mute their ideological preferences through the petition-selection process; that is, they are more political on matters that the public cannot see. Supreme Court justices have not moderated their ideological preferences over the past two decades; instead, those preferences appear to have grown stronger and more divisive. We conclude by briefly discussing the explanations for the court's growing polarity.

AN OVERVIEW OF THE DETERMINANTS OF
PETITION SELECTION AND CASE OUTCOMES

Two extreme theories about judges' behavior exist (Edwards and Livermore 2009). The "legalist" theory asserts that judges mechanically apply the law to the facts, while the "political science" theory argues that a judge's political ideology has a predominant influence on his or her rulings.

Epstein, Landes, and Posner (2013b) suggest a middle ground wherein ideology is a component in judicial behavior that increases in influence as a judge moves up the judicial hierarchy and gains more independence. In this framework, however, ideology does not rule out other possible influences on judges' rulings. We draw on this third approach to model the court's selection of petitions to hear (that is, the decision to grant a petition a *writ of certiorari*, or "granting cert") and justice rulings on business-related cases that are heard by SCOTUS (that is, case-outcome votes). We provide an overview of the relevant influences and their measurement on those two decision junctures.

Case-Outcomes Model

Data on U.S. Supreme Court business case outcomes during the Rehnquist court and the Roberts court up through 2011 are available in Epstein, Landes, and Posner's (2013a) Business Litigant Dataset (BLD). This dataset consists of all cases that were orally argued before the U.S. Supreme Court and that involved a business entity as either a respondent or a petitioner, but not both. Because BLD was constructed using Harold Spaeth's well-known U.S. Supreme Court Database, it contains detailed information on the legal characteristics, history, and outcomes of Supreme Court disputes, as well as data on the votes of each justice (Spaeth et al. 2014). Due to petition data constraints that are discussed in greater detail below, we limit our case-outcomes analyses to the 198 business cases that were submitted to and heard by SCOTUS between 1996 and 2011. The Spaeth data classifies the substantive issues that are raised in Supreme Court cases into broad categories, with the category "economic activity" the most frequent but not the only category that is relevant for business cases. For example, the category "federal taxation" could characterize the substantive issues of a business case. We capture further differences in the content of business cases by using their categories when they are petitioned before the court.

Following Epstein, Landes, and Posner (2013a), we classify any vote in favor of the business litigant as "probusiness" and any vote in favor of the nonbusiness party as "antibusiness." Although it is possible for one company to win at the expense of the interests of the larger business community, this classification scheme is superior to alternative definitions of a "business win" because it is more transparent, relies less on the subjective coding judgments of the researcher, and allows for the analysis of a wider range of business-related cases.[10]

We estimate separate models for the Roberts and Rehnquist courts to determine the distinct ideological preferences of the justices on those courts. For each court, we initially follow Epstein, Landes, and Posner (2013a) by specifying the probability of a probusiness vote as a function of: (a) an indicator for each justice serving on the court, which captures the ideological preferences of that justice rather than the justice's legal "philosophy";[11] (b) an indicator of whether the lower court from which the case was appealed reached a probusiness ruling; (c) a series of dummy variables indicating whether the solicitor general filed an *amicus* brief on behalf of the business litigant or the nonbusiness litigant; (d) an indicator of whether the federal government was the nonbusiness party in the case; and (e) an indicator variable of whether the substantive issues of a case fall within the scope of Spaeth's "economic activity" category.

In an alternative set of specifications, we replace the individual justice indicators with a single ideology binary measure that identifies justices as either Conservative\Moderate or Liberal according to Epstein, Landes, and Posner's (2013b) classification system, which they explain in detail in chapter 2 of their book. Importantly, their methodology determines justices' ideologies based on their actual votes in cases, as opposed to the ideology of the president who appointed them. In addition, the ideological status of a justice does not change over time.

Finally, as robustness checks, we expanded the specification of the case-outcomes model to include: (f) eleven topical dummies that categorize petitions to the Supreme Court according to the main legal questions and substantive matters of the dispute, which can be used to differentiate between the subject matter of the business cases heard by the court;[12] and (g) a series of lower-court dummies, which are described in greater detail below.

Petition-Selection Model

In principle, there are two selection decisions that may be relevant for our analysis: the SCOTUS justices' selection of cases from the pool of lower-court appeals and the selectivity behavior of litigants to include their case in the pool of SCOTUS petitions. Assembling a data set and estimating a model of the petition decisions by litigants would be a very formidable task of questionable value to our analysis given that all litigants who lose at lower courts have the right to petition the Supreme Court to hear their case and that many business litigants take advantage of this right, especially because the cost to those litigants of submitting a petition is not high. Moreover, we are not aware of any theoretical or empirical evidence that there is any systematic bias in the cases that business litigants choose to appeal, and, given that we are comparing the Roberts court (2005–2011) to the latter half of the Rehnquist court (1996–2005), we limit the possibility that differences in the types of cases that make it into the SCOTUS pool of petitions are driving our results. In particular, it seems highly unlikely that the types of cases being processed by the lower courts during the end of the Rehnquist court are categorically different from those circulating through the lower courts during the Roberts court.

Thus, we focus on estimating the determinants of case selection by the Roberts and Rehnquist courts using the online Bloomberg BNA Supreme Court Today dataset.[13] The Bloomberg database contains a myriad of information on virtually all paid cert petitions filed with the Supreme Court between 1996 and 2011.[14] However, because the format of the database is not conducive to statistical analysis and data must be downloaded separately for each individual petition, we constructed a sample of 2,768 petitions that were randomly selected from the Bloomberg database.[15] In addition, the 198 cases in our Business Litigant Database that are used to estimate the case-outcomes model can be treated as a choice-based sample in estimating the petition-selection model.

Thus, although a petition generally has a very low probability of being accepted (see below), we can construct a sample that includes a much larger fraction of petitions that have been accepted. In addition, by combining the choice-based sample with the random sample of 2,768 petitions, we can improve the efficiency of the parameter estimates that are obtained by estimating only the random sample of petitions. Hence, we first estimate our model with the random sample and then combine it with the choice-based sample as a robustness check.

As noted, we are not aware of a previous Supreme Court petition-selection model that explains how the justices select petitions. Covert and Wang (2020) stress that the Office of the Solicitor General is the most influential litigant that appears before the court and is more successful at the petition stage than are other litigants; thus, it is important to control for the office's influence in a petition model.

Four justices must vote to accept a petition to hear a case, but the votes of individual justices to hear a case are generally not known. The court typically hears about 1 percent of the nearly nine thousand appeals that they receive each year.[16] Feldman and Kappner (2017) collected a large sample of petition decisions from 2001 to 2015 for descriptive purposes, but they did not estimate a model to explain those decisions.[17]

We reviewed the extant literature on the factors that are most relevant for explaining the justices' case-selection decisions and specified the probability that a petition is granted a hearing with the Supreme Court as a function of: (a) thirteen lower-court indicators and a reference category that identify the court system whose decision is being appealed;[18] (b) a lawyer quality dummy that indicates whether any of the lawyers filing the petition are "top Supreme Court advocates," which we define to be litigators who have argued at least ten cases before the Supreme Court by 2010 and who were found by Feldman and Kappner (2017) to generally have the highest cert-acceptance rates in their sample;[19] (c) a second lawyer performance dummy that identifies top Supreme Court advocates who were working as the U.S. solicitor general when the federal government filed the petition; (d) an indicator for whether the court invited the solicitor general to submit a brief analyzing the petition and expressing the views of the United States;[20] (e) a series of court-calendar dummies indicating whether the decision to grant or deny a petition was made during the court's summer recess, the May or June lists, or one of the seven argument sessions;[21] and (f) a count variable measuring the size of the Supreme Court's docket in a given year.[22]

ECONOMETRIC MODEL

The econometric model jointly estimates the determinants of case selection and case outcomes, with a particular focus on determining the effect of the ideological preferences of the Roberts and Rehnquist court justices on the outcomes of business-related cases, accounting for the nonrandom selection of petitions. Nontechnical readers can skip the derivation of the model and the discussion of our identifying assumptions and turn to the estimation results, where we present the descriptive data and the estimated parameters for the justices' ideological preferences.

Formally, we let g index the two courts, with $g = 1$ for the Rehnquist court and $g = 2$ for the Roberts court. For a given case i before court g, there are up to nine votes by the justices on that court. We let y_{ij} denote the vote of justice j on case i, with y_{ij} equal to 1 if the vote is probusiness and 0 otherwise. Thus, the justice case-outcomes vote under court g is given by the following binary response model:

$$y_{ij} = I\left(y_{ij}^{*} \equiv \alpha + \gamma_i^g D_j^L + \omega_i^g D_j^C + \mathbf{X}_i \mathbf{B}^g + e_{ij}^g > 0\right), \tag{1}$$

where $I(\cdot)$ is an indicator function that is equal to 1 if the inside argument is true and is equal to zero otherwise; D_j^L is a liberal (or moderate) L ideology and D_j^C is a conservative C ideology dummy for justice j; and $\mathbf{X}_i$ is a vector of exogenous influences on the case outcome discussed previously, $\mathbf{B}$ is a vector of parameters, and e is an error term.[23]

The justices' ideological preferences toward a case, captured by the parameters γ_i^g and ω_i^g, would be expected to vary across cases because cases have different characteristics, many of which are unobserved. Given that there are at most nine votes for a case, it is infeasible for us to use fixed effects by interacting case dummies with ideological dummies to control for the variation in the ideological preferences across cases. We therefore adopt a random-effects specification and model γ_i^g and ω_i^g as two correlated random coefficients; as noted later, the joint distribution of the two random coefficients can be correlated with the case-selection process because unobserved case characteristics may affect both ideological preferences and case selection. Importantly, this specification captures the influence of a justice on other justices with the same ideology.[24] A simpler specification that uses only justice fixed effects cannot capture this influence.

Because we include an intercept α in the specification, the mean of ω_i^g is normalized to zero and γ_i^g can be written as $\gamma_i^g = \bar{\gamma}^g + \eta_i^g$, where η_i^g denotes a random term with zero mean. Given this specification, the estimates of $\bar{\gamma}^g$ measure for a given court g the average probusiness bias of liberal or moderate justices compared with the probusiness bias of conservative justices.

Selectivity Bias

A probit or logit regression to estimate equation (1) suffers from sample-selection bias because estimation is based only on the cases that the Supreme Court agreed to hear and ignores the information provided by the cases that the court declined to hear. Let S_i denote the binary indicator for case selection, which is equal to 1 if case i is granted a hearing by the Supreme Court and 0 otherwise. Thus, the case-selection model under court g is specified as:

$$s_i = I\left(s_i^* \equiv \mathbf{Z}_i \boldsymbol{\delta}^g + v_i^g > 0\right), \tag{2}$$

where $\mathbf{Z}_i$ is a vector of observed exogenous influences on case selection discussed previously (some of which are not included in $\mathbf{X}_i$), $\boldsymbol{\delta}$ is a vector of parameters, and v is an error term.

Formally, the selectivity issue arises because we can observe a case outcome y_{ij} only when $s_i = 1$:

$$\Pr(y_{ij}=1|s_i=1)=\Pr(y_{ij}^*>0|s_i^*>0).\tag{3}$$

The random coefficients in equation (1), η_i^g and ω_i^g, are likely to be correlated with the error term, η_i^g, because unobserved case characteristics that affect case selection also affect how justices' preferences are revealed in the merits-ruling stage of the process. Thus, maximizing the log-likelihood of the unconditional probability $\Pr(y_{ij}^*>0)$ as a probit or logit estimation with random coefficients leads to inconsistent parameter estimates.

If we assume joint normality of η_i^g, ω_i^g and v_i^g, such that

$$\mathbf{\Gamma}_i\equiv\left(\eta_i^g,\omega_i^g\right)'=\mathbf{\theta}^g v_i^g+\mathbf{\mu}_i^g,\tag{4}$$

where $\mathbf{\mu}_i^g\sim N(0,\Sigma_{2\times2})$ and $v_i^g\sim N(0,1)$, and if the latent variable y_{ij}^* is observable, we can specify the conditional expectation function

$$E\left(y_{ij}^*|s_i=1\right)=\alpha+\bar\gamma^g D_j^L+\mathbf{X}_i\mathbf{B}^g+\mathbf{D}_j\times\mathbf{\theta}^g\times E\left(v_i|v_i>-\mathbf{Z}_i\mathbf{\delta}^g\right),\tag{5}$$

where $\mathbf{D}_j=\left(D_j^L,D_j^C\right)$. It would appear that equation (5) can be estimated to obtain consistent parameter estimates by the usual two-step control-function type approach (Heckman 1976): first estimate a probit selection model to obtain the inverse Mills ratio and then regress y_{ij}^* on the explanatory variables along with interactions of the inverse Mills ratio and the ideological dummies to control for the unobserved influences on selection. However, that approach cannot be applied here because we observe only the binary case outcome y_{ij}. Given the joint normality assumption in equation (4) and the condition given by equation (3), we have

$$P(y_{ij}=1|s_i=1)$$

$$=\int_{e_{ij}^g}\left[\int_{v_i^g}\left[\int_{u_i^g}I\!\left(e_{ij}^g>-\gamma^g D_j^L-\mathbf{X}_i\mathbf{B}^g-\left(\mathbf{D}_j v_i^g\right)\!\mathbf{\theta}^g-\mathbf{D}_j\mathbf{u}_i^g\right)f\!\left(\mathbf{u}_i^g\right)\!d\mathbf{u}_i^g\right]f\!\left(v_i^g|v_i^g>-\mathbf{Z}_i\mathbf{\delta}^g\right)\!dv_i^g\right]de_{ij}^g$$

$$\neq\int_{e_{ij}^g}\left[\int_{u_i^g}I\!\left(e_{ij}^g>-\gamma^g D_j^L-\mathbf{X}_i\mathbf{B}^g-\left(\mathbf{D}_j E\!\left(v_i^g|v_i^g>-\mathbf{Z}_i\mathbf{\delta}^g\right)\right)\!\mathbf{\theta}^g-\mathbf{D}_j\mathbf{u}_i^g\right)f\!\left(\mathbf{u}_i^g\right)\!d\mathbf{u}_i^g\right]de_{ij}^g\tag{6}$$

The last inequality is the result of Jensen's Inequality because the indicator function is nonlinear.

Because we cannot use the standard two-step approach to control for selectivity bias, we instead derive the joint distribution of the endogenous variables $P(\mathbf{y}_i,s_i)$, where $\mathbf{y}_i=(y_{i1},...,y_{i9})'$, and we estimate the parameters in equation (1) by Maximum Simulated Likelihood Estimation (MSLE). As noted, this appears to be the first application, to the best of our knowledge, of a methodology to correct for selectivity bias when both the selectivity and outcome equations are discrete. We extend this application to allow the selection error to be correlated with the random coefficients in the outcome model.

We identify the case-outcomes model with selectivity by assuming the distribution of η_i^g, ω_i^g and v_i^g is joint normal.[25] Dropping the court superscript to simplify the exposition yields:

$$
(v_i,\omega_i,\eta_i)' \sim MVN\left(\mathbf{0},\begin{bmatrix} 1 & \rho_1\sigma_\omega & \rho_2\sigma_\eta \\ \rho_1\sigma_\omega & \sigma_\omega^2 & \rho_3\sigma_\omega\sigma_\eta \\ \rho_2\sigma_\eta & \rho_3\sigma_\omega\sigma_\eta & \sigma_\eta^2 \end{bmatrix}\right) = MVN\left(\mathbf{0},\begin{bmatrix} 1 & \boldsymbol{\Omega}_{12} \\ \boldsymbol{\Omega}_{12}' & \boldsymbol{\Omega}_{22} \end{bmatrix}\right) = MVN(\mathbf{0},\boldsymbol{\Omega}); \quad (7)
$$

e_{ij} is assumed to have a logistic distribution with variance normalized to $\pi^2/3$.

To summarize, then, our econometric model consists of: two binary response models, a binary probit model of petition selection and a binary mixed-logit model of probusiness voting on cases selected by SCOTUS; a cross-model correlation that is represented by equation (7); correlations among different justices' votes on a case that are captured by random individual effects, ω_i and η_i, and their correlation; and justice ideological preferences that influence case outcomes that are allowed to vary, as indicated by equation (7), according to unobserved case characteristics that affect both case selection and case outcomes.

Deriving the Data Likelihood

After dropping the court superscript, we define $\mathbf{W}_i \equiv (\mathbf{X}_i, \mathbf{Z}_i)$ and $\boldsymbol{\Theta} \equiv (\bar{\gamma}, \mathbf{B}, \boldsymbol{\Omega}, \boldsymbol{\delta})$. For any case i in the Business Litigation Database, the complete data likelihood of voting outcomes $\mathbf{y}_i \equiv (y_{i1},...,y_{i9})'$ and case selection s_i is:

$$
P(\mathbf{y}_i, s_i | \mathbf{W}_i, \mathbf{D}_j, \boldsymbol{\Theta}) = P(\mathbf{y}_i | s_i = 1, \mathbf{W}_i, \mathbf{D}_j, \boldsymbol{\Theta}) P(s_i = 1 | \mathbf{Z}_i, \boldsymbol{\delta}). \quad (8)
$$

Note, we assume that $P(s_i = 1 | \mathbf{Z}_i, \boldsymbol{\delta}) = \Phi(\mathbf{Z}_i\boldsymbol{\delta})$, where $\Phi(\cdot)$ indicates the standard normal distribution function.

The conditional probability $P(\mathbf{y}_i | s_i = 1, \mathbf{W}_i, \mathbf{D}_j, \boldsymbol{\Theta})$ is given by

$$
\begin{aligned}
P(\mathbf{y}_i | s_i = 1, \mathbf{W}_i, \mathbf{D}_j, \boldsymbol{\Theta}) &= \int_{v_i} P(\mathbf{y}_i | s_i = 1, \mathbf{W}_i, \mathbf{D}_j, v_i, \boldsymbol{\Theta}) f(v_i | s_i = 1) dv_i \\
&= \int_{v_i} P(\mathbf{y}_i | s_i = 1, \mathbf{W}_i, \mathbf{D}_j, v_i, \boldsymbol{\Theta}) f(v_i | v_i > -\mathbf{Z}_i\boldsymbol{\delta}) dv_i \\
&= \int_{v_i}\left(\int_{\Gamma_i} P(\mathbf{y}_i | s_i = 1, \mathbf{W}_i, \Gamma_i, \mathbf{D}_j, v_i, \boldsymbol{\Theta}) f(\Gamma_i | v_i) d\Gamma_i\right) f(v_i | v_i > -\mathbf{Z}_i\boldsymbol{\delta}) dv_i \\
&= \int_{v_i}\left(\int_{\Gamma_i}\left[\prod_j P(y_{ij} | s_i = 1, \mathbf{W}_i, \Gamma_i, \mathbf{D}_j, v_i, \boldsymbol{\Theta})\right] f(\Gamma_i | v_i) d\Gamma_i\right) f(v_i | v_i > -\mathbf{Z}_i\boldsymbol{\delta}) dv_i
\end{aligned} \quad (9)
$$

where given our mixed logit specification, $P\big(y_{ij}\big|s_i = 1, \mathbf{W}_i, \mathbf{D}_i, \mathbf{D}_j, v_i, \mathbf{\Theta}\big)$ has a simple binary logit functional form. According to the specification (7), $f\big(\mathbf{\Gamma}_i\big|v_i\big)$ is a bivariate normal density. The density function $f\big(v_i\big|v_i > -\mathbf{Z}_i\mathbf{\delta}\big)$ is a truncated normal that is truncated below $-\mathbf{Z}_i\mathbf{\delta}$ (because $s_i = 1$). When sample selection is not correlated with the case-outcomes equation, the integration in (9) does not depend on v_i because $f\big(\mathbf{\Gamma}_i\big|v_i\big) = f\big(\mathbf{\Gamma}_i\big)$. In that case, the parameters in the case-outcomes equation can be estimated consistently by maximizing the log of the likelihood function defined in (9).

Estimation

We combine the Business Litigation Database on case outcomes, which is denoted by Ψ_{BLD}, with the Bloomberg data set on case petitions, which is denoted by Ψ_{BNA}, to estimate the parameters in $\mathbf{\Theta}$. The log of the data likelihood takes the following form:

$$
\ln L(\mathbf{\Theta}) = \sum_{i \in \Psi_{BLD}} \ln P\big(\mathbf{y}_i\big|s_i = 1, \mathbf{W}_i, \mathbf{D}_j, \mathbf{\Theta}\big) + \sum_{i \in \Psi_{BLD}} \ln \Phi\big(\mathbf{Z}_i\mathbf{\delta}\big) + \\
\sum_{i' \in \Psi_{BNA}} \big[I\big(s_i = 1\big)\ln \Phi\big(\mathbf{Z}_{i'}\mathbf{\delta}\big) + I\big(s_i = 0\big)\ln\big(1 - \Phi\big(\mathbf{Z}_{i'}\mathbf{\delta}\big)\big)\big]
\tag{10}
$$

However, as noted, the parameters in the case-selection equation can be estimated by an enriched sample that contains both Ψ_{BLD} and Ψ_{BNA}, which oversamples the share of business cases that the Supreme Court selects to hear. We therefore take two approaches to estimation. In the baseline estimations, we use only the Bloomberg random sample to estimate the selection parameters so that the baseline estimator is:

$$
\hat{\mathbf{\Theta}} \equiv \arg\max_{\mathbf{\Theta}} \ln L(\mathbf{\Theta}) = \sum_{i \in \Psi_{BLD}} \ln P\big(\mathbf{y}_i\big|s_i = 1, \mathbf{W}_i, \mathbf{D}_j, \mathbf{\Theta}\big) + \\
\sum_{i' \in \Psi_{BNA}} \big[I\big(s_i = 1\big)\ln \Phi\big(\mathbf{Z}_{i'}\mathbf{\delta}\big) + I\big(s_i = 0\big)\ln\big(1 - \Phi\big(\mathbf{Z}_{i'}\mathbf{\delta}\big)\big)\big]
\tag{11}
$$

As a robustness check, we combine the Bloomberg random sample with the choice-based sample that we summarized earlier and use Manski and Lerman's (1977) Weighted Exogenous Sample Maximum Likelihood (WESML) estimation as applied to joint models by McFadden, Winston, and Boersch-Supan (1985), to estimate the parameters from:

$$
\tilde{\mathbf{\Theta}} \equiv \arg\max_{\mathbf{\Theta}} \ln L(\mathbf{\Theta}) = \sum_{i \in \Psi_{BLD}} \ln P\big(\mathbf{y}_i\big|s_i = 1, \mathbf{W}_i, \mathbf{D}_j, \mathbf{\Theta}\big) + \sum_{i \in \Psi_{BLD}} \varpi_1 \ln \Phi\big(\mathbf{Z}_i\mathbf{\delta}\big) + \\
\sum_{i' \in \Psi_{BNA}} \big[I\big(s_{i'} = 1\big)\varpi_1 \ln \Phi\big(\mathbf{Z}_{i'}\mathbf{\delta}\big) + I\big(s_{i'} = 0\big)\varpi_0 \ln\big(1 - \Phi\big(\mathbf{Z}_{i'}\mathbf{\delta}\big)\big)\big]
\tag{12}
$$

where $\varpi_1 = \dfrac{\% \text{ of cases granted hearing in the Bloomberg Sample}}{\% \text{ of cases granted hearing in the enriched Sample}}$, and ϖ_0 is defined

similarly to reweight the cases not selected by the Supreme Court. This estimator yields consistent parameter estimates.[26]

Estimation of the model requires evaluating the log-likelihood function given by equation (11) or the pseudo-log-likelihood function given by equation (12) at each iteration of the optimization procedure.[27] In those functions, the conditional probability $P(\mathbf{y}_i | s_i = 1, \mathbf{W}_i, \mathbf{D}_j, \mathbf{\Gamma})$, which is given in equation (9), can be evaluated only numerically because the probability involves integrations with respect to both $\mathbf{\Gamma}_i$ given v_i and v_i itself. We use Monte-Carlo integration to approximate the probability, where the Monte-Carlo approximation to equation (9) is given by

$$P(\mathbf{y}_i | \mathbf{W}_i, \mathbf{D}_j, \mathbf{\Theta}) \approx \frac{1}{R_v} \sum_{r_v=1}^{R_v} \left[\frac{1}{R_\Gamma} \sum_{r_\Gamma=1}^{R_\Gamma} \prod_{j=1}^{9} P\left(y_{ij} | \mathbf{W}_i, \mathbf{\Gamma}_i^{r_\Gamma}\left(v_i^{r_v}\right), \mathbf{D}_j, \mathbf{\Theta}\right) \right] \qquad (13)$$

where $v_i^{r_v}$ represents the r_vth random draw of v_i from the truncated normal distribution $TN_{(-\mathbf{z}_i \delta, +\infty)}(0,1)$ and $\mathbf{\Gamma}_i^{r_\Gamma}\left(v_i^{r_v}\right)$ represents the r_Γth random draw of $\mathbf{\Gamma}_i$ from the bivariate normal distribution conditional on $v_i^{r_v} \sim N\left(v_i^{r_v} \times \mathbf{\Omega}_{12}', \mathbf{\Omega}_{22} - \mathbf{\Omega}_{12}' \times \mathbf{\Omega}_{12}\right)$. R_v and R_Γ are the total number of random draws for v_i and $\mathbf{\Gamma}_i$ respectively.

The computational burden of evaluating equation (13) is considerable because of the nesting structure in the Monte-Carlo integrations. To reduce computation time, we used the Halton sequence (Train 2009) to simulate random draws when we implemented the integrations. The estimation results we report are based on 150 Halton draws; we performed robustness checks on the baseline results presented later by increasing the number of draws to 300, and we found that the results changed very little. We also provided a computational check by re-estimating the model using a simpler two-step approach, which is a less efficient but consistent estimator, by first obtaining consistent estimates of the parameter vector δ from a binary probit for case selection and then maximizing equation (13) given $\hat{\delta}$, a consistent estimate of δ. We found that the point estimates of the parameters were very close to those that we obtained from the efficient estimation approach that maximizes equation (13) with respect to δ and the other parameters simultaneously. Finally, we accounted for simulation error by reporting Huber sandwich robust standard errors in all estimations.

IDENTIFICATION

We seek to estimate the joint probabilities of Supreme Court justices' votes on a case and whether a case is selected by SCOTUS. Because we cannot exploit a natural or quasinatural experiment to estimate the joint probabilities, we identify the probabilities by excluding from the case-outcomes model predictors of petition selection that are uncorrelated with the justices' rulings on the merits. We provide a careful institutional justification for the exclusion restrictions that is informed by the legal literature, and we perform robustness checks by estimating alternative models that relax some of those restrictions. Below, we discuss the factors that we assume are orthogonal to justice voting on the case merits.

Monthly Calendar Dummies and Docket Size

Monthly calendar dummies and docket size capture the impact of changes in the justices' workload on their petition decisions. During the past several decades, the volume of Supreme Court petitions has steadily risen from about two thousand petitions in 1960 to a little under nine thousand in 2012 (Federal Judicial Center 2012). The task of processing thousands of petitions each year places a clear and substantial burden on the justices and their law clerks, and legal scholars have documented a variety of ways in which petition volume has affected both the quality of judicial review and the composition of cases ultimately heard by the Supreme Court.[28]

Particularly relevant to our analysis are the findings of Cordray and Cordray (2004), which indicate that cert-acceptance rates are dramatically lower during the summer recess and the months of February and March. This variation cannot be explained by systematic differences in case characteristics, because petitions must be filed within 90 days of the lower-court ruling and there is no reason to suspect that lower-court decisions on more meritorious cases are more likely to occur in certain months of the year. Furthermore, once the appeal is filed, the highly structured and largely automated process of reviewing and disposing of petitions leaves little room for manipulation (either by the justices or by the contestants involved), meaning that the assignment of petition decisions to calendar months is largely a random process.[29]

The observed monthly variation in cert-acceptance rates appears to be driven by work pressures that arise from the structuring of the court's calendar. For instance, the justices' workload peaks in February and March, when they are scheduled to not only hear a full set of arguments, but also to write their opinions for all the cases heard in the first four sessions of the term. At the same time, incentives for granting new petitions reach an annual low in February and March, primarily because January is the last session during which new cases can be added to the court's docket for the current term, and the justices have ample time to fill up next term's argument docket. Similar "institutional" forces can also explain the negative downturn in grant rates during the summer recess. In particular, Cordray and Cordray (2004, p. 209) explain that, "During the summer recess, the Court acts on almost no petitions for certiorari, and thus allows three months of filings to accumulate for disposition en masse upon their return in the fall. As a result, in each of the nine terms we canvassed from 1996 to 2002, the Court dealt with, on average, more than 1,600 petitions for certiorari at the end of the summer recess, as compared to an average of 574 petitions during each of the other periods."[30]

In sum, the month dummies and docket size variable primarily capture the effects of exogenous resource constraints and idiosyncrasies in the court's schedule on petition selection. Clearly, those influences do not affect the probusiness voting tendencies of justices on specific cases and they are unlikely to be correlated with unobserved influences on case-outcome votes.

Participation of the Solicitor General and Top Advocate

Court resource constraints also justify our assumption that the top advocate dummy and the indicator of whether the solicitor general (SG) is the petitioner are purely exogenous influences on petition selection. Because justices must review thousands of petitions each year, they have limited time to devote to any given petition.[31] Consequently, justices look to a variety of indicators to determine the importance of a petition and whether it should be approved. One "marker" of quality and legal significance is whether the petition was submitted by the solicitor general (Cordray and Cordray 2008). Due to the nature of the SG's client (that is, the United States), *writs for certiorari* from the SG's office generally merit the attention of the Supreme Court. In addition, as pointed out by Cooper (1990), the justices have confidence in the quality of those petitions because the SG's office has a reputation for rigorously screening and vetting its petitions, and because the solicitor general is a repeat player before the court. Days (1994) provides a history of the office and stresses that it enjoys a tradition of independence and that the solicitor general is not a "hired gun," but is ultimately responsible for advancing the "interests of the United States," which may, on occasion, conflict with a governmental entity.

A similar argument helps explain why SCOTUS grants petitions filed by certain seasoned Supreme Court advocates (many of whom were formerly employed in the SG's Office) at a significantly higher rate than they grant petitions filed by other lawyers. Lazarus (2008) reports that the Justices' clerks pay special attention to the petitions filed by prominent Supreme Court advocates because their reputations as top litigators convey an important message about the significance of the legal issues being presented and the credibility of the assertions being made. Thus, much in the same way that the solicitor general's petitions carry an experience-based stamp of quality assurance, the name of a top Supreme Court advocate on a petition acts as a beacon of potential cert-worthiness that helps distinguish it from the thousands of other competing appeals.

Of course, it is possible that the high acceptance rates for SG and top-advocate petitions are driven, in part, by political considerations. If, for example, the court has a probusiness orientation, but the current U.S. administration is enacting more private sector regulations, then the justices may actively seek out SG petitions to limit the scope of government regulation. However, because we include in our case-outcomes model an indicator for whether the federal government was a party in the case, we largely control for potential correlations between the SG-petitioner dummy in our petition-selection model and the error term in our case-outcomes model.

It could also be argued that the top Supreme Court advocate dummy should affect the case outcome and therefore be included in that model and not contribute to identification. However, we found in chapter 6 that such advocates actually had a statistically insignificant effect on the probability of winning a case before the Supreme Court when they represented the government, and we provided evidence that suggested that the top advocates working for the government were subject to resource constraints that limited their effectiveness except in the most important cases. Accordingly, when we included the top Supreme Court advocate dummy in the case-outcomes model, its coefficient was statistically insignificant and the other parameter estimates were barely affected.

Invitation to the Solicitor General to Submit a Brief

On rare occasions, the court will solicit the perspective of the solicitor general's office on the cert-worthiness of a petition through a call for the views of the solicitor general (CVSG). Extant research suggests that the CVSG is another information-gathering tool that the court uses to take advantage of the solicitor general's independence and objectivity (Days 1994) and unmatched expertise in federal policy and complex regulatory matters. For example, Thompson and Wachtell (2009) find that 91 percent of the CVSG cases reviewed between 1997 and 2004 involved complex regulatory and statutory schemes, while only 7 percent involved significant issues of constitutional law. This statistical breakdown is consistent with the justices' competence in dealing with questions of constitutionality, their relative unfamiliarity with regulatory systems, and the solicitor general's obvious comparative advantage in advising the court on issues related to federal regulation. The authors also observe that, although the solicitor general's response to a CVSG is almost always accompanied with a suggestion for how the court should rule on the case (assuming the petition is accepted), the court's ultimate decision on the merits is uncorrelated with the SG's recommendations. Finally, Thompson and Wachtell point to a plethora of anecdotal evidence that decouples the CSVG from any political motivations, further supporting our treatment of the CSVG indicator as exogenous to the final votes in our case-outcomes model.[32]

Lower-Court Dummies

It is well known that the Supreme Court is particularly prone to reverse the rulings of certain appellate courts—most notably, the Ninth Circuit and the U.S. Court of Appeals for the Federal Circuit on patent disputes.[33] Prominent explanations for high reversal rates include ideological differences between lower-court judges and Supreme Court justices, as well as variation in circuit size.[34] Notable differences in the subject matter and the number of cases disposed by circuit courts have also been documented (Hofer 2010), and this variation may account for part of the variation in cert-approval rates across appellate courts.

Although variation in cert-granting rates may, in part, be due to the policy preferences of SCOTUS justices, it is important to note that we control for whether the lower-court's ruling on a case was probusiness in our case-outcomes model. This, in turn, enables the lower-court dummies in our petition-selection model to capture cert-granting factors that are unrelated to the probusiness inclinations of the Supreme Court justices. As a robustness check, however, we include the lower-court dummies in an alternative specification of our case-outcomes model.[35]

ESTIMATION RESULTS

Descriptive information about the voting behaviors of the Supreme Court justices provides some initial insights into their ideological preferences. In table 7-1, we break down the Rehnquist and Roberts courts' votes on the 198 cases in the Business Litigant Database that were granted a hearing with the Supreme Court between 1996 and 2011. There is a clear ideological divide in the Rehnquist court justices' preferences: the share of liberal justices' (Souter, Stevens, Ginsberg, Breyer) votes that are probusiness is almost uniform at 37 percent, while the share of moderate and conservative justices' (Kennedy, Scalia, Thomas, O'Connor, Rehnquist) votes that are probusiness is at least 48 percent. The ideological divide grows in the Roberts court, with four of the five liberal justices voting probusiness less than 44 percent of the time (Kagan's share, which is based on a relatively small number of votes, is an outlier at 55 percent)

TABLE 7-1. Summary of Justices' Votes

	Rehnquist Court (1996–2005)		Roberts Court (2005–2011)	
	Total Number of Votes	Number of Votes Probusiness (%)	Total Number of Votes	Number of Votes Probusiness (%)
A. M. Kennedy (Conservative)	126	60 (48)	72	44 (61)
A. Scalia (Conservative)	124	66 (53)	72	44 (61)
C. Thomas (Conservative)	125	64 (51)	71	44 (62)
D. H. Souter (Liberal)	123	45 (37)	42	18 (43)
E. Kagan (Liberal)	—	—	11	6 (55)
J. P. Stevens (Liberal)	125	46 (37)	54	18 (33)
R. B. Ginsburg (Liberal)	125	47 (38)	72	29 (40)
S. A. Alito (Conservative)	—	—	68	43 (63)
S. D. O'Connor (Moderate)	120	59 (49)	2	0 (0)
S. G. Breyer (Liberal)	123	45 (37)	68	29 (43)
S. Sotomayor (Liberal)	—	—	26	9 (35)
W. H. Rehnquist (Conservative)	124	59 (48)	—	—
J. Roberts (Conservative)	—	—	70	40 (57)
Total number of votes	1115	491 (44)	628	324 (52)
Total number of cases	126	—	72	—

and four of the five conservative justices voting probusiness in more than 60 percent of relevant cases (Roberts' share is 57 percent).

Table 7-2 shows that the justices' ideological preferences have continued to diverge since Elena Kagan joined the Roberts court in 2010, as the incidence of probusiness voting among conservative justices (82 to 91 percent) rose to nearly twice the rate among liberal justices (46 to 56 percent). Of course, the descriptive data do not account for differences in the cases that the Rehnquist and Roberts justices heard, differences in the cases that the Roberts court has heard since 2010, or other nonideological influences on the justices' voting behaviors. Our econometric model controls for those effects on the justices' votes, thus enabling us to provide a more accurate characterization of the justices' ideological preferences and how they have evolved.

Case-Outcomes and Petition-Selection Models

We estimate separate models of case outcomes and petition selection and then present estimates of the joint model of those decisions to show the effects of controlling for case selectivity. Table 7-3 presents the results of a simple binary logit estimation of the case-outcomes equation that does not control for either case selection or justice preference heterogeneity. Generally, the coefficients for the individual justices indicate that their ideological preferences influence their probabilities of voting in favor of business to varying degrees. From the first two columns, we can see that probusiness voting propensities do not differ significantly between conservative justices and the conservative chief justice, who serves as the base case in each model. In contrast, the liberal justices' individual coefficients are negative and have some statistical reliability, indicating that their ideological preferences increase the likelihood (compared with the chief justice) that they will vote against the business entity. Note that the magnitude and statistical reliability of the liberal justices' ideology effects increase from the Rehnquist court to the Roberts court, suggesting a rise in court polarity. To be sure, different chief justices serve as the base in each model, but liberal justices' ideologies are still being compared with the ideology of a conservative chief justice.

We crystalize this finding in columns 3 and 4 of the table by replacing the individual justices' dummies with a liberal ideology indicator that is defined to equal 1 if a justice is liberal and 0 otherwise. The estimated coefficients on this variable indicate that the liberal justices in both the Rehnquist and Roberts courts are more likely than their moderate and conservative counterparts to vote against business. Importantly, the effect is statistically significant, imply-

TABLE 7-2. More Detailed Summary of Justices' Votes during Roberts Court

	In the Period of D. H. Souter (2005–2009)		In the Period of S. Sotomayor (2009–2011)		In the Period of E. Kagan (2010–2011)	
	Total Number of Votes	Number of Votes Probusiness (%)	Total Number of Votes	Number of Votes Probusiness (%)	Total Number of Votes	Number of Votes Probusiness (%)
A. M. Kennedy (Conservative)	42	27 (64)	26	15 (58)	11	10 (91)
A. Scalia (Conservative)	42	24 (57)	26	17 (65)	11	10 (91)
C. Thomas (Conservative)	41	25 (61)	26	16 (62)	11	9 (82)
D. H. Souter (Liberal)	42	18 (43)	—	—	—	—
E. Kagan (Liberal)	—	—	9	4 (44)	11	6 (55)
J. P. Stevens (Liberal)	42	15 (36)	10	2 (20)	—	—
R. B. Ginsburg (Liberal)	42	16 (38)	26	9 (35)	11	6 (55)
S. A. Alito (Conservative)	38	24 (63)	26	16 (62)	11	10 (91)
S. D. O'Connor (Moderate)	2	0 (0)	—	—	—	—
S. G. Breyer (Liberal)	38	18 (47)	26	8 (31)	11	5 (46)
S. Sotomayor (Liberal)	—	—	26	9 (35)	9	5 (56)
J. Roberts (Conservative)	40	21 (53)	26	16 (62)	11	10 (91)
Total number of votes	369	188 (51)	227	112 (49)	91	71 (73)
Total number of cases	42	—	26	—	11	—

TABLE 7-3. Simple Logit Estimates of Case-Outcomes Equation (Probability of Probusiness)

Variables	(1) Subsample of the Rehnquist court	(2) Subsample of the Roberts court	(3) Subsample of the Rehnquist court	(4) Subsample of the Roberts court
Constant	0.8363 (0.2640)	0.5734 (0.3195)	0.9591 (0.1957)	0.7686 (0.2216)

Justice dummies (Rehnquist is the base in models estimated on a subsample of the Rehnquist court and Roberts is the base in models estimated on a subsample of the Roberts court.

Variables	(1)	(2)	(3)	(4)
A. M. Kennedy (Conservative)	0.0232 (0.2828)	0.2287 (0.3663)		
A. Scalia (Conservative)	0.2919 (0.2848)	0.2287 (0.3663)		
C. Thomas (Conservative)	0.1962 (0.2837)	0.2716 (0.3685)		
D. H. Souter (Liberal)	−0.5359 (0.2889)	−0.6293 (0.4253)		
E. Kagan (Liberal)	—	−0.0681 (0.7109)		
J. P. Stevens (Liberal)	−0.5356 (0.2874)	−1.1111 (0.4027)		
R. B. Ginsburg (Liberal)	−0.4935 (0.2869)	−0.7618 (0.3661)		
S. A. Alito (Conservative)	—	0.3061 (0.3734)		
S. D. O'Connor (Moderate)	0.1066 (0.2865)	—		
S. G. Breyer (Liberal)	−0.5404 (0.2888)	−0.6400 (0.3699)		
S. Sotomayor (Liberal)	—	−1.0099 (0.5132)		

Ideology dummy

Variables	(1)	(2)	(3)	(4)
Liberal ideology dummy	—	—	−0.6492 (0.1377)	−0.9767 (0.1800)

Variables	(1) Subsample of the Rehnquist court	(2) Subsample of the Roberts court	(3) Subsample of the Rehnquist court	(4) Subsample of the Roberts court
Control variables				
Dummy variable: lower court ruled in favor of business	−0.7584 (0.1839)	−0.9602 (0.2866)	−0.7585 (0.1837)	−0.9386 (0.2851)
Dummy variable: federal government is nonbusiness litigant	−0.6399 (0.1919)	0.2298 (0.2459)	−0.6397 (0.1918)	0.2122 (0.2439)
Dummy variable: Solicitor General submitted *amicus* brief in favor of business petitioner	0.2587 (0.2374)	0.9390 (0.3060)	0.2578 (0.2372)	0.9482 (0.3044)
Dummy variable: Solicitor General submitted *amicus* brief in favor of nonbusiness petitioner	−1.9130 (0.2751)	−0.6255 (0.3551)	−1.9088 (0.2748)	−0.6313 (0.3542)
Dummy variable: Solicitor General submitted *amicus* brief in favor of business respondent	3.0377 (0.7514)	0.6319 (0.4130)	3.0359 (0.7513)	0.6099 (0.4097)
Dummy variable: Solicitor General submitted *amicus* brief in favor of nonbusiness respondent	−0.8509 (0.2505)	−1.2594 (0.2770)	−0.8505 (0.2503)	−1.2478 (0.2756)
Dummy variable: economics topic	−0.2512 (0.1453)	0.2010 (0.1878)	−0.2514 (0.1452)	0.2094 (0.1869)
Log-likelihood	−635.56	−373.84	−636.31	−375.81
Number of cases	126	72	126	72
Number of observations	1115	628	1115	628

ing that the two most recent courts are polarized to some extent along partisan lines.[36] However, although the magnitude of the coefficients for the liberal ideology dummy increases between the Rehnquist and Roberts courts, we cannot conclude that the Supreme Court is becoming increasingly polarized because the difference between the liberal ideology coefficients is not statistically significant at conventional levels.

The control variables have plausible effects on case outcomes and reveal similarities and differences between the Rehnquist and Roberts courts. For example, conditional on agreeing to hear a business case, both courts are more likely to rule against business if the lower court ruled in favor of it. In addition, antibusiness votes are more likely to occur if the solicitor general submits an *amicus* brief in favor of the nonbusiness entity, regardless of whether the nonbusiness party is the petitioner or the respondent in the case. However, when the federal government is a litigant in a business case, the Rehnquist court is less likely to rule in favor of business, while the rulings of justices in the Roberts court are not affected. Furthermore, although both courts are more likely to rule in favor of business if the solicitor general's *amicus* brief favors the business entity, the effect of the brief is statistically significant only in the Rehnquist court when the business entity is the respondent, while the effect is statistically significant only in the Roberts court when the business entity is the petitioner.

We also estimated simple probit petition-selection models for each court in two ways: (1) using only the Bloomberg sample of petitions, and then (2) combining the Bloomberg sample with the BLD sample and estimating the model by WESML to control for the oversampling of business cases that the Supreme Court agreed to hear. We present the estimation results for those models in appendix table A7-1. Generally, they validate empirically the variables that we discussed previously as influencing the Supreme Court's decision to hear a case. For example, a petitioned case that was previously heard by the Ninth Circuit Court, which we noted has been called the "rogue circuit" due to the high reversal rates of its rulings by the Supreme Court, has a higher likelihood of being heard by the Rehnquist and Roberts courts than do cases from other circuit courts (the effect is statistically insignificant only when we estimate the model with the Bloomberg sample for the Roberts court). Cases brought to either the Rehnquist or Roberts court by top Supreme Court advocates, including those who are serving as the U.S. solicitor general, are more likely to be heard than are cases brought by other petitioners. And the likelihood that a petition is approved by either court increases when SCOTUS justices ask the solicitor general to express the views of the United States on the case.

The estimates also suggest that the Rehnquist and Roberts courts differ in how they manage their caseloads. In particular, the Roberts court is less likely to grant a petition as the number of cases on its docket increases, but the Rehnquist court's decision to hear a case is not significantly correlated with its docket size. Similarly, while the probability that the Rehnquist court approves a petition does not vary significantly across the court's calendar, the Roberts court is less likely to approve a petition if it makes its decision during the summer session.

Joint Model of Case Outcomes and Case Selection

We now present estimates of the joint mixed-logit case-outcomes model and the probit petition-selection model, using as our base case the Bloomberg subsample to estimate the selection model. The estimator for this joint model is given by the likelihood function in equation (11); for sensitivity purposes, we also report estimates using the combined Bloomberg and the BLD samples to estimate the selection model with the pseudo-likelihood function given in equation (12). The joint estimation of case outcomes and petition selection is validated statistically by the estimated correlations of the selection error term and the ideology dummy variables in columns 1 and 2 of table 7-4, which exceed their standard errors and are statistically significant in all but one case. The statistically significant coefficients for the standard deviations of the conservative/moderate and liberal ideology dummy variables for all of the models in the table provide statistical justification for estimating the case-outcomes model by mixed-logit.

As we found previously when we estimated only the case-outcomes model, the estimated coefficients for the moderate and conservative justices are not statistically significantly different from the chief justice's coefficients for both the Rehnquist and Roberts courts. However, we do find for the joint model that the coefficients for the liberal justices on the Rehnquist court do not even exceed their standard errors, meaning that the coefficients for all the justices on that court are not statistically significantly different from the chief justice's base coefficient. In other words, business case outcomes in the Rehnquist court do not appear to be influenced by differences in the justices' politically based ideological preferences. In contrast, the coefficients for the liberal justices on the Roberts court are negative, statistically significant, and roughly of the same magnitude, indicating that differences in the justices' political ideologies strongly influence the rulings of the Roberts court, even after controlling for case selection and preference heterogeneity.

Columns 3 and 4 of table 7-4 present the joint-model results when we re-

TABLE 7-4. Joint Estimation of Mixed-Logit Case-Outcome Model
and Probit Case-Selection Model

Variables	(1) Mixed logit with control for sample selection on subsample of Rehnquist court	(2) Mixed logit with control for sample selection on subsample of Roberts court	(3) Mixed logit with control for sample selection on subsample of Rehnquist court	(4) Mixed logit with control for sample selection on subsample of Roberts court
Part 1: Case-Outcomes Equation				
Constant	2.8010 (1.3275)	1.6081 (1.2006)	4.3172 (1.4235)	2.7233 (1.4282)
Justice and ideology dummies (Rehnquist as the base in models on subsample of the Rehnquist court and Roberts as the base in models on subsample of the Roberts court.				
A. M. Kennedy (Conservative)	0.1198 (0.5202)	0.8175 (0.7418)		
A. Scalia (Conservative)	0.9548 (0.5314)	0.8175 (0.7418)		
C. Thomas (Conservative)	0.6777 (0.5255)	0.9637 (0.7588)		
D. H. Souter (Liberal)	−0.3368 (0.8343)	−2.9337 (1.2229)		
E. Kagan (Liberal)	—	−3.0797 (1.5531)		
J. P. Stevens (Liberal)	−0.4304 (0.8355)	−3.9674 (1.2254)		
R. B. Ginsburg (Liberal)	−0.2859 (0.8313)	−3.1729 (1.1684)		
S. A. Alito (Conservative)	—	0.8317 (0.7455)		
S. D. O'Connor (Moderate)	0.3077 (0.5271)	—		
S. G. Breyer (Liberal)	−0.4352 (0.8361)	−3.0045 (1.1731)		
S. Sotomayor (Liberal)	—	−3.0296 (1.3385)		
Mean of liberal ideology dummy	—	—	−1.2839 (0.6740)	−4.7475 (1.2079)
Standard deviation of conservative/moderate ideology dummy	6.6314 (1.0202)	8.1809 (1.5127)	6.4444 (0.9552)	7.8631 (1.9059)
Standard deviation of liberal ideology dummy	6.8372 (1.3107)	3.8474 (0.8171)	5.1914 (0.7749)	4.0222 (0.9633)

Variables	(1) Mixed logit with control for sample selection on subsample of Rehnquist court	(2) Mixed logit with control for sample selection on subsample of Roberts court	(3) Mixed logit with control for sample selection on subsample of Rehnquist court	(4) Mixed logit with control for sample selection on subsample of Roberts court
Correlation between conservative/moderate and liberal ideology dummy	0.6035 (0.0678)	0.4031 (0.1456)	0.5897 (0.0877)	0.6536 (0.1016)
Correlation between selection error and conservative/ moderate ideology dummy	0.7882 (0.0842)	−0.2837 (0.1012)	0.3461 (0.1263)	−0.3987 (0.1170)
Correlation between selection error and liberal ideology dummy	0.2674 (0.1167)	0.2548 (0.2083)	0.0300 (0.1368_	0.1135 (0.1724)
Law variables				
Dummy of lower court ruled in favor of business	−4.6736 (1.3474)	−1.2649 (1.4197)	−3.4832 (1.0039)	−1.0990 (1.4430)
Dummy of federal government is nonbusiness litigant	−2.3399 (1.6176)	−0.5023 (1.2512)	−5.1020 (1.3870)	1.4258 (1.3066)
Dummy of Solicitor General submitted *amicus* brief in favor of business petitioner	−0.0743 (1.6844)	4.3603 (1.2699)	−1.0884 (1.4527)	5.4504 (1.6837)
Dummy of Solicitor General submitted *amicus* brief in favor of nonbusiness petitioner	−5.4166 (1.8916)	−2.4784 (1.3156)	−9.5795 (2.1456)	−2.1486 (1.4341)
Dummy of Solicitor General submitted *amicus* brief in favor of business respondent	9.3134 (3.4880)	4.3911 (1.6947)	7.4362 (2.2434)	3.8868 (1.7797)
Dummy of Solicitor General submitted *amicus* brief in favor of nonbusiness respondent	−4.7554 (1.8921)	−3.5744 (1.3368)	−5.4733 (1.3271)	−3.3499 (1.8787)
Dummy of economic topic	−1.0262 (0.9549)	0.0231 (0.7125)	−0.0285 (0.7838)	0.7245 (0.8951)

continued

TABLE 7-4. CONTINUED

Variables	(1) Mixed logit with control for sample selection on subsample of Rehnquist court	(2) Mixed logit with control for sample selection on subsample of Roberts court	(3) Mixed logit with control for sample selection on subsample of Rehnquist court	(4) Mixed logit with control for sample selection on subsample of Roberts court
Part 2: Case-Selection Equation				
Constant	−2.1136 (0.8419)	1.7606 (1.9245)	−1.8058 (0.7576)	2.0230 (1.8823)
Lower Court Dummy 2	−0.0146 (0.2622)	0.3945 (0.3353)	0.0052 (0.2720)	0.4004 (0.3067)
Lower Court Dummy 4	0.4089 (0.2561)	−0.2276 (0.4676)	0.3910 (0.2399)	−0.2616 (0.4149)
Lower Court Dummy 6	0.4988 (0.1959)	0.2735 (0.3506)	0.4840 (0.1822)	0.2299 (0.3204)
Lower Court Dummy 7	0.0420 (0.3049)	0.4755 (0.2439)	0.1474 (0.2638)	0.4835 (0.2251)
Lower Court Dummy 8	0.4524 (0.2214)	0.5415 (0.2518)	0.5481 (0.2103)	0.5816 (0.2679)
Lower Court Dummy 9	0.3515 (0.1655)	0.2887 (0.2435)	0.3643 (0.1543)	0.3377 (0.2496)
Lower Court Dummy 11	0.2375 (0.2159)	−0.2912 (0.6416)	0.3162 (0.2078)	−0.2129 (0.6439)
Lower Court Dummy 13	0.2053 (0.3532)	0.2783 (0.4829)	0.1658 (0.3399)	0.3047 (0.4964)
Dummy of top Supreme Court advocates	1.1694 (0.1892)	0.9259 (0.2327)	1.1264 (0.1929)	1.0140 (0.2380)
Dummy of top Supreme Court advocates working as the U.S. Solicitor General	0.5407 (0.3072)	2.1588 (0.6405)	0.5079 (0.2762)	2.0394 (0.6670)
Indicator for whether SCOTUS invited the Solicitor General to express the views of the United States	1.0789 (0.3066)	0.9974 (0.3398)	1.0511 (0.3437)	0.9078 (0.3398)
Annual number of cases on SCOTUS docket (in thousands)	0.0215 (0.0968)	−0.3724 (0.1732)	−0.0136 (0.0883)	−0.3599 (0.1554)
Dummy of decided in February session	−0.1745 (0.2659)	−0.6020 (0.3855)	−0.2048 (0.2248)	−0.7101 (0.3469)
Dummy of decided in March session	−0.0861 (0.2140)	−0.1414 (0.2858)	−0.1190 (0.2061)	−0.2298 (0.2851)

Variables	(1) Mixed logit with control for sample selection on subsample of Rehnquist court	(2) Mixed logit with control for sample selection on subsample of Roberts court	(3) Mixed logit with control for sample selection on subsample of Rehnquist court	(4) Mixed logit with control for sample selection on subsample of Roberts court
Dummy of decided in Summer session (July–September)	−0.1307 (0.1581)	−0.6431 (0.2821)	−0.1937 (0.1561)	−0.6974 (0.2819)
Dummy of decided in November session	−0.2137 (0.2167)	−0.6053 (0.2880)	−0.3482 (0.2036)	−0.6874 (0.2624)
Log-likelihood	−650.49	−393.08	−652.79	−395.67
Number of cases in outcome equation	126	72	126	72
Number of observations in outcome equation	1,115	628	1,115	628
Number of cases in selection equation	1,733	1,035	1,733	1,035
Total number of observations	2,848	1,663	2,848	1,663

Notes: The selection model is estimated based on the Bloomberg subsample. The models are estimated by mixed-logit based on 150 Halton draws. Huber sandwich robust standard errors reported in parentheses.

place the individual justice indicators with a single liberal ideology dummy. Interestingly, this parsimonious specification indicates that liberal justices in the Rehnquist court are statistically significantly less likely (at the 90 percent level) than their moderate and conservative colleagues to vote probusiness. This finding of a statistically significant ideological effect in the Rehnquist court conflicts with the statistically insignificant individual justice coefficients in column 1 of table 7-4, although it is consistent with earlier results produced by the simple binary logit model of case outcomes (column 3 of table 7-3). Importantly, however, column 4 of table 7-4 shows that the coefficient on the liberal justices' dummy in the Roberts court is negative, highly significant, and nearly four times larger than its counterpart in the Rehnquist court. Thus, both specifications of the joint model indicate that the Supreme Court has become much more polarized along partisan lines under Chief Justice Roberts.

Taken together, the preceding estimation results coalesce around two main findings. First, the influences of political ideology on justice voting behaviors are both greater and, within a given court, exhibit greater variation in the Roberts court than in the Rehnquist court. Second, controlling for petition selection is critical to accurately estimating and comparing court polarity. In particular, marked differences in the polarization of the Roberts and Rehnquist courts emerged only when we correctly controlled for petition selection. This result suggests that the petition-selection behaviors of the Roberts court have worked to mute the ideological preferences of its liberal and conservative justices, while the Rehnquist court's petition-selection behaviors have worked in the opposite direction by bringing forward cases that elicit and reveal the ideological divisions among its member justices.[37]

Robustness

We explored the robustness of our findings that show the Supreme Court's increasing polarization in several ways. First, we re-estimated the joint model using the combined Bloomberg and BLD sample to estimate the selection model. As shown in appendix table A7-2, the estimated coefficients for the case-outcomes model under this specification are generally consistent with the estimates we obtained for the specification of case outcomes in table 7-4.[38] We also assessed the possibility that the Rehnquist and Roberts courts have different ideological preferences and degrees of polarization simply because different justices serve on each court. More specifically, we addressed this concern by re-estimating the joint model using the subsample of justices who served on both courts. Appendix table

A7-3, which contains the estimated coefficients for this specification, shows that the liberal ideology dummy in the Rehnquist court is statistically insignificant and that the coefficient on the liberal ideology dummy in the Roberts court model remains largely unchanged, indicating that justices who served on the Rehnquist court have become more ideologically motivated under the Roberts court.

Finally, recall that our identification strategy to estimate the joint model involved omitting the lower-court dummy variables from the case-outcomes equation. As noted earlier, it could be argued that those variables should also be included in the specification of case outcomes. Thus, in appendix table A7-4, we present estimated coefficients for a specification of the case-outcomes model that includes lower-court dummy variables, meaning that our petition-selection model is identified only by the month calendar dummies, docket size, the top advocate petitioner dummy variable, the solicitor general petitioner dummy variable, and an indicator for whether SCOTUS invited the solicitor general to submit a brief. We argued that those variables are clearly exogenous to rulings on case merits. In this final specification, we also included in the case-outcomes model a series of case topic dummies that classify cases according to their legal and substantive content. The case topic fixed effects control for case hetero-geneity and the possibility that vote outcomes vary systematically across case topics.[39] We find that the coefficients for the liberal ideology dummy variables are not affected much by those changes. We have therefore found that our esti-mates of the effect of the justices' ideological preferences on case outcomes are robust to changes in the samples that we use to estimate the petition-selection specification, the justices that are included in the samples, and the specification of the case-outcomes model.

Quantitative Implications and Qualifications

We have stressed that the estimates of justices' ideological preferences are af-fected by case selectivity and that the endogenous decision to approve a petition should be jointly estimated with case outcomes. Table 7-5 provides quantitative evidence to clarify and underscore those points by showing how controlling for case selection influences the conservative and liberal justices' predicted proba-bilities of voting in favor of business on a typical business case. In particular, when we do not control for case selection (column 1), the probability that con-servative justices on the Rehnquist court will vote in favor of business is 13 per-centage points higher than the probability that liberal justices will vote in favor of business, while the difference between the conservative and liberal justices'

TABLE 7-5. Comparison of the Predicted Probability of Voting Probusiness across Models

	(1) Simple logit without control for case selection on full sample of justices (Model 3 and 4 of Table 3)	(2) Simple logit without control for case selection on subsample of justices serving both courts	(3) Mixed logit with control for case selection on full sample of justices (Model 3 and 4 of Table 5)	(4) Mixed logit with control for case selection on subsample of justices serving both courts (Model 1 and 2 of Table 7)
Rehnquist Court				
Conservative justices ($p1$)	0.50	0.51	0.44	0.45
Liberal justices ($p2$)	0.37	0.37	0.36	0.39
Probability of $p1 > p2$	0.99	0.99	0.96	0.95
Roberts Court				
Conservative justices ($p1$)	0.61	0.61	0.65	0.65
Liberal justices ($p2$)	0.40	0.40	0.38	0.37
Probability of $p1 > p2$	0.99	0.99	0.99	0.99

probabilities of voting in favor of business is 21 percentage points in the Roberts court. When we control for case selection (column 3), the difference between the conservative and liberal justices' probabilities of voting in favor of business is 8 percentage points for the Rehnquist court and 27 percentage points for the Roberts court—a statistically significant difference.

We obtain similar differences between the conservative and liberal justices' probusiness voting probabilities when we focus only on those justices who served on both courts (columns 2 and 4). Thus, controlling for case selection reduces the estimated polarization of the Rehnquist court justices' ideological preferences but increases the polarization of the Roberts court justices' ideological preferences, with the overall finding that polarization has sharply increased between the two most recent and, based on historical evidence, the most ideologically divided of all U.S. Supreme Courts.

Although we have limited our analysis to business cases, which currently account for roughly 40 percent of the court's docket (Rosen 2013), we believe that our estimates of ideology serve as a lower bound on the true extent of polarization because business cases are often decided on statutory rather than constitutional grounds. Thus, because justices tend to have entrenched, preconceived views on questions of constitutionality (Rosen 2013), expanding our sample to include nonbusiness cases that involve constitutional issues would likely increase our estimates of court polarization.

Another potential limitation of our analysis is that we focus only on the two most recent courts. However, we have indicated that concerns about polarization have become increasingly stronger during the past two decades. Thus, comparing the Roberts court to earlier (pre-Rehnquist) courts would likely only strengthen our finding that polarization has sharply increased under the Roberts court.[40]

DISCUSSION

We have concluded that justices deviate from purely legalistic behavior and allow their political ideology to influence their decisions. Chief Justice Roberts has warned that such behavior raises serious concerns if it leads to extreme polarization and partisanship, although he has asserted that his court does not behave in this manner.

Our findings challenge Justice Roberts' characterization of his court's behavior. In particular, we have found that justices on the Roberts court have strong and divided ideological preferences that affect their rulings on business cases and mirror the polarization in Congress (McCarty, Poole, and Rosenthal 2006) and the partisanship of the presidency. Bartels and Johnston (2013) argue that because the Supreme Court's justices are unelected, serve life terms, and are virtually free from public accountability, it is crucial for the court to maintain a reputation among the public as impartial, trustworthy, and above the unrelenting politics that characterizes and compromises the two other branches of government. Unfortunately, the sharp increase in polarization that we documented may be affecting the court's reputation, as suggested by a September 2016 Gallup poll, which found that 45 percent of Americans had a "great deal" or a "fair amount" of faith in the Supreme Court—the lowest share of Americans to express trust in the judicial branch since Gallup first asked the question in 1976.[41]

Why has the court become more politicized? A number of forces appear to be at work, including advocacy groups providing greater input to the legal process and the growing politicization of Congress, the president, and, more generally, the legal world. At the same time, Posner (2008) points out that judges and academics, who were once close, have grown apart as academic law—influenced in part by social science and economics—has become increasingly critical of the subjectivity involved in judicial decisionmaking.[42] The declining importance of academic feeder judges discussed in chapter 3 is additional evidence of the growing distance between judges and academics. Posner's point indicates that problems in the legal profession may again be affecting government performance.

Chief Justice Roberts has broadly indicated that the greatest danger of po-larization, as reflected by a steady flow of 5-4 decisions, is that it threatens the "rule of law," which could have significant economic implications.[43] As noted, given the addition of Justices Gorsuch and Kavanaugh to the court, Justice Roberts is currently considered the swing vote. But he has had limited success, at best, in reducing polarization on the court.[44] In fact, polarization is likely to increase given that Justice Barrett has replaced Justice Ginsburg and that the Democrats may eventually try to pack the court and expand its size.

Narrow decisions are considered by Supreme Court observers to be the most political and therefore the most likely to be overturned by later courts. Polariza-tion may also adversely affect the behavior of the justices' law clerks by making them reluctant to recommend certain cert-worthy petitions that would not be well received by partisan justices.

In sum, polarization makes it more difficult for the court to work out rea-sonable compromises and to reach durable agreements on important matters affecting the nation. Unfortunately, our findings support growing concern among the public and legal specialists that the justices' lack of accountability may have created a court whose members' ideological divide mirrors that of so-ciety's, instead of a court whose members provide wisdom to help guide the evolution of American society to improve its material and moral quality of life.

TABLE A7-1. Estimation Results of Petition Selection Model (Probability of Being Approved)

Parameters in Selection Model	(1) Simple Probit on Bloomberg subsample during the period of the Rehnquist court	(2) Simple Probit on Bloomberg subsample during the period of the Roberts court	(3) WESML on subsample of the Rehnquist court (including both Bloomberg subsample and BLD subsample)	(4) WESML on subsample of the Roberts court (including both Bloomberg subsample and BLD subsample)
Constant	-2.0380 (0.8624)	1.9961 (1.8010)	-1.5856 (0.9389)	0.7962 (1.9629)
Lower Court Dummy 1	—	—	0.3860 (0.4233)	0.1861 (0.6968)
Lower Court Dummy 2	0.0042 (0.2899)	0.2906 (0.2892)	0.1861 (0.3071)	0.7287 (0.3210)
Lower Court Dummy 3	0.0589 (0.3502)	0.2124 (0.3838)	0.2476 (0.3650)	0.3580 (0.4612)
Lower Court Dummy 4	0.3412 (0.2553)	-0.3121 (0.4654)	0.4014 (0.2937)	0.0418 (0.4897)
Lower Court Dummy 5	0.2715 (0.2196)	-0.3221 (0.4321)	0.2819 (0.2560)	-0.3628 (0.6132)
Lower Court Dummy 6	0.5793 (0.2293)	0.2528 (0.3010)	0.4978 (0.2444)	0.4817 (0.3598)
Lower Court Dummy 7	0.0597 (0.3056)	0.5218 (0.2909)	0.3867 (0.2972)	0.7409 (0.3513)
Lower Court Dummy 8	0.4994 (0.2558)	0.5272 (0.3616)	0.5918 (0.2725)	0.6114 (0.4646)
Lower Court Dummy 9	0.4081 (0.1895)	0.2382 (0.2449)	0.6289 (0.2077)	0.5711 (0.2809)
Lower Court Dummy 10	-0.2829 (0.4503)	0.0883 (0.4714)	-0.0332 (0.4262)	0.3619 (0.5042)
Lower Court Dummy 11	0.3473 (0.2268)	-0.2875 (0.4190)	0.3232 (0.2690)	0.4035 (0.3657)*continued*

TABLE A7-1 CONTINUED

Parameters in Selection Model	(1) Simple Probit on Bloomberg subsample during the period of the Rehnquist court	(2) Simple Probit on Bloomberg subsample during the period of the Roberts court	(3) WESML on subsample of the Rehnquist court (including both Bloomberg subsample and BLD subsample)	(4) WESML on subsample of the Roberts court (including both Bloomberg subsample and BLD subsample)
Lower Court Dummy 12	−0.3702 (0.5802)	−0.2065 (0.4783)	0.4917 (0.3740)	0.1795 (0.4836)
Lower Court Dummy 13	0.2502 (0.4372)	0.2808 (0.4400)	0.2628 (0.4801)	0.5228 (0.5037)
Dummy of top Supreme Court advocates	1.1768 (0.2355)	0.9854 (0.2400)	1.3549 (0.2451)	1.4328 (0.2369)
Dummy of top Supreme Court advocates working as the U.S. Solicitor General	0.9679 (0.4344)	1.8329 (0.6873)	0.9089 (0.4503)	1.1075 (0.5289)
Indicator for whether SCOTUS invited the Solicitor General to express the views of the United States	1.1705 (0.4505)	0.6446 (0.4157)	1.7903 (0.4029)	1.1734 (0.4086)
Annual no. of cases on SCOTUS docket (in thousands)	0.0163 (0.0970)	−0.3666 (0.1909)	−0.0543 (0.1043)	−0.2624 (0.1480)
Dummy of decided in January session	−0.0468 (0.2693)	−0.2972 (0.3070)	0.3107 (0.3230)	−0.2519 (0.3729)
Dummy of decided in February session	−0.2784 (0.3094)	−0.9296 (0.4790)	−0.1365 (0.3772)	−0.7504 (0.5272)

Dummy of decided in March session	-0.1995	-0.4396	-0.0669	-0.3920
	(0.2923)	(0.3637)	(0.3628)	(0.4460)
Dummy of decided in April session	-0.0537	-0.4401	0.0959	-0.2593
	(0.2835)	(0.3781)	(0.3531)	(0.4411)
Dummy of decided in May session	-0.4285	-0.7354	0.1212	-0.5188
	(0.3340)	(0.3877)	(0.3548)	(0.2428)
Dummy of decided in June session	-0.3033	-0.1516	-0.0216	0.0554
	(0.2819)	(0.3010)	(0.3388)	(0.3627)
Dummy of decided in Summer session	-0.2496	-0.9356	-0.0849	-0.6086
	(0.2574)	(0.3209)	(0.3220)	(0.2613)
Dummy of decided in October session	0.1596	-0.2477	0.3079	-0.2131
	(0.2857)	(0.3389)	(0.3574)	(0.4193)
Dummy of decided in November session	-0.2204	-0.8923	0.1559	-0.4479
	(0.3007)	(0.3985)	(0.3481)	(0.4096)
Log-likelihood	-260.67	-158.62	-228.01	-130.64
Number of observations	1,697	1,017	1,865	1,107

Notes: Huber sandwich robust standard errors reported in parentheses.

TABLE A7-2. Robustness Checks: Joint Estimation of Mixed-Logit
Case-Outcomes Model and Probit Case-Selection Model

Variables	(1) Mixed logit with control for sample selection on subsample of Rehnquist court	(2) Mixed logit with control for sample selection on subsample of Roberts court
Constant	5.5695 (1.1404)	3.3165 (1.4895)
Mean of liberal ideology dummy	−1.7092 (0.8784)	−5.6606 (1.2241)
Standard deviation of conservative/ moderate ideology dummy	6.3281 (0.8660)	7.0422 (1.4031)
Standard deviation of liberal ideology dummy	4.9800 (0.7679)	4.5366 (0.9313)
Correlation between conservative/ moderate and liberal ideology dummy	0.5851 (0.0538)	0.5922 (0.1091)
Correlation between selection error and conservative/moderate ideology dummy	−0.0078 (0.1190)	−0.3002 (0.0999)
Correlation between selection error and liberal ideology dummy	0.0391 (0.1161)	0.2378 (0.1258)
Dummy of lower court ruled in favor of business	−3.3560 (0.9192)	−1.9499 (1.4776)
Dummy of federal government is nonbusiness litigant	−3.8810 (0.9272)	1.3408 (1.1422)
Dummy of solicitor general submitted amicus brief in favor of business petitioner	−1.1567 (1.1418)	5.3745 (1.7223)
Dummy of solicitor general submitted amicus brief in favor of nonbusiness petitioner	−7.5675 (1.3817)	−2.5675 (1.2744)
Dummy of solicitor general submitted amicus brief in favor of business respondent	6.2962 (2.0716)	2.1809 (1.4600)
Dummy of solicitor general submitted amicus brief in favor of nonbusiness respondent	−4.6294 (1.2893)	−4.0472 (1.8942)
Dummy of economic topic	−2.4573 (0.7757)	1.5659 (0.9809)

Notes: The selection model is estimated based on combined sample of Bloomberg and BLD by WESML. The models are estimated by mixed-logit based on 150 Halton draws. Huber sandwich robust standard errors reported in parentheses.

TABLE A7-3. Robustness Checks: Joint Estimation of Mixed-Logit Case-Outcomes Model and Probit Case-Selection Model on the Subsample of Justices Serving Both Courts

Variables	(1) Mixed-logit with control for sample selection on subsample of Rehnquist court	(2) Mixed-logit with control for sample selection on subsample of Roberts court
Constant	3.3177 (1.3065)	2.3634 (1.4885)
Mean of liberal ideology dummy	−0.8635 (0.7036)	−4.1260 (1.4507)
Standard deviation of conservative/ moderate ideology dummy	7.0545 (1.2603)	5.8860 (1.3727)
Standard deviation of liberal ideology dummy	4.8685 (0.8248)	3.6559 (0.9833)
Correlation between conservative/ moderate and liberal ideology dummy	0.6393 (0.0951)	0.6007 (0.1459)
Correlation between selection error and conservative/moderate ideology dummy	0.1607 (0.1540)	−0.4614 (0.1625)
Correlation between selection error and liberal ideology dummy	−0.3987 (0.1744)	0.1563 (0.2582)
Dummy of lower court ruled in favor of business	−1.1666 (1.0046)	−1.2962 (1.4809)
Dummy of federal government is nonbusiness litigant	−3.4255 (1.3501)	0.8048 (1.4770)
Dummy of solicitor general submitted amicus brief in favor of business petitioner	0.4107 (1.4728)	3.9246 (1.3854)
Dummy of solicitor general submitted amicus brief in favor of nonbusiness petitioner	−8.8758 (2.7223)	−2.3508 (2.3761)
Dummy of solicitor general submitted amicus brief in favor of business respondent	4.9079 (2.8453)	2.3607 (2.0504)
Dummy of solicitor general submitted amicus brief in favor of nonbusiness respondent	−6.1006 (1.7604)	−2.6100 (1.5831)
Dummy of economic topic	−1.1574 (0.8247)	1.0085 (0.9848)

Notes: The selection model is estimated based on the Bloomberg subsample. The models are estimated by mixed-logit based on 150 Halton draws. Huber sandwich robust standard errors reported in parentheses. Justices included in the estimations are: A. M. Kennedy, A. Scalia, C. Thomas, D. H. Souter, J. P. Stevens, R. B. Ginsburg, and S. G. Breyer.

TABLE A7-4. Robustness Checks of Adding Case Topic and Lower Court Fixed Effects: Joint Estimation of Mixed-Logit Case-Outcomes Model and Probit Case-Selection Model

Variables	(1) Mixed logit with control for sample selection on subsample of Rehnquist court	(2) Mixed logit with control for sample selection on subsample of Roberts court
Constant	4.4045 (2.7764)	2.8191 (2.1400)
Mean of liberal ideology dummy	−1.0040 (0.6013)	−5.1686 (1.2534)
Standard deviation of conservative/ moderate ideology dummy	8.6551 (1.6164)	9.5883 (2.1310)
Standard deviation of liberal ideology dummy	5.9190 (0.9341)	2.3038 (0.6250)
Correlation between conservative/ moderate and liberal ideology dummy	0.7825 (0.0435)	0.8140 (0.1277)
Correlation between selection error and conservative/moderate ideology dummy	0.0448 (0.0617)	−0.4142 (0.1188)
Correlation between selection error and liberal ideology dummy	−0.0587 (0.0832)	0.1221 (0.2710)
Dummy of lower court ruled in favor of business	−2.1376 (0.9353)	−2.0276 (1.4885)
Dummy of federal government is nonbusiness litigant	−6.6409 (1.4342)	−0.2087 (1.2293)
Dummy of solicitor general submitted *amicus* brief in favor of business petitioner	−0.3641 (1.0878)	5.4587 (1.3216)
Dummy of solicitor general submitted *amicus* brief in favor of nonbusiness petitioner	−10.5239 (1.9762)	0.3378 (1.7038)
Dummy of solicitor general submitted *amicus* brief in favor of business respondent	5.8586 (2.4971)	7.1721 (2.5242)
Dummy of solicitor general submitted *amicus* brief in favor of nonbusiness respondent	−8.0782 (1.6168)	−0.8091 (1.4355)
Dummy of economic topic	−3.2435 (0.9212)	0.1611 (0.9433)
Case topic dummies included?	Yes	Yes
Lower court dummies included?	Yes	Yes

Notes: Huber sandwich robust standard errors reported in parentheses. The selection model is estimated on the Bloomberg subsample.

EIGHT

A SYNTHESIS

The preceding chapters have provided a critical perspective on the legal profession by exploring important issues that arise during the lifecycle of a lawyer, beginning in law school and culminating, for a select minority, in being appointed to the U.S. Supreme Court. In the process, we have identified shortcomings of the profession that stem from the ability of the state to regulate entry through occupational licensing requirements and to allow the American Bar Association to institute regulations governing law school accreditation and law firm competition. To summarize the findings:

- Chapters 2 and 3 covered law schools, which, subject to ABA regulations, offer a course of study that fails to consider the heterogeneous interests of prospective lawyers and the public's demand for legal services; provides very specialized training that does not expose students to valid approaches by other disciplines for analyzing and solving legal problems and does not adequately prepare students for working with people who have training in those disciplines; and requires the completion of a long (three years), expensive program. People who could provide valued legal services are discouraged from enrolling in law school because the rate of return is too low or because they are credit constrained, while many law school graduates who might otherwise pursue careers in public interest law incur significant debt and find that their career options are limited to employment at higher-paying law firms or corporations in order to pay off that debt.

- Chapter 4 covered law firms, which are protected by ABA regulations from competition that could be provided by corporations and foreign law firms, and shows that they have created a working environment that reflects the vast inefficiencies of a regulated industry while providing a poor foundation for attorneys to improve government performance should they temporarily take a policymaking position in the public sector.

- Chapters 5, 6, and 7 covered the legal workforce in government, which does not attract the academically strongest law school graduates because it is compromised by a significant earnings penalty, cannot use the full capabilities of the lawyers in the Office of the Solicitor General because of resource constraints, and is raising concerns in many quarters because of the increasing ideological polarity among Supreme Court justices.

In this chapter, we argue that the profession's shortcomings have contributed to the public's limited access to justice, the federal government's inefficient policy performance, and potentially harmful outcomes of Supreme Court decisions.

ACCESS TO JUSTICE

There are notable differences in who has access to legal justice in the United States from the Supreme Court to the lower courts. For example, Covert and Wang (2020) indicate that former members of the solicitor general's office, who mainly work at law firms catering to moneyed interests, have outsized success at seeking *certiorari* for cases before the Supreme Court. When justices were interviewed about the matter, they thought that having those lawyers handle many of the cases that they heard was helpful and came without significant cost. Zirin (2019) explains in his book, subtitled *A Portrait of Donald Trump in 3,500 Lawsuits*, how the president has used the legal system for decades as a weapon against his adversaries, including people who provided him with goods and services, and has brought lawsuits in lower courts simply as a matter of sport.

At the same time, access to affordable civil legal services is increasingly out of reach across the United States. More than 80 percent of people with low incomes as well as many middle-income Americans receive inadequate assistance when facing critical civil legal issues, such as child custody and support, debt collection, eviction, and foreclosure.[1] Approximately 76 percent of civil matters in one major study of ten major urban areas had at least one self-represented party.[2] Moreover, in rural areas, there are often few, if any, lawyers to address the public's legal needs.[3] As a result of those and related problems, the United States ties for 99th out of 126 countries in terms of the accessibility and affordability of civil legal services.[4]

The law profession has become increasingly aware that the public's access to legal services is lacking, as evidenced by a discouraging ABA commission report on the future of legal services[5] and by Judge Richard Posner's realization that the way his court was treating self-represented litigants "wasn't right."[6] Gibney (2019) reports the typical costs for the plaintiff or initiator of common legal events, which many people cannot afford:

- Simple contract: $300–$1,500

- Contested divorce: $15,000–$30,000 + judgment

- Contract litigation: $91,000

- Simple bankruptcy: $1,500–$5,000

- Employment dispute: $10,000–$50,000

- Medical malpractice: $10,000–$100,000

- Automobile tort: $17,500–$50,000

What about legal assistance? The reality is that most Americans must expect to bear their own legal expenses or do without legal services. More than sixty million Americans qualify for legal aid, should they need it. However, in 2016, public legal aid budgets totaled just $1.6 billion, of which the federal government supplied 25 to 35 percent via the Legal Services Corporation.[7] The Legal Services Corporation (2017) concluded that 86 percent of civil legal problems reported by low-income Americans in 2016 were not addressed with adequate or professional legal help.

Juetten (2018) proclaimed that the law profession's legal monopoly has failed the public by not serving 80 percent of the known market, while Hadfield (2010) indicates that, at most, 1 to 2 percent of all legal effort consists of pro bono service to the poor. In theory, class action lawsuits do afford justice, but individual compensation is often small, and since 2010, the Supreme Court has overturned almost 70 percent of class action decisions made by appeals courts by either reversing or vacating those decisions.[8]

Rebecca Sandefur takes a new approach in her 2019 article "Access to What?" by arguing that although access to justice is restricted, resolving problems lawfully does not necessarily require a lawyer's assistance. We would add that access to justice often does not require the assistance of highly trained lawyers because even nonlawyers would be an improvement over the current situation. As specific examples of the problem, Oppel Jr. and Patel (2019) point out that a public defender for the poor in Louisiana had 194 felony cases, with 113 clients formally charged. In total, he needed to do the work of five full-time lawyers to serve all of his clients. Agan, Freedman, and Owens (2018) report that a large fraction of felony defendants in large urban jurisdictions are represented by publicly provided legal counsel that are assigned to their case rather than by defense attorneys that the defendants retained on their own. Based on data in Bexar County, Texas, the authors found that such defendants are convicted more often and that they receive harsher sentences than do defendants represented by retained counsel because assigned attorneys appear to lack incentives to provide effective representation.

The legal profession bears responsibility for the public's limited access to justice because the high entry barriers that it has created in legal education and practice, the declining rates of return to a legal education, and the pressure on law school graduates to obtain high-paying jobs in the private sector are severely restricting the supply of people who could ably assist the broad public with their legal problems. As a result, many people who would benefit from legal assistance either obtain inadequate assistance or no assistance at all.

GOVERNMENT POLICY PERFORMANCE

Government failure in economic and social policies has generated huge costs to society (Winston 2006, 2021b; Schuck 2014), but explanations for that failure that are supported by persuasive empirical evidence are generally not available. For example, lobbying by interest groups has often been claimed to be a primary source of government failure. Baumgartner et al. (2009), however, conducted an extensive study of lobbying resources and outlays and concluded that they do not have much effect on policy outcomes. To the extent that lobbying for or against a specific policy helped a special interest, it did so by maintaining the status quo.[9]

Lawyer-legislators are a rare example where it is quite clear that a particular interest group (lawyers) can strongly affect a number of laws, such as liability, which significantly benefit members of their profession. However, does the legal profession deserve any blame for the social costs of the broader array of inefficient government policies, including economic regulations, public production, treatment of externalities, and the pursuit of social goals, such as reducing poverty and providing merit goods?

Given that extensive government policy failures clearly exist, we consider the circumstantial evidence that suggests that lawyers may be an important part of the problem. Lawyers are at the center of policymaking by virtue of being the most represented profession in Congress; laying claim to an entire branch of government, the courts; and accounting for the majority of presidents and vice-presidents. At the same time, their success at getting elected to public office—attributable to their network connections with affluent people and their ability to raise funds from them (Bonica 2017)—does not suggest that lawyers naturally empathize with the broad American public or that they are committed to thinking rigorously about public policies that would enhance resource allocation and redistribute income to achieve social goals effectively.

Lawyers from the private sector are appointed to fill high-level government positions because of their political and ideological appeal. We noted earlier that work at a major private sector law firm representing the interests of large corporations is an important qualification for an appointment to the federal judiciary (Fallon and Kang 2019). President Trump has packed the federal courts of appeal with big law firm partners whose values are most likely to reflect those of corporations (Kim 2018). Those types of appointments may lead to biased procorporate rulings, which may not enhance social welfare and may follow ideological lines, as in the Supreme Court. Fallon and Kang suggest that lawyers who are selected to be judges should represent other interests, such as workers, but that may simply shift ideologically based policy in a different direction. We believe that improvements in legal training and the cultural environment of the legal profession could have positive effects on public policy, both by providing lawyers with different skills and by attracting different types of people to become lawyers.

Although it is not entirely clear how lawyers in government approach the formation of policy, Miller (1995) points to their emphasis on procedure and advocacy and the prosecutorial style of congressional hearings instead of on a systematic search for truth. Lawyers also have a predilection with writing laws and regulations and with producing huge volumes that run in the thousands of pages yet nonetheless result in ambiguities and a constant stream of legal challenges instead of initiating clear and effective policies that help to resolve social problems. For example, the Federal Register exceeds some forty thousand pages, the Dodd-Frank Act spawned an additional fourteen thousand pages on top of its initial 2,300 pages, and the Affordable Care Act amounted to 2,700 pages and 1,327 waivers. Clear and precise writing of laws and regulations would confirm that less is more.

Finally, Bonica, Chilton, and Sen (2015) argue that lawyers have ideological biases, which can strongly influence their positions on public policy because they have not been trained to develop an analytical approach to analyze alternative policies. As noted in Posner (2008), cost-benefit analysis is one such approach. And even when their ideology does not necessarily come into play, lawyers are prone to dismiss potentially important policy considerations that go beyond a legal standard because they lack technical training and appear to have little interest in understanding technical arguments that may inform policy positions.

Gibney (2019) laments that it is common to hear lawyers and law professors try to excuse various acts of ignorance by singing the refrain that "lawyers don't do math."[10] Yet lawyers' lack of technical training limits their ability as practitioners and as judges to assess technical issues in legal disputes whose resolution revolves around those issues, and it also limits the sophistication of the technical arguments that can be made during a trial. Consider the following problems that arise among lawyers who have become judges and the reaction of judges to certain arguments by lawyers.

- As noted, when Justice Roberts was confronted with a basic statistical argument showing that Wisconsin's voting districts had been warped by political gerrymandering, he characterized the argument as "sociological gobbledygook."

- Justices at the Georgia Supreme Court were considering whether to revive a challenge based on alleged statistical anomalies in the election of the lieutenant governor. McDonald (2019) reported that at the hearing, Justice Sarah Hawkins Warren said, "We are all lawyers. We are all judges. You are making us shudder with math," while Justice Nels Peterson said, "I am one of many people who went to law school because I was told there would be no math. Yet here it is." In fairness, the justices appeared to be grappling with the matter, but it was also clear that they did not have the training to assess the technical arguments or to determine which expert to believe.

- The Federal Communications Commission decided to eliminate newspaper, broadcast, and television and radio cross-ownership rules, which could allow more media mergers. In reaching its decision, it claimed to have considered the effect on both racial and gender diversity, but it also claimed that no data on female ownership were available. This led the U.S. Court of Appeals for the Third Circuit to vacate the order, noting that the analysis on ownership by racial minorities was "so insubstantial that it would receive a failing grade in any introductory statistics class."[11]

As indicated by a 2019 survey, federal judges appear to be recognizing some of their technical limitations, as two-thirds of them said that they needed additional training in e-discovery rules and practices.[12]

The likelihood of government failure is increased by the self-selection of lawyers who go into government. As we found in chapters 5 and 6, the government does not attract the most able lawyers graduating from the nation's leading law schools, and when it recruits top lawyers from the private sector for a few years, the performance of those lawyers may be compromised by the government's resource constraints. President Trump's ongoing criticisms of lawyers when they are defending the government in court have been demoralizing, and they are likely to make it even more difficult for the government to attract talented attorneys (Barber 2019). U.S. Attorney General William Barr piled on by equating his own Department of Justice prosecutors to preschoolers and headhunters.[13]

The potential problems caused by self-selection are exacerbated when government lawyers are opposed by lawyers who work at law firms and who are strongly supported by other able attorneys and by significant resources. Moreover, those lawyers have great financial incentives to prevail on behalf of their clients in legal matters against the government regardless of the social welfare consequences.

We are not aware of systematic empirical evidence on the effect of the relative quality of government and private sector lawyers on the outcome of specific policy disputes; however, some circumstantial evidence is suggestive:

- The U.S. Department of Justice tried the AT&T antitrust case entirely with staff lawyers, and the case was resolved with a consent decree whose terms were initially proposed by AT&T. However, when DOJ sued Microsoft and went to trial, it hired one of the best private antitrust litigators, David Boies, and won the case. The case was settled following the appeal, but the government undoubtedly strengthened its position by winning the initial case.

- Although the vast majority of merger cases are settled, until the U.S. Justice Department successfully challenged H&R Block's proposed merger with TaxAct in 2012, it had not won a merger challenge in eight years.[14]

- Federal agencies (and their lawyers) that are responsible for regulating banks have been widely criticized for failing to resist private lawyers' lobbying efforts on behalf of their financial clients to soften regulatory rules and enforcement.

- And, until the recent spate of successful prosecutions of insider trading, the federal government was not especially successful in high-profile cases involving white-collar defendants.

Winston (2021b) argues that policymakers who indulge their preferences, however formed, compound government failures because they rarely conduct retrospective policy assessments to learn from past mistakes. This criticism is likely to apply to lawyers involved in government policy because lawyers are trained to adhere to precedents, but they are not trained to conduct rigorous retrospective assessments of the welfare effects of those precedents. The result is that lawyers contribute significantly to status quo bias, which Winston concludes is the strongest explanation for government failure because it inhibits learning, enables significant economic inefficiencies in a given area to persist and interact with inefficiencies in other areas, and makes it extremely difficult for the government to reform its inefficient policies by implementing efficient ones. Society, of course, has other goals besides economic efficiency, but persistent inefficiencies make it much more difficult for society to accomplish those goals.

OUTCOMES OF SUPREME COURT DECISIONS

The Supreme Court occupies a very powerful position in the United States because its decisions are the final word on important issues that come before it. The court has transformed the country by, for example, settling presidential elections, legalizing abortion, advancing civil rights, and requiring prisoners to be advised of their rights before being questioned by police. However, we have found that the court's decisions on business cases have increasingly reflected ideological splits, which does not bode well for the effects of those decisions on the public. And they certainly do not accord with Justice Barrett's claim that that judges are not policymakers and that they must be resolute in setting aside any policy views they may hold.

The fact is that judges are policymakers, and ideology is a poor basis for policymaking because it can blind one to essential facts and it can cause one to overlook fundamental errors. Gabrielson (2017) reviewed several dozen Supreme Court cases from recent years and uncovered a number of false or wholly unsupported claims. Gabrielson then contacted the justices who wrote the majority opinions that contained the factual errors to respond to the specific criticisms, but they refused to do so.

It is admittedly difficult to show a causal relationship between the court's polarization and how it affects the efficiency and equity of specific policies and programs. At a minimum, one could envision the potential costs of polarization over time as the important decisions that the court made during, say, a Democratic administration are completely overturned by a different court during a subsequent Republican administration, or vice-versa, with the court abandoning a more socially desirable middle ground that forges decisions not marked by ideological splits. In terms of circumstantial evidence, one could point to, for example, antitrust policy that has not significantly improved consumer welfare (for example, Crandall and Winston 2003). More research is clearly needed to assess the effects of (and to identify possible reforms to mitigate) the Supreme Court's worrisome trend of ideological polarity.[15]

Gibney (2019) criticizes the justices for their lack of technical knowledge and support. He argues that clerks rarely have practical experience in fields other than law and cannot do much to correct judicial misapprehensions about, for example, commodity derivatives or semiconductor lithography. At the same time, justices have demonstrated a limited understanding of technology in arguments. For example, cell phones perplexed Justices Roberts and Scalia, both of whom wondered why anyone might have more than one cell phone other than for criminal behavior; Justice Sotomayor conflated Dropbox and iCloud and (inadvertently, we presume) coined the term iDrop; and Justice Roberts described intellectual property as complex because it involved "a lot of arrows."

SUMMARY

Our critique of the legal profession, guided by our empirical findings, economic perspectives, and institutional evidence, may have crossed a line because the legal profession is accustomed to regulating itself and is accustomed to lawyers such as legal academics and members of American Bar Association committees identifying areas where the profession could use improvement.

However, the arguments and evidence that we have summarized in this

chapter suggest that the legal profession as a whole has not paid sufficient attention to how it has contributed to the public's limited access to justice; vast inefficiencies in government policies; and an entire branch of the federal government
developing an ideological divide that significantly affects its decisions on crucial
issues facing the nation. In the final chapter, we turn to policy reforms to help
address those problems and to increase the legal profession's social benefits.

NINE

POLICY REFORMS TO IMPROVE THE LEGAL PROFESSION AND BENEFIT THE NATION

Notwithstanding the ABA's significant influence on legal practice in the United States, less than 13 percent of the nation's lawyers are dues-paying members of the ABA. (In contrast, some twenty thousand economists are dues-paying members of the American Economic Association, which amounts to a large fraction of the nation's professional economists.) The small percentage of lawyers who are members of the ABA may indicate that most lawyers choose to be free riders who benefit from the ABA's regulations that limit entry and competition in the legal profession, or it may indicate that most lawyers believe that the ABA has become too political.[1]

In the introduction, we summarized the concerns that many lawyers have expressed about the legal profession. A common recommendation from legal scholars is that regulations in the profession that monopolize its control over education and practice should be reformed to allow additional practitioners to provide legal services, thereby increasing the public's access to justice (Knake 2018; Barton and Bibas 2017). The Institute for the Advancement of the American Legal System is attempting to define minimum lawyer competency with an eye toward making recommendations on how to reform the bar exam or to possibly identify an alternative way to determine such competency. Finally, several American Bar Association standing committees have issued a joint resolution urging the ABA to encourage U.S. jurisdictions to consider innovative approaches to the "access to justice crisis" to help the more than 80 percent of people below the poverty line and the many middle-income Americans who lack meaningful access to effective civil legal services.[2]

Some states have taken preliminary steps to improve access to legal services and promote innovation in providing legal services at affordable prices. For example:

- Arizona has recently approved nonlawyer ownership or investment in law firms and created a new category of nonlawyer licensee called legal paraprofessionals, who will be able to represent clients in court in matters such as family law and debt collection and landlord-tenant disputes. In addition, the University of Arizona started a two-year pilot project that licenses a small group of nonlawyers, known as licensed legal advocates, to give limited legal advice on civil matters stemming from domestic violence, including protective orders, divorce, child custody, consumer protection, and housing (Ward 2020).

- Washington has allowed limited license legal technicians to practice law in selected areas since 2014.[3]

- In 2019, Utah began licensing paralegal practitioners, who can practice without a lawyer's supervision in cases involving marriage and divorce, debt collection, and other matters. Utah also approved reforms in 2020 that allow for nonlawyer ownership or investment in law firms. An Office of Legal Services will evaluate nontraditional legal services that apply to provide service and oversee the applicants who are approved. Rocket Lawyer, an online platform that helps consumers create legal documents and connects them with a network of independent attorneys, is among the first applicants that has been approved.

- Effective 2021, Minnesota approved a pilot project that will permit legal paraprofessionals to provide legal services in landlord-tenant disputes and family law. The paraprofessionals may make court appearances but they must be supervised by a licensed attorney.

- New Mexico's Supreme Court has appointed a working group to consider whether the state should allow licensed legal technicians to provide civil legal services.

- California instituted a Task Force on Access through Innovation in Legal Services.[4] Half of the twenty-two members are not lawyers. Recommended reforms include relaxing UPL regulations, allowing nonlegal professionals to provide legal services under certain conditions, and eliminating the restriction on nonlawyer ownership of law firms (Tashea 2020). The State Bar of California Board of Trustees voted to establish a "regulatory sandbox" to create experiments that evaluate new methods of delivering legal services based on recommendations of the Task Force (Ambrogi 2020).

For its part, the federal government has, to a limited extent, challenged entry barriers to professional services. For example, the Federal Trade Commission filed a complaint that the North Carolina State Board of Dental Examiners' prohibition of nondentists from offering tooth whitening services and products without a dentistry license was anticompetitive. In *North Carolina State Board of Dental Examiners v. FTC*, the Supreme Court held that a state licensing board that is composed primarily of active market participants has state action immunity from antitrust law only when it is actively supervised by the state. Thus, the Board lost its antitrust immunity, but the state has not intervened to allow nondentists to practice. Leading federal policymakers from both political parties, such as President Trump and Senator Elizabeth Warren, have set their sights on reforming antitrust and strengthening enforcement against anticompetitive actions. Investigating the anticompetitive effects of occupational licensing in the legal and other professions and how it has imposed substantial costs on employment, consumers, and the U.S. economy should be included on their agenda.[5]

Economists have opposed occupational licensing in general (Han and Kleiner 2016; Blair and Chung 2018; and Mills and Timmons 2018), and in the legal profession in particular (Winston and Karpilow 2016), because it reduces employment, increases prices, and generates economic rents for those who work in the licensed occupation without improving service quality for consumers.

We have argued in this book that public policy toward the legal profession has not only generated large economic rents for lawyers and limited the public's access to legal services but may have also contributed to government policies and ideologically based decisions by the Supreme Court that have generated significant social costs. We suggest that deregulating the legal profession to facilitate a broader range of legal education programs and to stimulate greater competition in legal services could help to address those problems.

REFORMING LAW SCHOOL EDUCATION

As discussed in chapters 2 and 3, the problems with the legal profession begin with regulation of law school education programs and occupational licensing; all but a handful of states require aspiring lawyers to graduate from an ABA-accredited law school, which usually entails a three-year course of study, and most states require them to pass a bar examination to obtain a license to practice law.[6] Many capable individuals are either unwilling or unable to spend three years in law school and graduate with debts that can easily exceed $150,000, not to mention the opportunity cost of not earning income during that period. In addition, as we showed in chapter 2, the rate of return for law school graduates may be unattractive for those people who do not graduate from a top law school.

Eliminating occupational licensing in the legal profession would mean that those individuals who wish to provide legal services would not be required to graduate from an ABA-accredited law school and pass a state bar examination. At the same time, the ABA would be free to exist and accredit law schools, and states would be free to offer bar examinations. Individuals who wished to provide legal services would therefore have the option to complete a course of study at an ABA-accredited law school and take a state bar examination, or participate in an alternative legal educational program and practice law without a license from the state. Market forces would then direct the type of education and licensing that an individual would seek to acquire in order to provide particular legal services for consumers.

Importantly, law school education would evolve because alternative educational institutions would be allowed to enter the market for legal education, and incumbent law schools would be incentivized and able to revise their curriculum to respond to the diverse preferences of potential lawyers and employers without having to be concerned about receiving the ABA's imprimatur. Expanding on our overview in chapter 3, the following new types of educational institutions and programs could develop.[7]

- Specialized vocational law schools and online programs in specific areas of law. Students could complete such programs in less than a year and could expand the provision of low-cost and effective legal services because they were not under pressure upon graduation to seek a high-paying job to pay off large debts that they would have accumulated by attending an expensive three-year law school.

- "Corporate" law schools and programs that are developed in part by law firms to prepare certain students to practice law at their firms upon graduation.

- Undergraduate law programs that would enable college undergraduates to major in and receive a bachelor's degree in law. Some of those graduates could immediately practice in certain areas of the law that do not require more advanced coursework and professional experience: other graduates could enroll in a law school offering a J.D. degree and complete it in less than three years. Undergraduate law degree and accelerated J.D. degree programs exist, for example, in European countries.

- Law schools that offer new integrative multidisciplinary degree programs, which are distinct from a traditional law school curriculum and are designed for prospective lawyers who want to follow certain career paths. For example, law schools in combination with other university departments could offer a program that blends law, economics, political science, and policy analysis for lawyers who want to work in government; law, policy analysis, and STEM disciplines for lawyers who want to advise policymakers and judges on technical matters or who want to work in the private sector on legal issues involving science and technology; and law and medicine for lawyers who want to work in government and the private sector on health-related legal issues.[8] Undoubtedly, other multidisciplinary law degree programs would be developed as the demand for lawyers with skills in other disciplines develops.

As a final point, the increased competition in legal education and greater interaction between law school faculty and faculty in other university departments could potentially address the criticisms raised in chapter 3 that law school faculty should simultaneously improve their academic standards and their knowledge of actual legal practice.

COUNTERARGUMENTS AND RESPONSES

The main counterargument to eliminating occupational licensing and deregulating legal education is that potential clients have imperfect information about a lawyer's competence; thus, regulations are necessary to ensure access to attorneys who have received certain training and certification. However, Winston and Karpilow (2016) present evidence that the ABA regulations do little to improve lawyer quality and that many clients fail to receive adequate legal services.[9] The authors also point out that various institutions such as AVVO have emerged to inform consumers about the quality and reputation of lawyers. It is likely that more institutions would emerge in a deregulated environment.

Newcomb (2019) reports survey evidence indicating that 95 percent of consumers said that online reviews help them to determine which attorney to hire. In addition, a product manager at Martindale-Hubbell, a legal services information company, found that 83 percent of those consumers checked reviews before doing anything else about a legal matter. And new information services continue to be developed. For example, Justice Toolbox is a recent startup that helps consumers choose lawyers through a free website that compiles the lawyers' win rates in state courts.

Finally, the ABA's Section of Legal Education and Admissions to the Bar has recently adopted a tighter bar pass standard that requires at least 75 percent of a law school's graduates who sit for the bar exam to pass within two years of graduation. However, the ABA has not provided any evidence that this tighter standard will improve the quality of legal services to the public or that it will increase the returns from a legal education. On the other hand, the new standard could decrease the supply of lawyers by reducing the number of accredited law schools.

STIMULATING COMPETITION AMONG LAW FIRMS

Under ABA requirements, firms that sell legal services must be owned and managed by lawyers who are licensed to practice law in the United States, meaning that corporations and foreign law firms cannot compete with U.S. law firms. We have argued in chapter 4 that entry into the legal profession should be deregulated to allow corporations and foreign law firms to compete with U.S. law firms, which have developed a poor culture partly because they have been insulated from such competition. We singled out firms that combined legal, finance, and accounting services as potentially strong competitors for big law firms that specialize in corporate law. As noted, a few states have recently approved nonlawyer ownership of or investment in law firms on an experimental basis.

Although firms in many other industries operate ethically as public corporations, the exclusion of corporations providing legal services from being organized as public corporations has been justified on the grounds that corporate entities have an incentive to represent their shareholders instead of their clients. Because it is the only jurisdiction in the United States that since 1991 permits nonlawyer ownership of a law firm, known as an Alternative Business Structure

Firm, Washington, D.C., serves as an empirical test for the legal industry. As reported by Gershman (2016), there is no evidence of disciplinary action ever being taken against nonlawyers or lawyers in D.C. because they were pressured into ethics violations by their nonlawyer partners.

EFFECTS OF POLICY REFORMS

The combination of deregulating entry into the legal profession by allowing nonlawyers, corporations, and foreign law firms to provide legal services, and various institutions to offer alternative legal educational programs, is likely to stimulate several responses by individuals, firms, and educational institutions that could potentially improve access to legal services and government policy.

Access to Legal Services

Access to legal services is likely to improve for three reasons. First, the new opportunity to obtain legal training at a lower cost would increase the investment returns and thereby expand the supply and heterogeneity of people who provide legal services. Some may serve the public as solo practitioners and others may work at law firms or public sector institutions.

Second, intensified competition among legal providers may help to address the workplace problems at law firms discussed in chapter 4, such as gender and racial bias and health-related problems, that may have forced some lawyers to leave the profession or to take early retirement. If incumbent law firms' workplace environments improve, or if new (for example, corporate law firms) offer a more appealing workplace environment, then fewer lawyers may leave or retire early from the legal profession, which would increase the supply of legal service providers. Importantly, improved workplace environments may also enable lawyers who wish to expand their pro bono or other services to improve the public's access to legal services to do so.

Finally, the now classic effect of deregulation that results in greater competition and decreases in costs would lead to lower prices for most legal services, which would increase access to those services. Additional entry and cost and price declines would result from deregulation spurring innovation and greater technological advances in the legal profession. Evidence also exists that greater competition could reduce discrimination in legal practice as it does in other areas. Libgober (2019) conducted a field experiment in which he sent emails to lawyers signed by people with "white-sounding" names and by people with "Black-sounding" names seeking legal representation. He found that lawyers in California were less likely to respond to the emails from the assumed Black clients than they were from those they assumed to be white clients, while lawyers in Florida did not differ much in their response rates to potential Black and white clients. Libgober pointed out that differences in competition could explain the difference in behavior by lawyers in California and Florida. Specifically, there are 20 percent more lawyers per capita in Florida than in California, and Florida lawyers also earn less on average than those in California do; thus, they have greater incentives to attract new business regardless of a potential client's race.

In a fully deregulated environment, competition would become even more intense than the current level of competition because of the entry of new legal service firms and legal practitioners. Costs would fall as legal service providers improve their operational efficiencies, possibly by working more closely with nonlawyers, and as they hire lower-cost lawyers from vocational and corporate law schools and lawyers who have only an undergraduate law degree.

Improving Government Policy

Government policy could also improve as several factors come into play. First, the reduction in lawyers' rents should reduce the government earnings penalty discussed in chapter 5 and help the government to attract more able lawyers. In the process, this may help the government reduce its resource constraints, as shown in chapter 6, because it would be better able to assign litigators to cases that are better aligned with their expertise. For its part, the government should make greater efforts to reform the civil service system, which constrains hiring, firing, and salary determination of government workers who are not political appointees, to assemble a workforce that would provide more effective support for its litigators.

Second, greater competition among legal service providers that improves the culture of law firms to make them more efficient, innovative, and congenial toward all of their employees could help government performance if lawyers from those firms impart those values when they take leave from the private sector to work in government.

Third, the development of multidisciplinary law programs could greatly improve the training of lawyers who commit to work in government. Lawyers who obtain a broad analytical, multidisciplinary education may be more effective at helping policymakers appreciate rigorous policy-based arguments and they may be more likely to advance those arguments themselves when they are able to recommend policies as either elected officials or in high-ranking positions in a governmental department or agency.

Fourth, Posner (2008) argues that judges should make more pragmatic, policy-based decisions and that lawyers with the type of education described above could help them do so. Lawyers with such an education are also likely to take a less ideological approach to resolving cases; thus, if they became a justice on the Supreme Court, they could help to reduce the ideological polarity pointed out in chapter 7 by their own (less ideological) perspective.

A less ideological court is more likely to be receptive to forming and working with a panel of independent experts from appropriate academic disciplines to improve its understanding of, and the decisions it makes about, cases that involve increasingly complex social and technical issues. Fisher and Larsen (2019) argue that in a digital era, "virtual briefings" are provided online to influence justices and their law clerks outside of traditional briefing rules. The participation of experts who do not represent parties or who have not even filed a brief in the case represents to a certain extent a potentially influential "expert panel." For example, the authors show that the Twitter patterns of law clerks indicate that they are paying close attention to producers of virtual briefings and that the threads of those online arguments are starting to appear in the court's decisions. The expert panels that we recommend would extend the influence of online experts and would facilitate more targeted discussion.[10]

During a time when there is likely to be serious consideration among political leaders about packing the court, we suggest an alternative approach: pack the court with economists who serve on expert panels to provide advice to all justices about the efficiency and distributional effects of potential rulings.

COVID-19: STRENGTHENING THE CASE FOR DEREGULATION

The novel coronavirus, which was first confirmed to have infected Americans in January 2020, and the associated disease, COVID-19, has strongly affected the circumstances and behavior of the American public, some of which could greatly benefit from legal assistance; current and prospective law students; law schools; and law firms in ways that on closer examination strengthen the case for deregulating the legal profession.

The American public faces significant challenges in adjusting to and ultimately overcoming the harmful effects of the COVID-19 pandemic. Many vulnerable individuals would benefit greatly from legal assistance to cope with stressful problems related to their domestic relationships, housing, education, employment, health, imprisonment, and other important matters. Plaintiffs' lawyers are seeking opportunities to bring class action lawsuits in some of those areas. However, less affluent groups are unlikely to benefit much from those actions and to get effective, if any, legal representation—a state of affairs that reinforces the importance of deregulating entry into the legal profession to increase access to justice.

Current law students are taking courses online, and they should not be subjected to ABA regulations on how many credits they can receive from such courses. Some states are providing regulatory relief to recent law school graduates by granting them licenses for limited practice under lawyer supervision until they can take the bar exam. And the Utah Supreme Court, and perhaps others, has waived the bar exam requirement for recent graduates. However, those actions only hint that more extensive changes will be necessary, because both current and prospective law students are rethinking their career options. Just before the onset of the pandemic, there were 25 percent fewer students attending law school than there were at the peak in 2010 (Li, Yao, and Liu 2020). Further declines in law school enrollment are likely as job prospects become dimmer, causing the supply of lawyers to decrease and access to justice to be even more out of reach for many. Deregulation to allow nonlawyers to provide legal services and to allow various institutions to offer alternative education programs could help to counter that disturbing trend.

The Great Recession caused significant financial harm to the legal industry, and the economic fallout from the COVID-19 pandemic may be similar. Law firms are saving money in the short term by curtailing discretionary travel and overtime, but some firms are letting go valuable staff, such as associates, which entails a loss in human capital investment. The legal industry is reaching out to litigation funders to prepare for greater economic woes, which hints that greater involvement with potential funders may be necessary. Law firms could have been better able to weather the financial storm of the pandemic as partners with other types of firms that have diverse sources of revenues to withstand large negative economic shocks. Deregulating entry to legal practice to allow corporations and foreign entities to provide legal services in the United States would facilitate such partnerships and allow law firms to evolve in a global environment where legal, accounting, and finance issues are increasingly interrelated. Indeed, given their various client bases and practices throughout the world, the largest law firms have been able to increase their profitability despite the COVID-19–impaired economy.

Although it is too early to assess how government policy has served the public during the pandemic, one ongoing concern with the legal profession that has reared its ugly head is that plaintiffs' lawyers are quickly preparing class action lawsuits against medical providers and employers. Liability concerns have led Congress to legislate liability protection for N95 mask manufacturers that feared they would face lawsuits if health-care workers wearing masks got sick. Concerns of liability lawsuits have discouraged some manufacturers who do not usually make masks from assisting during the coronavirus. Firms may be targeted for lawsuits if they reopen and workers and consumers get sick, thus hampering the economic recovery. Deregulation that leads to a less self-regulated and less self-aggrandized legal profession may lead to improved public policies, such as liability reform that enables society to deter harmful behavior and provide compensation in a more efficient and equitable manner.

IS REFORM OF THE LEGAL PROFESSION REALLY DESIRABLE? IF SO, IS IT POSSIBLE?

Economics is characterized as an imperial science because of its aggressiveness in addressing—some might say interfering with—central problems in neighboring academic disciplines without any invitation (Stigler 1984). An example of economic imperialism is our critique of the controversial claim by well-known law professor Alan Dershowitz. During President Trump's impeachment trial, where he was investigated for offering inappropriate quid pro quos to a foreign nation, Dershowitz asserted: "Every public official that I know believes that his election is in the public interest. And if a President does something which he believes will help him get elected in the public interest, that cannot be the kind of quid pro quo that results in impeachment."[11]

Much of the legal community took issue from a legal perspective with Dershowitz's position, but an economic perspective that stresses choice and preferences perhaps provides a more compelling, and more damning, critique. Dershowitz essentially assumes that the public has revealed a preference to reelect President Trump, and he then works backward to conclude that Trump's behavior must have been in the public interest. However, if Trump were not reelected, as turned out to be the case, and his behavior was a factor in his defeat, then Dershowitz's effort to justify Trump's behavior on the grounds that it was motivated by his belief that his election would enhance the public interest collapses because, in fact, the public rejected that belief by revealing its preference and voting him out of office. Dershowitz would have benefited from the choice and preferences module in an introductory economics course, which explains that preferences, including consumer and public, are only revealed ex-post, and not necessarily known ex-ante.

This type of argument that brings the tools and perspective of economics to bear on an adjacent topic might provoke some lawyers to suggest that our book should have been titled: *The Trouble with Economists*. However, we have used the basic economic concepts of choice and preferences subject to constraints to shed light on important problems that many lawyers have already identified with the profession's institutions. We have then expanded on their potentially serious implications—less well-off people having limited access to legal services and policy failures at the highest levels of government—and we have recommended policy reforms.

The existence of limited access to legal services and government policy failures is indisputable, as is the desirability of implementing solutions to address them. Will the deregulatory policies in education and industry competition that we have advocated have their intended effects on the legal profession? It is clearly difficult to provide a definitive answer at this point, but there is little doubt that the legal profession's anticompetitive features have made it much less innovative, competitive, and welfare-enhancing than it could be. Recent concerns about race relations in the United States apply to the legal profession, as recent studies of the experiences of Blacks in law schools and law firms reveal that the profession could greatly improve the training and career development of Black lawyers.

Unless the legal profession is profoundly different from other industries, unleashing competition to address the preceding issues is likely to increase the industry's efficiency, reduce discrimination that does exist, and enable the public to realize significant and, in all likelihood, unexpected benefits.

Of course, economists' well-known argument that replacing regulations with a market solution will produce large social benefits generally does not move policymakers to act quickly, especially when some of those policymakers are members of the very profession that is criticized for inhibiting market forces. And although we believe that some lawyers are supportive of the deregulatory policies that we propose, industries that are subject to entry barriers, whether created by occupational licensing requirements or regulations, generally do not support policies that would erode those barriers; thus, the legal industry is unlikely to support deregulating itself.[12]

However, as pointed out by Robinson (2015), lawyers' dominance in politics is declining—for example, they are a minority in the Senate for the first time ever, and their share in the House is down to one-third. At the same time, lawyers are still a very strong force in government. Importantly, public frustration with "establishment" government may lead to people with increasingly more diverse backgrounds and who are open to making a fresh assessment of the monopoly protection that lawyers have enjoyed for so long being elected to government positions. Momentum for reform that goes beyond the recent encouraging actions and investigations by certain states could be built by first conducting experiments at the state level that significantly loosen ABA regulations and licensing requirements. Then the expected results of those experiments that show that access to legal services has improved as a result of those reforms could be used to motivate even more extensive deregulatory reform.

Deregulation has completely transformed U.S. industries and generated trillions of dollars of social benefits (Litan 2014). It is not unreasonable to imagine that if the legal profession were deregulated, it could help the nation to achieve greater fairness and efficiency far more than the economics profession could ever hope to do.

REFERENCES

Abrams, Edward S., and Samuel P. Engel. 2015. "Does Law School Still Make Economic Sense? An Empirical Analysis of Big Law Firm Partnership and the Relationship to Law School Attended." *Buffalo Law Review* 63: 609–83.

Adler, Jonathan H. 2008. "Getting the Roberts Court Right: A Response to Chemerinsky." *Wayne Law Review* 54 (Fall): 983–1013.

Adler, Jonathan H., ed. 2016. *Business and the Roberts Court.* Oxford University Press.

Agan, Amanda, Matthew Freedman, and Emily Owens. 2018. "Is Your Lawyer a Lemon? Incentives and Selection in the Public Provision of Criminal Defense." National Bureau of Economic Research, Working Paper 24579, Cambridge, MA, May.

Altonji, Joseph G., Todd E. Elder, and Christopher R. Taber. 2005. "Selection on Observed and Unobserved Variables: Assessing the Effectiveness of Catholic Schools." *Journal of Political Economy* 113 (January): 151–84.

Alvare, Dana J. 2018. "Vying for Lead in the 'Boys' Club': Understanding the Gender Gap in Multidistrict Litigation Leadership Appointments." Temple University.

Ambrogi, Robert. 2020. "California Bar Takes Giant Step Towards Regulatory Sandbox." *LawSites*, May 15.

Antilla, Susan. 2019. "Insurers Grow Wary of High-Risk Executives in Wake of #MeToo Movement." *CNBC.Com*, December 26.

Arcidiacono, Peter, Jane Cooley, and Andrew Hussey. 2008. "The Economic Returns to an MBA." *International Economic Review* 49 (August): 873–99.

Artz, Benjamin, Colin P. Green, and John S. Heywood. 2020. "Does Performance Pay Increase Alcohol and Drug Use?" *Journal of Population Economics* (forthcoming).

Azmat, Ghazala, and Rosa Ferrer. 2017. "Gender Gaps in Performance: Evidence from Young Lawyers." *Journal of Political Economy* 125 (October): 1306–355.

Barber, C. Ryan. 2019. "A Very Difficult Time: Challenges for Career Lawyers at Trump's DOJ." *Law.Com*, July 15.

Barnes, Robert. 2020. "John Roberts's Supreme Court Power Hinges on Trump's Reelection. But Not in the Way you Might Think." *Washington Post*, July 17.

Bartels, Brandon L., and Christopher D. Johnston. 2013. "On the Ideological Foundations of Supreme Court Legitimacy in the American Public." *American Journal of Political Science* 57 (January): 184–99.

Barton, Benjamin H., and Stephen Bibas. 2017. *Rebooting Justice: More Technology, Fewer Lawyers, and the Future of Law*. New York: Encounter Books.

Baumgartner, Frank R., Jeffrey M. Berry, Marie Hojnacki, David C. Kimball, and Beth L. Leech. 2009. *Lobbying and Policy Change: Who Wins, Who Loses, and Why*. University of Chicago Press.

Bazelon, Emily. 2018. "When the Supreme Court Lurches Right." *New York Times Magazine*, August 22.

Becker, Gary Stanley. 1964. *Human Capital: A Theoretical and Empirical Analysis, with Special Reference to Education*. University of Chicago Press.

Becker, Sascha O., and Andrea Ichino. 2002. "Estimation of Average Treatment Effects Based on Propensity Scores." *The Stata Journal* 2, no. 4: 358–77.

Bertrand, Marianne, Claudia Goldin, and Lawrence F. Katz. 2010. "Dynamics of the Gender Gap for Young Professionals in the Financial and Corporate Sector." *American Economic Journal: Applied Economics* 2 (July): 228–55.

Bhatia, Kedar. 2012. "Top Supreme Court Advocates of the Twenty-First Century." *Journal of Legal Metrics* 1, no. 3: 561–82.

Biddle, Jeff E., and Daniel S. Hamermesh. 1998. "Beauty, Productivity, and Discrimination: Lawyers' Looks and Lucre." *Journal of Labor Economics* 16 (January): 172–201.

Biggs, Andrew, and Jason Richwine. 2011. "Comparing Federal and Private Sector Compensation." AEI Economic Policy Working Paper 2011-02, Washington, D.C., June.

Biskupic, Joan. 2019. "What the Supreme Court Is Doing Behind Closed Doors." *CNN*, April 26, www.cnn.com/2019/04/26/politics/supreme -court-closed-doors/index.html.

Biskupic, Joan, Janet Roberts, and John Shiffman. 2012. "Echo Chamber: A Small Group of Lawyers and its Outsized Influence at the U.S. Supreme Court." *Reuters Special Report*, December 8.

Black, Dan A., and Jeffrey A. Smith. 2006. "Estimating the Returns to College Quality with Multiple Proxies for Quality." *Journal of Labor Economics* 24 (July): 701–28.

Black, Ryan C., and Ryan J. Owens. 2020. "The Influence of Personalized Knowledge at the Supreme Court: How (Some) Former Law Clerks Have the Inside Track," *Political Research Quarterly*, forthcoming.

Black, Ryan, Sarah Treul, Timothy Johnson, and Jerry Goldman. 2011. "Emotions, Oral Arguments, and Supreme Court Decision Making." *Journal of Politics* 73 (April): 572–81.

Blakely, Susan Smith. 2018. *What Millennial Lawyers Want: A Bridge from the Past to the Future of Law Practice*. Aspen: Wolters Kluwer.

Blair, Peter Q., and Bobby W. Chung. 2018. "How Much of Barrier to Entry is Occupational Licensing?" National Bureau of Economic Research working paper 25262, Cambridge, MA, December.

Blank, Rebecca M. 1985. "An Analysis of Workers' Choice between Employment in the Public and Private Sectors." *Industrial and Labor Relations Review* 38 (January): 211–24.

Blau, Peter M., and Otis Dudley Duncan. 1967. *The American Occupational Structure*. New York: Wiley.

Bonica, Adam. 2017. "Why Are There So Many Lawyers in Congress?" Political Science Working Paper, Stanford University, January.

Bonica, Adam, Adam S. Chilton, and Maya Sen. 2016. "The Political Ideologies of American Lawyers." *Journal of Legal Analysis* 8, no. 2: 277–335.

Bonica, Adam, Adam S. Chilton, Jacob Goldin, Kyle Rozema, and Maya Sen. 2019. "Legal Rasputins? Law Clerk Influence on Voting at the US Supreme Court." *Journal of Law, Economics, and Organization* 35 (March): 1–36.

Boskin, Michael J. 1974. "A Conditional Logit Model of Occupational Choice." *Journal of Political Economy* 82 (March–April): 389–98.

Brehm, John O., and Scott Gates. 1999. *Working, Shirking, and Sabotage.* University of Michigan Press.

Brewer, Dominic J., Eric R. Eide, and Ronald G. Ehrenberg. 1999. "Does It Pay to Attend an Elite Private College? Cross-Cohort Evidence on the Effects of College Type on Earnings." *Journal of Human Resources* 34 (Winter): 104–23.

Brodherson, Marc, Laura McGee, and Mariana Pires dos Reis. 2017. *Women in Law Firms*, McKinsey and Company, October.

Bunton, Derwyn. 2016. "When the Public Defender Says, 'I Can't Help,'" *New York Times*, February 19.

Burk, Bernard A., Jerome M.Organ, and Emma B. Rasiel. 2019. "Competitive Coping Strategies in the American Legal Academy: An Empirical Study." *Nevada Law Journal* (forthcoming).

Caplan, Lincoln. 2016. *American Justice 2016: The Political Supreme Court.* University of Pennsylvania Press.

Card, David. 1999. "The Causal Effect of Education on Earnings." *Handbook of Labor Economics* 3, North-Holland Press, 1801–63.

Chemerinsky, Erwin. 2014. *The Case Against the Supreme Court.* New York: Viking Press.

Chemerinsky, Erwin. 2008. "The Roberts Court at Age Three." *Wayne Law Review* 54 (Fall): 947–80.

Chen, Vivia. 2019. "What Makes Lawyers Happy? Money, Honey." *Law.Com*, January 31.

Chilton, Adam, Jonathan Masur, and Kyle Rozema. 2019. "Rethinking Law School Tenure Standards." Social Science Research Network Working Paper, https://papers.ssrn.com/sol3/papers.cfm?abstract_id=3200005.

Cleveland, Grover E. 2018. "Helping First-Generation Lawyers Thrive." *Law Practice Today*, April 13, www.lawpracticetoday.org/article/helping-first-generation-lawyers/.

Cohen, Alma, and Crystal S. Yang. 2018. "Judicial Politics and Sentencing Decisions." National Bureau of Economic Research Working Paper 24615, Cambridge, MA, May.

Cooper, James. 1990. "The Solicitor General and the Evolution of Activism." *Indiana Law Journal* 65, no. 3: 675–96.

Cordray, Margaret, and Richard Cordray. 2008. "Strategy in Supreme Court Case Selection: The Relationship between Certiorari and the Mertis." *Ohio State Law Journal* 69: 1–51.

Cordray, Margaret, and Richard Cordray. 2004. "The Calendar of the Justices:

How the Supreme Court's Timing Affects Its Decisionmaking." *Arizona State Law Journal* 36: 183–255.

Cosslett, Stephen R. 1981. "Maximum Likelihood Estimator for Choice-Based Samples." *Econometrica* 49: 1289–1316.

Council of Economic Advisors. 2015. *Occupational Licensing: A Framework for Policymakers.* The White House, Washington, D.C.

Covert, Darcy, and A. J. Wang. 2020. "The Loudest Voice at the Supreme Court: The Solicitor General's Dominance of Amicus Oral Argument." Unpublished manuscript, Yale University Law School.

Crandall, Robert W., and Clifford Winston. 2003. "Does Antitrust Policy Improve Consumer Welfare? Assessing the Evidence." *Journal of Economic Perspectives* 17 (Fall): 3–26.

Dale, Stacy B., and Alan B. Krueger. 2014. "Estimating the Effects of College Characteristics over the Career Using Administrative Earnings Data." *Journal of Human Resources* 49 (Spring): 323–58.

Daly, Anne, Don Fleming, and Phil Lewis. 2004. "Is a Legal Education a Better Investment than an Economics Degree?" *Australasian Journal of Economics Education* 1, no. 2: 183–97.

Days III, Drew S. 1994–1995. "In Search of the Solicitor General's Clients: A Drama with Many Characters." *Kentucky Law Journal* 83: 485–503.

De Haan, Ed, Simi Kedia, Kevin Koh, and Shivaram Rajgopal. 2015. "The Revolving Door and the SEC's Enforcement Outcomes: Initial Evidence from Civil Litigation." Journal of Accounting and Economics 60 (November–December): 65–96.

Deo, Meera E. 2019. *Unequal Profession: Race and Gender in Legal Academia.* Stanford University Press.

Devins, Neal, and Lawrence Baum. 2014. "Split Definitive: How Party Polarization Turned the Supreme Court into a Partisan Court." William and Mary Law School Working Paper no. 09-276, May.

Edwards, Harry T., and Michael A. Livermore. 2009. "Pitfalls of Empirical Studies that Attempt to Understand the Factors Affecting Appellate Decisionmaking." *Duke Law Journal* 58: 1895–989.

Ehrenberg, Ronald G. 1989. "An Economic Analysis of the Market for Law School Students." *Journal of Legal Education* 39 (December): 627–54.

Eisenberg, Theodore, Geoffrey Miller, and Roy Germano. 2017. "Attorneys' Fees in Class Actions: 2009–2013." *New York University Law Review* 92 (October): 937–70.

Epstein, Lee, William Landes, and Richard Posner. 2013a. "How Business Fares in the Supreme Court." *Minnesota Law Review* 97: 1431–472.

Epstein, Lee, William Landes, and Richard Posner. 2013b. *The Behavior of Federal Judges: A Theoretical and Empirical Study of Rational Choices*. Harvard University Press.

Epstein, Lee, William Landes, and Richard Posner. 2012. "Are Even Unanimous Decisions in the United States Supreme Court Ideological?" *Northwestern University Law Review* 106, no. 2: 699–714.

Epstein, Richard. 2013. "The Myth of a Pro-Business SCOTUS." Hoover Institution, Stanford University, July 9, www.hoover.org/research/myth -pro-business-scotus.

Falk, Justin. 2012. "Comparing Benefits and Total Compensation in the Federal Government and the Private Sector." *The BE Journal of Economic Policy and Analysis* 12 (October): 1–37.

Fallon, Brian, and Christopher Kang. 2019. "No More Corporate Lawyers on the Federal Bench." *The Atlantic*, August 21.

Federal Judicial Center. 2012. "Supreme Court of the United States: Caseload, 1878–2012," www.fjc.gov/history/caseload.nsf/page/caseloads_Sup_Ct_ totals.

Feldman, Adam, and Alexander Kappner. 2017. "Finding Certainty in Cert: An Empirical Analysis of the Factors Involved in Supreme Court Certiorari Decisions from 2001–2015." *Villanova Law Review* 61: 795–843.

Fisher, Jeffrey L., and Allison Orr Larsen. 2019. "Virtual Briefing at the Supreme Court." *Cornell Law Review* (forthcoming).

Flood, John, and Lachlan Robb. 2018. "Professions and Expertise: How Machine Learning and Blockchain are Redesigning the Landscape of Professional Knowledge and Organization." Griffith Law School Research Paper No. 18–20.

Frakes, Michael D., and Melissa F. Wasserman. 2017. "Is the Time Allocated to Review Patent Applications Inducing Examiners to Grant Invalid Patents? Evidence from Microlevel Application Data." *Review of Economics and Statistics* 99 (July): 550–63.

Friley, Jesselyn. 2017. "The 'M' in MLP: A Proposal for Expanding the Roles of Clinicians in Medical-Legal Partnerships." *Yale Law Journal* 126: 1225–240.

Gabrielson, Ryan. 2017. "It's a Fact: Supreme Court Errors Aren't Hard to Find." *ProPublica*, October 17.

Garicano, Luis, and Luis Rayo. 2016. "Why Organizations Fail: Models and Cases." *Journal of Economic Literature* 54 (March): 137–92.

George, Tracey, and Lee Epstein. 1992. "On the Nature of Supreme Court Decision Making." *American Political Science Review* 86, no. 2: 323–37.

Gershman, Jacob. 2016. "Nonlawyer Ownership of Law Firms Is a Bad Idea, Say Bar Groups." *Wall Street Journal*, May 12.

Gibney, Bruce Cannon. 2019. *The Nonsense Factory: The Making and Breaking of the American Legal System*. New York: Hachette Books.

Gittleman, Maury, and Brooks Pierce. 2012. "Compensation for State and Local Government Workers." *Journal of Economic Perspectives* 26 (Winter): 217–42.

Goddeeris, John H. 1988. "Compensating Differentials and Self-Selection: An Application to Lawyers." *Journal of Political Economy* 96 (April): 411–28.

Goldin, Claudia. 2014. "A Grand Gender Convergence: Its Last Chapter." *American Economic Review* 104 (April): 1091–119.

Greene, Jenna. 2014. "FTC's Winning Streak Provokes Questions About Process." *National Law Journal*, January 6.

Griswold, Erwin. 1975. "Rationing Justice—The Supreme Court's Caseload and What the Court Does Not Do." *Cornell Law Review* 60: 335–54.

Hadfield, Gillian K. 2020. "Legal Markets." *Journal of Economic Literature* (forthcoming).

Hadfield, Gillian K. 2010. "Higher Demand, Lower Supply? A Comparative Assessment of the Legal Resource Landscape for Ordinary Americans." *Fordham Urban Law Journal* 37: 129–56.

Han, Suyoun, and Morris M. Kleiner. 2016. "Analyzing the Influence of Occupational Licensing Duration on Labor Market Outcomes." National Bureau of Economic Research Working Paper 22810, Cambridge, MA, November.

Hansen, Lars Peter. 1982. "Large Sample Properties of Generalized Method of Moments Estimators." *Econometrica* 50 (July): 1029–54.

Hart, Henry. 1959. "The Supreme Court, 1958 Term—Forward: The Time Chart of the Justices." *Harvard Law Review* 100: 101.

Heckman, James J. 1976. "The Common Structure of Statistical Models of Truncation, Sample Selection and Limited Dependent Variables and a Simple Estimator for Such Models." *Annals of Economic and Social Measurement* 5, no. 4: 475–92.

Heckman, James J., Lance J. Lochner, and Petra E. Todd. 2003. "Fifty years of Mincer Earnings Regressions." National Bureau of Economic Research Working Paper 9732, Cambridge, MA, May.

Heckman, James J., and Burton Singer. 1984. "A Model for Minimizing the Impact of Distributional Assumptions in Econometric Models for Duration Data." *Econometrica* 52 (March): 271–320.

Henderson, Todd. 2017. "Do Lawyers Make Better CEOs than MBAs?" *Harvard Business Review*, August 24.

Henderson, William. 2017. "The Legal Profession's Last Mile Solution." *Law. Com*, July 10.

Hernandez, Gabriel Orum. 2016. "The Startup Scene: Frustrations and Futures for Venture Capitalists in Legal Technology." *Legaltech News*, October 20.

Hodkinson, Paul. 2019. "Would Mandatory Psychologist Appointments Reduce Burnout in Big Law?" *Law.Com*, July 23.

Hofer, Roy. 2010. "Supreme Court Reversal Rates: Evaluating the Federal Courts of Appeals." *Landslide* 2, no. 3 (January–February).

Holden, Richard, Michael Keane, and Matthew Lilley. 2017. "Peer Effects on the United States Supreme Court." University of New South Wales working paper.

Howard, Philip. 2019. *Bureaucracy vs. Democracy: Examining the Bureaucratic Causes of Public Failure, Economic Waste, and Voter Alienation* (forthcoming).

Iaryczower, Matias, and Matthew Shum. 2012. "The Value of Information in the Court: Get it Right, Keep it Tight." *American Economic Review* 102 (February): 202–37.

Isaacson, Daniella. 2016. "Why Don't Law Firms Innovate? Clients Don't Make Them." *Law.Com*, August 18.

Jacobi, Tonja, and Matthew Sag. 2019. "The New Oral Argument: Justices as Advocates." *Notre Dame Law Review* 94.

Johnson, Timothy, Paul Wahlbeck, and James Spriggs II. 2006. "The Influence of Oral Arguments on the U.S. Supreme Court." *American Political Science Review* 100 (February): 99–113.

Juetten, Mary. 2018. "How Can We Reform Legal Education? Try Spotlighting the Outcomes." *ABA Journal*, November 9.

Kane, Thomas J., and Cecilia Elena Rouse. 1995. "Labor-Market Returns to Two- and Four-Year College." *American Economic Review* 85 (June): 600–614.

Kaplan, David A. 2018. *The Most Dangerous Branch: Inside the Supreme Court's Assault on the Constitution*. New York: Crown Publishing.

Katz, Daniel Martin, Michael James Bommarito, and Josh Blackman. 2014. "Predicting the Behavior of the Supreme Court of the United States: A General Approach," http://ssrn.com/abstract=2463244 or http://dx.doi .org/10.2139/ssrn.2463244.

Kim, Ellis. 2018. "President Trump Is Packing the Courts with Law Firm Partners." *American Lawyer*, November 20.

Kiser, Randall. 2019. *American Law Firms in Transition: Trends, Threats, and Strategies.* Chicago: American Bar Association Publishing.

Kleiner, Morris, and Evgeny S. Vorotnikov. 2018. "At What Cost? State and National Estimates of the Cost of Occupational Licensing." Institute for Justice, Washington, D.C., https://ij.org/wp-content/uploads/2018/11/Licensure_Report_WEB.pdf.

Knake, Renee Newman. 2019. "The Legal Monopoly." *Washington Law Review* (forthcoming).

Krill, Patrick, Ryan Johnson, and Linda Albert. 2016. "The Prevalence of Substance Use and Other Mental Health Concerns about American Attorneys." *Journal of Addiction Medicine* 10 (January/February): 46–52.

Kronman, Anthony T. 1993. *The Lost Lawyer: Failing Ideals of the Legal Profession.* Harvard University Press.

Krueger, Alan B., and David Schkade. 2008. "Sorting in the Labor Market: Do Gregarious Workers Flock to Interactive Jobs?" *Journal of Human Resources* 43 (Fall): 859–83.

Lahav, Alexandra D., and Peter Eiegelman. 2019. "The Curious Incident of the Falling Win Rate: Individual vs. System-Level Justification and the Rule of Law." *UC Davis Law Review* (forthcoming).

Lauderdale, Benjamin, and Tom Clark. 2012. "The Supreme Court's Many Median Justices." *American Political Science Review* 106, no. 4: 847–66.

Law, David, and David Zaring. 2010. "Law Versus Ideology: The Supreme Court and the Use of Legislative History." *William and Mary Law Review* 51, no. 4: 1653–747.

LawGeex. 2018. "Comparing the Performance of Artificial Intelligence to Human Lawyers in the Review of Standard Business Contracts." February, www.lawgeex.com.

Lazarus, Richard. 2008. "Advocacy Matters Before and Within the Supreme Court: Transforming the Court by Transforming the Bar." *Georgetown Law Journal* 96, no. 5: 1487–564.

Lazear, Edward P., and Paul Oyer. 2013. "Personnel Economics." In *The Handbook of Organizational Economics*, edited by Robert Gibbons and John Roberts, 479–519. Princeton University Press.

Legal Services Corporation. 2017. "The Justice Gap: Measuring the Unmet Civil Legal Needs of Low-Income Americans." June, www.lsc.gov/sites/default/files/images/TheJusticeGap-FullReport.pdf.

Levine, Stewart. 2016. "The Best Lawyer You Can Be: A Guide to Physical, Mental, Emotional, and Spiritual Wellness." American Bar Association.

Li, Miranda, Phillip Yao, and Goodwin Liu. 2020. "Who's Going to Law School? Trends in Law School Enrollment Since the Great Recession." *U.C. Davis Law School* (forthcoming).

Libgober, Brian. 2019. "Getting a Lawyer While Black: A Field Experiment." *Lewis and Clark Law Review* 24: 1–53.

Liebenberg, Roberta D., and Stephanie A. Scharf. 2019. *Walking Out the Door: The Facts, Figures, and Future of Experienced Women Lawyers in Private Practice.* American Bar Association, www.alm.com/intelligence/solutions-we -provide/business-of-law- solutions/analyst-reports/walking-out-the-door/.

Lim, Claire S. H. 2015. "Media Influence on Courts: Evidence from Civil Case Adjudication." *American Law and Economics Review* 17: 87–126.

Lim, Youngski. 2000. "An Empirical Analysis of Supreme Court Justices' Decision Making." *Journal of Legal Studies* 29, no. 2: 721–52.

Lindley, Joanne, and Stephen Machin. 2014. "The Rising Post-College Wage Premium in America and Britain." Unpublished paper, November.

Liptak, Adam. 2018. "A Case for Math, not "Gobbledygook" in Judging Partisan Voting Maps." *New York Times*, January 15.

Litan, Robert E. 2014. *Trillion Dollar Economists.* Hoboken, NJ: John Wiley and Sons.

Lovelace, Ryan. 2019. "Past, Present, and Future Nominations Revolving Around Big Law." *National Law Journal*, March 8.

MacEwen, Bruce, and Janet Stanton. 2017. "What Makes the Elite NYC Legal Market so Different?" Adam Smith, Esq, New York.

Manski, Charles F., and Steven R. Lerman. 1977. "The Estimation of Choice Probabilities from Choice-Based Samples." *Econometrica* 45 (November): 1977–88.

Martin, Andrew D., and Kevin M. Quinn. 2007. "Assessing Preference Change on the U.S. Supreme Court." *Journal of Law, Economics, and Organization* 23, no. 2: 365–85.

Matter, Ulrich, and Alois Stutzer. 2015. "The Role of Lawyer-Legislators in Shaping the Law: Evidence from Voting on Tort Reforms." *Journal of Law and Economics* 58, no. 2: 357–84.

McCarty, Nolan, Keith T. Poole, and Howard Rosenthal. 2006. *Polarized America: The Dance of Ideology and Unequal Riches.* Cambridge, MA: MIT Press.

McDonald, R. Robin. 2019. "Ga. Justices Home in on Discovery, Statistical Anomalies in Lt. Governor's Election Fight." *Law.Com*, May 7.

McFadden, Daniel, Clifford Winston, and Axel Boersch-Supan. 1985. "Joint

Estimation of Freight Transportation Decisions Under Nonrandom Sampling." In *Analytical Studies in Transport Economics*, edited by Andrew F. Daughety, 137–57. Cambridge University Press.

McGinnis, John O. 1992. "Principle Versus Politics: The Solicitor General's Office in Constitutional and Bureaucratic Theory." *Stanford Law Review* 44, no. 2: 799–814.

McLellan, Lizzy. 2020. "Lawyers Reveal True Depth of Mental Health Issues." *Law.Com*, February 19.

Merritt, Deborah Jones. 2015. "What Happened to the Class of 2010? Empirical Evidence of Structural Change in the Legal Profession." Public Law and Legal Theory Working Paper No. 290, Ohio State University Moritz College of Law, March.

Miller, Mark C. 1995. *The High Priests of American Politics: The Role of Lawyers in American Political Institutions*. University of Tennessee Press.

Mills, Anna, and Edward J. Timmons. 2018. "Bringing the Effects of Occupational Licensing into Focus: Optician Licensing in the United States." *Eastern Economic Journal* 44 (January): 69–83.

Mitch. 2017. "Tipping the Scales of Justice: The Role of the Nonprofit Sliding Scale Law Firm in the Delivery of Legal Services." University of Wisconsin Law School Legal Studies Research Paper Series No. 1424.

Muro, Mark, Jacob Whiton, and Robert Maxim. 2019. "What Jobs Are Affected By AI?" Brookings Institution Metropolitan Policy Program, November.

National Association for Law Placement Foundation. 2020. *Women of Color: A Study of Law School Experiences*. NALP and Center for Women in Law, University of Texas, Austin.

Nelson, Scott. 2009. *Opposing Cert: A Practitioner's Guide*. Washington, D.C.: Public Citizen Litigation Group, www.citizen.org/documents/OpposingCertGuide.pdf.

Newcomb, Kelly. 2019. "How Lawyers Can Make Positive and Negative Online Reviews Work for Them." *ABA Journal*, January 17.

O'Flaherty, Brendan, and Aloysius Siow. 1995. "Up or Out Rules in the Market for Lawyers." *Journal of Labor Economics* 13 (October): 709–35.

Oppel Jr., Richard A., and Jugal K. Patel. 2019. "One Lawyer, One Day, 194 Felony Cases." *New York Times*, February 3.

Oster, Emily. 2019. "Unobservable Selection and Coefficient Stability: Theory and Evidence." *Journal of Business and Economic Statistics* 37, no. 2: 187–204.

Oyer, Paul, and Scott Schaefer. 2009. "The Returns to Attending a Prestigious Law School." Unpublished paper, Stanford Graduate School of Business.

Pagliero, Mario. 2011. "What Is the Objective of Professional Licensing? Evidence from the US Market for Lawyers." *International Journal of Industrial Organization* 29 (July): 473–83.

Pagliero, Mario. 2010. "Licensing Exam Difficulty and Entry Salaries in the US Market for Lawyers." *British Journal of Industrial Relations* 48 (December): 726–39.

Peery, Destiny, Paulette Brown, and Eileen Letts. 2020. *Left Out and Left Behind: The Hurdles, Hassles, and Heartaches of Achieving Long-Term Legal Careers for Women of Color.* Chicago: American Bar Association.

Peppers, Todd C., and Micheal W. Giles. 2012. "Of Potted Plants and Political Images: The Supreme Court and the State of the Union Address." *Kansas Journal of Law and Public Policy*, no. 1: 4981.

Polantz, Katelyn. 2016. "Survey: What It Takes to Become a New Partner." *The American Lawyer*, November 7.

Posner, Richard A. 2008. *How Judges Think*. Harvard University Press.

Priest, George L., and Benjamin Klein. 1984. "The Selection of Disputes for Litigation." *Journal of Legal Studies* 13, no. 1: 1–55.

Public Information Office of the Supreme Court of the United States. 2014. "A Reporter's Guide to Applications Pending before the Supreme Court of the United States," www.supremecourt.gov/publicinfo/reportersguide .pdf.

Randazzo, Sara, and Nicole Hong. 2018. "At Law Firms, Rainmakers Accused of Harassment Can Switch Jobs with Ease." *Wall Street Journal*, July 30.

Ready, Frank. 2020. "Why Can't Tech Kill the Billable Hour at Law Firms?" *Law.Com*, March 12.

Rishikof, Harvey, I. Scott Messenger, and Michael Jo. 2009. "The Liberal Tradition of the Supreme Court Clerkship: Its Rise, Fall, and Reincarnation." *Vanderbilt Law Review* 62: 1749–814.

Rivera, Lauren A. 2015. *Pedigree: How Elite Students Get Elite Jobs*. Princeton University Press.

Robinson, Nick. 2015. "The Declining Dominance of Lawyers in U.S. Federal Politics." Research paper, Harvard Law School Center on the Legal Profession.

Rosen, Jeffrey. 2013. "Can the Judicial Branch be a Steward in a Polarized Democracy?" *Daedalus* 142 (Spring): 25–35.

Rosen, Sherwin. 1992. "The Market for Lawyers." *Journal of Law and Economics* 35 (October): 215–46.

Rozema, Kyle. 2020. "Does the Bar Exam Protect the Public?" https://papers .ssrn.com/sol3/papers.cfm?abstract_id=3612481.

Ruger, Theodore W., Pauline T. Kim, Andrew D. Martin, and Kevin M. Quinn. 2004. "The Supreme Court Forecasting Project: Legal and Political Science Approaches to Predicting Supreme Court Decisionmaking." *Columbia Law Review* 104: 1150–210.

Sandefur, Rebecca L. 2019. "Access to What?" *Daedalus* 148 (Winter): 49–55.

Scheindlin, Shira A., Carrie H. Cohen, Tracee E. Davis, Bernice K. Leber, Sharon M. Porcellio, Lesley F. Rosenthal, and Lauren J. Wachtler. 2017. "If Not Now, When? Achieving Equality for Women Attorneys in the Courtroom and in ADR." Report of the Commercial and Federal Litigation Section, New York State Bar Association, July.

Schneider, Andrea Kupfler. 2002. "Shattering Negotiation Myths: Empirical Evidence on the Effectiveness of Negotiations Style." *Harvard Negotiation Law Review* 7: 148–233.

Schrag, Philip G., and Charles W. Pruett. 2011. "Coordinating Loan Repayment Assistance Programs with New Federal Legislation." *Journal of Legal Education* 60 (May): 583–615.

Schuck, Peter H. 2014. *Why Government Fails So Often: And How It Can Do Better.* Princeton University Press.

Schwartz, Joshua I. 1988. "Two Perspectives on the Solicitor General's Independence." *Loyola of Los Angeles Law Review* 21, no. 4: 1119–66.

Scott, Kevin. 2006. "Supreme Court Reversals of the Ninth Circuit." *Arizona Law Review* 48: 341–54.

Segal, Jeffrey A., and Harold J. Spaeth. 2002. *The Supreme Court and the Attitudinal Model Revisited.* Cambridge University Press.

Seidman, Ilene. 2016. "The Bad Business of Ignoring the Justice Gap." *ABA Journal*, February 18.

Simkovic, Michael, and Frank McIntyre. 2014. "The Economic Value of a Law Degree." *Journal of Legal Studies* 43 (June): 249–89.

Simon, Michael, Alvin F. Lindsay, Loly Sosa, and Paige Comparato. 2018. "Lola v. Skadden and the Automation of the Legal Profession." *Yale Journal of Law and Technology* 20: 234–310.

Simons, Hugh A., and Nicholas Bruch. 2017. "Do Mergers Increase Profitability?" *Law.Com*, December 5.

Skerrett, Lauren E. 2020. "On Being A Black American Biglaw Associate." *Above the Law*, June 4.

Sloan, Karen. 2019. "New Report Shows Depression and Anxiety are Prevalent at Harvard Law." *Law.Com*, December 30.

Spaeth, Harold, Lee Epstein, Andrew Martin, Jeffrey Segal, Theodore Ruger, and Sara Benesh. 2014. The Supreme Court Database, http://Supremecourt database.org.

Spaeth, Harold, Lee Epstein, Ted Ruger, Keith Whittington, Jeffrey Segal, and Andrew Martin. 2013. "Supreme Court Database Codebook." The Supreme Court Database. http://scdb.wustl.edu/.

Springer, James V. 1984. "Some Suggestions on Preparing Briefs on the Merits in the Supreme Court of the United States." *Catholic University Law Review* 33 (Spring): 593–602.

Stigler, George J. 1984. "Economics: The Imperial Science?" *Scandinavian Journal of Economics* 86 (September): 301–13.

Strom, Roy. 2018. "Managing Partners' Frustration Mounts as Law Firm Innovation Stagnates." *The American Lawyer*, May 21.

Sunstein, Cass R. 2020. "Barrett's 'Originalism' Can Be Pure Politics," *Bloomberg Opinion*, October 13.

Tamanaha, Brian. 2012. *Failing Law Schools.* University of Chicago Press.

Tashea, Jason. 2020. "Nothing is Off-Limits for this California Bar Task Force." *Legal Rebels*, February 1.

Thompson, David, and Melanie Wachtell. 2009. "An Empirical Analysis of Supreme Court Certiorari Petition Procedures: The Call for Response and the Call for the Views of the Solicitor General." *George Mason Law Review* 16, no. 2: 237–302.

Thomsen, Jacqueline. 2020. " 'Politicians in Robes': Democrats Launch Push to Counter Conservatives' Judicial Strategy." *Law.Com*, May 27.

Train, Kenneth. 2009. *Discrete Choice Methods with Simulation.* 2nd ed. Cambridge University Press.

Tucker, Catherine. 2014. "The Effect of Patent Litigation and Patent Assertion Entities on Entrepreneurial Activity." Sloan School of Management Working Paper 5095-14, Cambridge, MA, June.

U.S. Chamber of Commerce Institute of Legal Reform. 2018. "Costs and Compensation of the U.S. Tort System." U.S. Chamber of Commerce, Washington, D.C., October.

United States Government Accountability Office. 2015. *Federal Workforce: Improved Supervision and Better Use of Probationary Periods are Needed to Address Substandard Employee Performance.* GAO-15-191, February.

Vossmeyer, Angela. 2015. "Analysis of Discrete Data Models with Endogeneity, Simultaneity, and Missing Outcomes." Ph.D. Diss., Department of Economics, University of California, Irvine.

Ward, Stephanie Francis. 2020. "Training for Nonlawyers to Provide Legal Advice Will Start in Arizona in the Fall." *ABA Journal*, February 6.

Ward, Stephanie Francis. 2019. "The Financial Costs for Firms When Women and Minority Lawyers Leave." *ABA Journal*, December 30.

Wasserman, Howard M. 2020. "Academic Feeder Judges." Florida International University Legal Studies Research Paper No. 20-02, January.

Wilkins, David B., Bryon Fong, and Ronit Dinovitzer. 2015. "The Women and Men of Harvard Law School: Preliminary Results from the HLS Career Study." HLS Center on the Legal Profession, https://clp.law.harvard.edu/assets/HLS-Career-Study-FINAL.pdf.

Williams, Joan C., Marina Multhaup, Su Li, and Rachel Korn. 2018. "You Can't Change What You Can't See: Interrupting Bias in the Legal Profession." ABA Commission on Women in the Profession and the Minority Corporate Counsel Association.

Winston, Clifford. 2021a. "Back to the Good or Were They the Bad Old Days of Antitrust? A Review Essay of Jonathan B. Baker's *The Antitrust Paradigm: Restoring a Competitive Economy.*" *Journal of Economic Literature* (forthcoming).

Winston, Clifford. 2021b. *Gaining Ground: Markets Helping Government.* Brookings Institution Press (forthcoming).

Winston, Clifford. 2006. *Government Failure Versus Market Failure: Microeconomic Policy Research and Government Performance.* Brookings Institution Press.

Winston, Clifford. 1998. "U.S. Industry Adjustment to Economic Deregulation." *Journal of Economic Perspectives* 12 (Summer): 89–110.

Winston, Clifford, Robert W. Crandall, and Vikram Maheshri. 2011. *First Thing We Do, Let's Deregulate All the Lawyers.* Brookings Institution Press.

Winston, Clifford, and Quentin Karpilow. 2016. "Should the U.S. Eliminate Entry Barriers to the Practice of Law? Perspectives Shaped by Industry Deregulation." *American Economic Review Papers and Proceedings* 5 (May): 171–76.

Women Lawyers on Guard. 2020. *Still Broken: Sexual Harassment and Misconduct in the Legal Profession.* Arlington, Virginia.

Yang, Crystal S. 2016. "Resource Constraints and the Criminal Justice System: Evidence from Judicial Vacancies." *American Economic Journal: Economic Policy* 8 (November): 289–332.

Zirin, James D. 2019. *Plaintiff in Chief: A Portrait of Donald Trump in 3,500 Lawsuits.* New York: All Points Books.

NOTES

1. The figures in this paragraph are from Robinson (2015) and the U.S. Political Stats are from CQ Press, https://library.cqpress.com/uspoliticalstats.

2. "Attorney Explains Legal Profession Above the Law on CBS News *60 Minutes* Hidden Camera," YouTube, February 22, 2016, www.youtube.com/watch?v=xY9S C8p4OFA.

3. Some recent extreme cases of UPL by individuals include an unlicensed jail-house lawyer (although the Vermont Supreme Court threw out the charges) and an unlicensed individual who had competently practiced law in estate planning for many years and had been promoted to partner in her law firm.

4. One could argue that legal services have been less effective than other industries at gaining favorable tax treatment because law firms do not get tax-specific benefits in the same way that other industries do, such as accelerated depreciation. However, the difference in tax treatment could be explained by the fact that law firms are not capital intensive.

5. Legal scholars such as Richard Posner and others who have contributed to law and economics research programs have strongly advocated the use of cost-benefit analysis. The University of Chicago's influence on antitrust theory has also given rise to greater consideration of costs and benefits in that area of law. Critics of Chicago's influence on antitrust laws simply assert that Chicagoans have strong ideological beliefs that markets work while ignoring empirical evidence on the matter and their own equally strong ideological beliefs that markets do not work (Winston 2021a).

6. In 2018, the Supreme Court in a 5-4 decision on *Gill v. Whitford* followed Roberts's lead by ruling that courts should stay out of disputes over partisan gerrymandering, with Roberts indicating that those disputes are too difficult for courts to decide.

Chapter 2

1. California is the most notable state to have its own law school accreditation process. Wisconsin allows graduates of the state's two major law schools to practice without taking a bar exam.

2. Karen Sloan, "Law Student Debt and Stress Levels on the Rise, Survey Finds," *National Law Journal*, February 29, 2016, reports that roughly 45 percent of law students expect to graduate owing more than $100,000 in student loans.

3. Austin, Christopher, and Dickerson (2017) provide evidence that LSAT scores are a good predictor of whether a law student will pass a state bar examination.

4. An exception is Lindley and Machin's (2014) paper providing estimates of post-college wage premiums in America and Britain.

5. There is some recent work by legal academics such as Tamanaha (2012) that argues that a legal education is no longer a sound investment, but this work generally does not perform an empirical analysis to support its conclusions.

6. We do not claim, nor do our data enable us to determine, whether law students get a greater return from attending a private rather than a public law school.

7. In 2018, the starting annual salary at large, corporate law firms in New York City jumped up to $190,000 after being held at $160,000 for many years. In addition, note that some new government lawyers, for example, those who work at the U.S. Department of Justice, earn much more than $65,000.

8. As is common among large-scale surveys, both the AJD and the B&B oversample certain segments of their respective populations. Accordingly, the data sets include sample weights that adjust for this oversampling to make the data sets nationally representative. Failure to account for the oversampling by not applying the weights could lead to skewed results. For example, the mean J.D. wage appears to be significantly higher when not accounting for the sample weights than it is when appropriately accounting for the weights. This is because the AJD intentionally oversamples J.D.s from private law firms, who tend to have higher wages than J.D.s employed by the public sector or by other private organizations.

9. The tiers are based on the rankings of law schools by *U.S News and World Report* that are used to classify law schools in the AJD.

10. The equality $\exp(\log x + 0.449) = 1.56x$ shows that increasing $\log x$ by .449 log points is equivalent to a 56 percent increase in the level of x. This is consistent with the summary statistics in table 2-1, which shows that the average wage for J.D.s, $109,000, is 56 percent greater than the average wage for non-J.D.s, $70,000.

11. We specified a lawyer indicator dummy, which was included in the CPS sample instead of the J.D. indicator variable, which was not included, with the difference that not all J.D. holders become lawyers. We also included a year indicator variable for each year of the CPS sample.

12. The hours of work variable is likely to be endogenous, but excluding it had little effect on our findings.

13. There are people with a J.D. who do nonlaw work, but we expect such work to be financially competitive with legal work. As empirical support, we found that the coefficient of a dummy variable for a "nonlaw job" in a wage regression estimated for the AJD sample was statistically insignificant.

14. "New Report Shows Most Law School Grads Passing Bar," American Bar Association, April 2019, www.americanbar.org/news/abanews/aba-news-archives/2019/04/new-report-shows-law-schools/.

15. For example, the average multistate bar exam score for February 2020 dropped to a new low, with the decrease attributable to repeat test-takers representing more than two-thirds of those taking the test. Debra Cassens Weiss, "Average Multistate Bar Exam Score Drops to New Low, Raising Concerns about Bar Pass Rates," *ABA Journal*, April 21, 2020, www.abajournal.com/news/article/multistate-bar-exam-score-drops-to-new-low-raising-concerns-about-bar-pass-rates.

16. Those states were California, Delaware, Louisiana, Nevada, and Virginia. For a complete discussion, see "Which States Have the Hardest Bar Exams?" JD Advising, www.jdadvising.com/states-hardest-bar-exams/.

17. Karen Sloan, "Associates Like Their Partners, but the Feeling Is Not Mutual, Study Finds," Law.com, April 02, 2020, www.law.com/2020/04/02/partners-say-associates-today-dont-work-as-hard-as-they-did/.

18. Hugh A. Simons, "Advice to Law Students in the Time of Covid-19: Your Path to Big Law," Law.com, March 21, 2020, www.law.com/2020/03/21/advice-to-law-students-in-the-time-of-covid-19-your-path-to-big-law/.

19. The sociology literature has termed this phenomenon "occupational inheritance." See, for example, Blau and Duncan (1967). Scholarly work on occupational inheritance generally finds a positive correlation between a parent's and child's occupation, though there is disagreement on the reason for this correlation.

20. To test this, we estimated a series of regressions, restricting the sample to individual law school tiers. We specified various subsets of the explanatory variables, including at least the lawyer parent variable in all regressions. We did not find that the lawyer parent variable had a statistically significant effect for any of the regressions or law school tiers.

21. The Hausman test statistic is 0.58, which is much smaller than the critical value at the 0.05 level of 30.14. Therefore, we fail to reject the null hypothesis that the OLS estimator is consistent.

22. We split up the sample and estimated separate models for each law school tier because we did not have three instruments that could distinguish how individuals choose which law school tier to attend.

23. As a robustness check of the nearest neighbor propensity score matching estimates, we also used kernel weighting. The results were similar.

24. As with any counterfactual analysis, one could question, for example, the estimates of a J.D. career earnings trajectory for non-J.D.s because non-J.D.s never go to

law school. Although it is difficult to resolve that issue, it does not appear to affect our findings that the J.D. premium clearly emerges, accounting for selection and the tuition and opportunity cost of law school.

25. A cubic polynomial is commonly used for this purpose because it is a very flexible function of experience. Using a cubic spline did not affect the main findings.

26. For comparison, we also estimated lawyer wages using a subsample of the CPS data. We restricted the age to thirty-two, which corresponds to roughly ten years after college graduation. We obtained the estimates by first regressing log wage on the explanatory variables used previously in our wage regressions. Then we predicted lawyer wages for each individual in the subsample and obtained a mean of $95,000, while the predicted average nonlawyer salary in the CPS subsample was $65,000.

27. We do not have information on scholarships or the cost actually paid by students to attend a given law school. However, scholarships amount to a transfer. Someone is bearing the cost of law school. Just because all of the costs are not borne by the student, they are still borne and should be considered in the return and not netted out. First-tier schools are the most generous in providing scholarships, so accounting for scholarships just increases the (private) advantage of going to a first-tier school. We do have information on whether family and friends helped shoulder the cost of law school, but that source should not affect the rate of return on a legal education given the funds are fungible. In general, to the extent that people pay less than the full cost of attending law school, their individual return is modestly better than we estimate, as total tuition cost is on the order of one-tenth of the net lifetime benefit from attending law school.

28. In 2020 dollars, average law school prices for the 1998 to 2000 law school cohorts were $21,000 per year. The top 20 schools charged $29,000 per year, middle-tier schools charged $20,000, and lower-tier schools charged $19,000.

29. The computation of net present values relies on estimates of J.D. and non-J.D. wages at one point in time and estimates of how those wages evolve over time. Each estimate has a standard error associated with it. We computed the standard errors for the net present value (NPV) calculations by taking draws for each parameter estimate from the appropriate distribution, as indicated by the standard errors of each individual estimate, and computing the net present value with those draws. We repeated this procedure one thousand times, at which point the standard errors converged, and we computed the standard errors of the NPV as the standard deviation of the sample of one thousand estimates.

30. This is the average age of retirement as of 2013, according to Gallup's Economy and Personal Finance Survey. The retirement age has been steadily increasing, thus it may be the case that individuals in our cohort will retire later still. A longer career will increase the estimated returns. However, the estimate is not terribly sensitive to career length given the heavy discounting of the distant future.

31. The internal rate of return of an investment is defined as the discount rate, which makes the benefits of the investment equal to 0. That is, in our context, the rate of return is r^*, where $NPV_{JD}(r^*,T) - NPV_{nonJD}(r^*,T) = 0$. An alternative way to interpret the 38 percent premium is that it is roughly equivalent to moving from the median of the non-J.D. earnings distribution to the 75th percentile.

32. There is a large literature on the returns to college education. For example, Card (1999) surveys twelve widely cited studies with estimates ranging from 5 to 15 percent.

33. Merritt (2015) provides a detailed analysis of the bleak employment market facing the law school class of 2010 based on early career outcomes. She concludes that structural shifts have occurred that raise troubling questions about the long-term career prospects for law school graduates.

34. The data on LSAT scores are from 509 reports submitted by accredited law schools to the ABA.

35. The data on the share of "at risk" students are from a Law School Transparency investigation, http://lawschooltransparency.com/reform/projects/investigations/2015/key-findings/.

36. The data on bar passage rates are from 509 reports submitted by accredited law schools to the ABA.

37. Aaron N. Taylor, Chad Christensen, and Louis M. Rocconi, "How a Decade of Debt Changed the Law Student Experience" (LSSSE Annual Results 2015), February 2016, Indiana University Center for Postsecondary Research, http://lawprofessors.typepad.com/files/lssse-annual-report-2015.pdf.

38. Individuals who are eventually employed as lawyers may have wages during their intervening years of employment that are greater than the wages of individuals who have only a bachelor's degree. We therefore performed a sensitivity analysis where we inflated by 20 percent the predicted wages of law school graduates during the intervening years between graduation and finding a job that requires or rewards a J.D. Because the delay occurs at the beginning of a J.D.'s career when wages and the premia are relatively low, and lasts for only a short time, the increased wages had a very limited effect—less than one percentage point—on the lifetime rate of return.

39. Law School Transparency, "Law School Costs," https://data.lawschooltransparency.com/costs/debt-income/?scope=schools.

Chapter 3

1. The full report is available at the ABA website: www.americanbar.org/content/dam/aba/administrative/legal_education_and_admissions_to_the_bar/reports/2015_june_report_of_the_aba_task_force_on_the_financing_of_legal_education.authcheckdam.pdf.

2. As noted, it is not clear whether those individuals use their legal training for their career in another sector.

3. Exceptions do exist throughout the country. For example, California has its own law school accreditation process, and Wisconsin allows graduates of the state's two major law schools to practice without taking a bar exam. Currently, seven states also allow individuals to become a lawyer by serving as an apprentice under the supervision of a practicing attorney or judge. The specific rules for obtaining a license to practice law through an apprenticeship vary from state to state.

4. ABA's accreditation standards also include a bar examination passage rate that a law school's graduates must achieve to stay accredited. The ABA aims for a 75 percent

passage rate, but there are loopholes, and, as noted, bar passage rates have been falling nationwide. The ABA may eliminate those loopholes, but it is not clear that the quality of legal practitioners is enhanced by its requirement of a minimum bar passage rate for a law school's graduates. In fact, certain law schools are being sued by some of their graduates, even though they passed the state bar, because they have been unable to obtain a job as a lawyer several years after graduating.

5. Recent examples of this gap are described by Seidman (2016), who points out that roughly two-thirds of those eligible for legal aid in Massachusetts are turned down because there are not enough legal aid attorneys, and by Bunton (2016), who discusses why the New Orleans public defender's office began to refuse new cases.

6. In fact, Winston, Crandall, and Maheshri (2011) provide examples of individuals who have provided effective legal services for many years without ever attending law school, only to be charged with the unauthorized practice of law.

7. Companies such as LegalZoom can help lower the cost of some legal services. However, LegalZoom is not a law firm, its employees are not acting as anyone's attorney, and the company is not providing legal advice to anyone. LegalZoom can provide self-help services at an individual's specific direction.

8. The United Kingdom, for example, sharply differentiates between legal services with barristers representing individuals and organizations in court and solicitors performing most of their work out of court in a law firm or other legal setting. Barristers are compensated more highly than solicitors because they are the leading advocates in a trial. Recently, nonlawyers have been able to expand their presence in the U.K. legal profession as a legal regulator has given Reed Smith, an international law firm, the approval to adopt an alternative business structure that allows the firm to have nonlawyer partners and receive outside investment. The different job classifications, however, do not necessarily increase access to legal services for low-income individuals.

9. Karen Sloan, "Help Wanted: Law Schools Need Professors," Law.com, October 3, 2019, www.law.com/2019/10/03/help-wanted-law-schools-need-professors/?slreturn=20191019121130.

10. Such courses are distinct from courses on analytical methods, covering statistics and regression analysis, which have been taught at the top law schools for many years.

Chapter 4

1. Some high-level federal government officials also come from state government. We discuss the constraints that affect the performance of government lawyers in later chapters.

2. Eisenberg, Miller, and Germano (2017) find that lawyers' fees as a percentage of a class action recovery tend to decrease as the size of the recovery increases.

3. Kiser (2019) believes that law firms face severe, chronic, and endemic problems that are rooted in several sources, and he suggests how law firms should change to adopt modern practices and to provide greater value to clients.

4. Hugh A. Simons, "How Many Excess Partners Does Your Firm Have?" Law.com, August 30, 2017, www.law.com/americanlawyer/almID/1202796892210/.

5. James Manyika and others, *Harnessing Automation for a Future that Works,*

McKinsey Global Institute, January 12, 2017, www.mckinsey.com/featured-insights/
digital-disruption/harnessing-automation-for-a-future-that-works; Caroline Hill,
"Deloitte Insight: Over 100,000 Legal Roles to Be Automated," Legal IT Insider,
March 16, 2016, www.legaltechnology.com/latest-news/deloitte-insight-100000-legal-
roles-to-be-automated/.

6. Debra Cassens Weiss, "Lawyers Have Duty to Stay Current on Technology's
Risks and Benefits, New Model Ethics Comment Says," August 6, 2012, *ABA Journal,*
www.abajournal.com/news/article/lawyers_have_duty_to_stay_current_on_tech
nologys_risks_and_benefits.

7. "2015 Law Firms in Transition: An Altman Weil Flash Survey," Altman Weil,
Inc., www.altmanweil.com/dir_docs/resource/1c789ef2-5cff-463a-863a-2248d23
882a7_document.pdf.

8. Lex Machina is an example of a technology company in Silicon Valley that com-
bines data and software to help corporate counsel and law firms craft and implement
legal strategies. The company began as a project at Stanford University and is currently
a division of LexisNexis, which contains a large database for legal and public-records
related information.

9. Dan Packel, "'This Is Not Greenberg Traurig': Firm Leader Touts New Innovation Venture," Law.com, June 12, 2019, www.law.com/americanlawyer/2019/06/12/
this-is-not-greenberg-traurig-firm-leader-touts-new-innovation-venture.

10. "Burnout Is Part of the Profession. How Can Attorneys Avoid It?" The Young
Lawyer Editorial Board, Law.com, February 26, 2019, www.law.com/americanlawyer/
2019/02/26/burnout-is-part-of-the-profession-how-can-attorneys-avoid-it.

11. Zach Schlein, "58% of Young Lawyers Think Legal Profession Is 'Less Desirable,'
Bar Survey Finds," Law.com, May 8, 2019, www.law.com/dailybusinessreview/2019/
05/08/58-of-young-lawyers-think-legal-profession-is-less-desirable-bar-survey-finds.

12. Debra Cassens Weiss, "Percentage of Equity Partners Continues to Shrink While
BigLaw Profits Increase," *ABA Journal,* May 7, 2019, www.abajournal.com/news/article/
percentage-of-equity-partners-continues-to-shrink-while-biglaw-profits-increase.

13. Vivia Chen, "American Law Firms with Zero Black Partners—How Is This
Possible in 2019?" Law.com, June 06, 2019, www.law.com/americanlawyer/2019/06/
06/am-law-firms-with-zero-black-partners-how-is-this-possible-in-2019.

14. "Report to the House of Delegates," ABA, www.americanbar.org/content/
dam/aba/images/abanews/2018-AM-Resolutions/300.pdf.

15. Christine Simmons, "170 GCs Pen Open Letter to Law Firms: Improve on Diversity
or Lose Our Business," Law.com, January 27, 2019, www.law.com/americanlawyer/2019/
01/27/170-gcs-pen-open-letter-to-law-firms-improve-on-diversity-or-lose-our-business.

16. The lack of diversity and gender bias issues is hardly limited to law firms. For
example, the American Economic Association has started to come to terms with bias
toward female and minority economists (www.aeaweb.org/about-aea/code-of-conduct).

17. In an earlier study, Levine (2016), drawing on evidence from the American
Bar Association Commission on Lawyer Assistance Programs and the Hazelden Betty
Ford Foundation, reported that 21 to 36 percent of lawyers are problem drinkers, 28
percent suffer from depression, 19 percent have anxiety, and 23 percent are impaired

by stress. Krill, Johnson, and Albert (2016) reported that alcohol use disorders among American attorneys occur at a higher rate than in other professions.

18. "Well-Being in the Legal Profession," ABA, Well-Being Pledge Campaign, www.americanbar.org/groups/lawyer_assistance/well-being-in-the-legal-profession/.

19. We stress that this view applies to lawyers who take leave from their law firm. Some law professors also take leave from their law school to take positions in government, which may broaden their scholarly perspectives and improve their research. We speculate, but certainly cannot prove, that legal academics who are exposed to alternative approaches to policy analysis and to quantitative methods are likely to contribute to more socially desirable government policies (or help to prevent socially undesirable policies) than are legal academics without that background.

Chapter 5

1. Our use of the term earnings penalty is not intended to be normatively loaded. It could also be thought of as a negative wage differential or wage gap. The use of the word "penalty" in this context indicates that a financial cost is associated with choosing to work as a lawyer in the government.

2. Gittleman and Pierce (2012) find that, on average, public sector workers in state government in various professions have compensation costs that are 3 to 10 percent greater than those for workers in the private sector, while in local government, the gap is 10 to 19 percent. The authors, however, do not report a comparison that is specific to lawyers in local and state government versus lawyers in the private sector. Instead, they combine lawyers with seven other professions.

3. For example, the president's annual salary of $400,000 puts a cap on federal government lawyers' earnings, but this figure vastly overstates the cap because the highest current annual salary for a lawyer who works for the president, the White House Counsel, is $183,000.

4. Very few lawyers begin their careers as an in-house counsel, and private law firms do not tend to hire associates from in-house positions. Of course, private sector lawyers may switch to an in-house position, but that switch is not included in the initial "After the JD" survey.

5. *After the JD II: Second Results from a National Study of Legal Careers*, American Bar Foundation and NALP Foundation for Law Career Research and Education, 2009, www.law.du.edu/documents/directory/publications/sterling/AJD2.pdf.

6. Labor supply is based on a utility function that includes wages, nonwage job characteristics, and personal characteristics as arguments. Thus, γ, the coefficient for G represents a penalty, because if a person with those observed and unobserved personal and job characteristics went to work in the private sector, their earnings would be greater. Apparently, the utility from working for the government compared with the private sector justifies working for the government.

7. Specifically, we use the Huber-White sandwich estimator to compute the standard errors in our second-stage earnings equation.

8. An exception is Biddle and Hamermesh (1998), who used a sample of lawyers to estimate the relationship between beauty and earnings.

9. Annual salaries for government lawyers are based on a schedule of pay classifications. For example, most entry level jobs for federal attorneys are classified by the GS-12 pay grade, which is currently about $64,000 per year at Step 1.

10. As a qualification, our model may underestimate the earnings penalty from working in government because we do not account for private sector lawyers' fringe benefits related to law firm perks, such as free meals, free tickets to sporting and other entertainment events, and the like.

11. In a sense, lawyers who work for private law firms for their entire career eventually become a partner or obtain similar job security. Of course, it is difficult to make partner at, say, the two hundred largest law firms in the United States, but it is easier to make partner at law firms outside of this elite group. Solo practitioners and partners at very small firms do not have the same job security as partners at larger firms because they are more vulnerable to economic downturns that may significantly affect their flow of business.

12. This is especially true when we perform our analysis using Wave 3 of the AJD survey, which includes lawyers in their eleventh year of their career who would have had more than sufficient time to become a partner or to obtain greater security at their place of work.

13. Our data provide respondents' answers to the questions of how many hours they worked in the previous week, and, where applicable, how many hours they billed in that week. Although weekly billable hours of work are important for private sector lawyers, there is no comparable measure for government lawyers, and private lawyers' weekly hours of work are highly correlated with their billable hours. In the interest of generating billable hours, it could be argued that lawyers in the private sector work much harder and have less downtime than do government lawyers. We explore this possible effect empirically by multiplying government lawyers' hours per week by two-thirds and re-estimating the earnings equation. We find that this adjustment has a modest effect on the earnings penalty.

14. Generally, the demand for lawyers that may affect earnings is driven to a large extent by time-related variables, such as macroeconomic and policy considerations, as well as industry and societal trends that may affect the demand for private sector lawyers. Those influences could be captured by annual time dummies, but because each AJD sample discussed below includes information about lawyers only for a specific number of years after they passed the bar examination, we do not include those dummies in our estimations.

15. It may also be appropriate to include demand variables in the model, such as the availability of government jobs, which varies with the state of the economy over time and could be captured with time dummies. But, as in the case of the earnings equation, we do not include those time dummies because each AJD sample includes information about lawyers only for a specific number of years after they passed the bar examination.

16. *After the JD: First Results of a National Study of Legal Careers*, NALP Foundation for Law Career Research and Education and the American Bar Foundation, 2004, www.americanbarfoundation.org/uploads/cms/documents/ajd.pdf.

17. *After the JD II*, American Bar Foundation and NALP Foundation for Law Career Research and Education, 2009.

18. Historically, lawyers' unemployment rates have been low. In 2002, less than 4 percent of lawyers surveyed by the AJD reported being unemployed; in the 2007 wave, this number hovered at about 5 percent. Unemployment among new law school graduates significantly increased following the Great Recession but has stabilized during the past few years. The novel coronavirus is likely to be another large shock to employment in the legal industry.

19. Robert Nelson and others, *After the JD, Wave 3: A Longitudinal Study of Careers in Transition, 2012–2013, United States,* Inter-university Consortium for Political and Social Research, www.icpsr.umich.edu/icpsrweb/ICPSR/studies/35480.

20. *After the JD II,* American Bar Foundation and NALP Foundation for Law Career Research and Education, 2009.

21. AJD Wave 1 contains a sample of 4,538 lawyers. Our analyses focused on the 3,411 reported working in either government or a private law firm. From among this subset, we dropped in sequence: (1) 276 lawyers who reported invalid salaries; (2) sixty-five who were missing on either race, age, or gender; (3) 295 who were missing on either the measure hours worked per week or the indicator for working full time; (4) nineteen who were missing on law school rank and 1,324 who were missing on law school GPA; (5) forty-one who were missing on at least one of our parental characteristics measures; (6) fifty-one who were missing on the debt measure; and (7) another eight who were missing on either the financial security or help society measures. This led to a final analysis sample of 1,332 lawyers working in government or at a private law firm. The final "clean" sample was not biased in any particular way, and, as we discuss later, the findings we obtained from it are consistent with those we obtained from a larger sample of University of Michigan law school graduates that had fewer instances of missing data.

22. We are not aware of any evidence that grade inflation is more prevalent at higher-ranked law schools. However, if graduates from higher-quality law schools tend to have higher GPAs than graduates from lower-quality law schools, that does not contradict the finding that the private sector hires lawyers of higher average quality. In any case, based on the University of Michigan sample, we find similar sectoral differences between GPAs, and we estimate an earnings penalty that is consistent with the estimate we obtain using the AJD sample.

23. Between 2005 and 2010, Congress passed several laws addressing the issue of student debt forgiveness, but those programs are too recent to affect AJD respondents. Between 1994 and 2008, roughly one-quarter to 40 percent of law schools had loan-forgiveness plans for graduates who worked in the public sector or who took other, low-paying jobs (Schrag and Pruett 2011). However, it is not clear how those plans contributed to equalizing the educational debt that was actually reported by AJD respondents who worked for government and private law firms.

24. AJD Wave 2 surveyed 3,705 lawyers. Our analyses focused on the 2,272 who reported working in either government or a private law firm. We used the same exclusion criteria employed for the AJD Wave 1 to arrive at a Wave 2 analysis sample of 904 lawyers.

25. Parental characteristics may arguably capture unobserved ability, but such abil-

ity is also likely to be highly correlated with observed ability as captured by the quality of the law school that the child attended and the child's GPA. For example, assume that the child's parent works for the government. What would that fact tell us about the quality of the child as a lawyer conditional on the child earning a 4.0 GPA at Harvard Law School?

26. The white category includes respondents that self-reported their racial group as both white and Hispanic (less than 4 percent of the whites in the sample).

27. Despite its statistical insignificance in our estimations, we kept the debt variable in the sector-choice specification because student debt levels are of particular interest in policy discussions, and therefore its effect is of interest.

28. Recall from chapter 2 that an individual's choice to become a lawyer is positively affected by having a lawyer parent, but we did not assess whether having a lawyer parent affected sector choice.

29. Our findings were not affected by whether the job satisfaction index included compensation as one of its factors.

30. In chapter 4, we noted that equity partners' happiness is associated with their compensation. This also appears to be true for the lawyers in the AJD sample, as a regression of their compensation on the job "satisfaction index" discussed above showed a positive and statistically significant relationship.

31. There may be concern that whether a lawyer that is employed full time is endogenous, but this variable has been found in other contexts (for example, Winston, Crandall, and Maheshri 2011) to be strongly determined by scheduling flexibility rather than earnings, especially for women. In any case, our estimate of the works in government dummy was not affected much by the inclusion of this variable.

32. Generally, summary statistics of the entire AJD sample indicate that differences in race earnings gaps are primarily due to minorities choosing to work in sectors such as public interest law that pay lower-than-average wages. Within a sector, racial or ethnic pay gaps have been found to be largely nonexistent. It is also important to note that the positive effect on earnings of being a racial or ethnic minority may not apply to lawyers who have been in practice for longer than, say, ten years because the *American Lawyer* reports that minorities constitute a tiny share of partners at the top 100 largest firms.

33. Because the mean and median earnings diverged for the highest earners in the AJD3, we re-estimated the full model using a linear instead of a log-linear earnings equation and obtained an estimated earnings penalty that was slightly lower, 53 percent, than the estimated penalty based on a log-linear earnings equation.

34. After eleven years into their careers, it is not clear that lawyers are choosing which sector to work in. Instead, their selection may be largely affected by unobserved characteristics.

35. Based on a sample of lawyers who we observed in AJD1 and AJD3, we estimated a model of earnings controlling for law school tier that identified lawyers who started in government and then switched to the private sector. We found that starting one's career in government had a negative effect on earnings. To be sure, there are lawyers who may raise their earnings in the private sector by starting their careers as law clerks in government. But the share of all federal and state and local government lawyers who

obtain those competitive clerkships is small. For example, each associate U.S. Supreme Court justice has no more than four clerks, while the Chief Justice may have five. State Supreme Courts are often composed of a fewer number of justices and law clerks. Finally, established lawyers who work for private law firms may increase their earnings by accepting a high-level government position and then returning to the private sector to resume their practice. But those lawyers tend to have more than the eleven years of work experience covered by the AJD sample; thus, we could not quantify that effect.

36. As noted, the AJD sample included weights to be consistent with a random sample. The Michigan sample did not include sampling weights, but as shown below, the responses in the two samples are broadly consistent, suggesting that the Michigan sample does not suffer from any particular sampling bias.

37. We were unable to conduct a similar analysis for lawyers who switched from working in the government in AJD2 to working for the private sector in AJD3 because only thirteen lawyers made that switch.

38. The government earnings penalty was not affected even though the government did not retain its intellectually strongest lawyers, probably because, as shown in table 5-5, the government also did not retain some of its intellectually weaker lawyers. On net, then, the average quality of public sector attorneys appears to have remained relatively constant across the AJD waves.

39. The problem of self-selection in government is hardly limited to lawyers. For example, Gregory Travis, "How the Boeing 737 Max Disaster Looks to a Software Developer," *Washington Post*, April 18, 2019, explains that as airplanes became more complex and the gulf between what the Federal Aviation Administration (FAA) could pay an engineer and what an aircraft manufacturer could pay grew larger, more and more of those engineers migrated from the public to the private sector. Soon, the FAA had no in-house ability to determine if an airplane's design and manufacture were safe.

Chapter 6

1. U.S. Department of Justice, About the Office, www.justice.gov/osg/about-office-1.

2. Our findings were not affected when we used alternative cut-off points for the number of cases a top advocate argued before the Supreme Court.

3. We define split-decision cases to be any case in which at least one justice votes for the petitioner and at least one justice votes for the respondent.

4. More specifically, we used Spaeth's *petitioner* and *respondent* variables to identify federal government and private parties. A party was labeled as the federal government if either the *petitioner* or *respondent* variable assumed one of the following values: 1, 27, 301, 302, 304, 305, 307–372, 374, 376–417.

5. Here, we used Spaeth's *petitionerState* and *respondentState* variables to identify state parties so as not to remove those. Some of the entities that are excluded from the "private" category include city, town, township, village, or borough governments, commissions, committees, and agencies. For more details on Spaeth's categorization of SCOTUS petitioners and respondents, see Spaeth et al. (2013).

6. For simplicity, we also excluded the few cases that are decided by an equally divided vote.

7. This specification is a more targeted approach to control for temporal effects than to use year fixed effects.

8. Natural court indicators are widely used in studies of Supreme Court outcomes; see, for example, Lim (2000). We also tried to capture ideological conflict between the court and the president because such conflict may hurt the performance of the solicitor general's office, which presumably shares the views of the president. We specified a dummy variable indicating whether the president is a Democrat because the majority of justices in our sample have been appointed by a president from the Republican Party since the 1980s. However, this dummy variable was statistically insignificant and did not affect our findings.

9. For instance, Donald B. Verrilli was a partner at Jenny & Block before serving the government as associate deputy attorney general and later solicitor general. Maureen E. Mahoney spent more than a decade litigating in the private sector at Latham & Watkins before working as deputy solicitor general (1991 to 1993). And Theodore B. Olson has, apart from his two government stints as assistant attorney general (1981 to 1984) and solicitor general (2001 to 2004), worked at the private law firm of Gibson, Dunn & Crutcher since 1965.

10. Epstein, Landes, and Posner (2013) and chapter 7 discuss the growing polarization of the Roberts court compared with the Rehnquist court in deciding business cases.

11. The government does have contracts with private law firms for legal services but not to provide representation in cases against a private sector entity before the Supreme Court.

12. Priest and Klein (1984, 52) apply their predictive model to antitrust cases before the Supreme Court and note evidence that government agencies as plaintiffs in antitrust prosecutions are successful much more than 50 percent of the time, which is consistent with our data. Lahav and Eiegelman (2019) provide recent evidence that is at variance with the Priest-Klein hypothesis by finding that the success rate for plaintiffs in adjudicated federal civil cases declined from roughly 70 percent in 1985 to 33 percent in 2009 and then stabilized. A reason for the falling win rate was not provided.

13. The characteristics of cases involving a top advocate are broadly similar to those not involving a top advocate with the exceptions that there was a somewhat higher percentage of criminal procedure cases not involving a top advocate and somewhat higher percentage of economic activity cases involving at least one top advocate.

14. We do not present clustered standard errors in the table because it is not clear what the natural clustering variable should be. For example, clustering on attorneys raises the question of which attorney, the prosecution or the defense? And what if there are multiple attorneys for a particular side? A plausible check on our estimated standard errors was to cluster on issue areas. When we did so, we found that the clustered standard errors were similar to, if not smaller than, the robust standard errors that we reported in table 6-3. For example, the standard error of the coefficient for top advocate attorney for the private sector decreased from 0.299 to 0.236.

15. As indicated in table 6-1, our sample includes eleven top advocate attorneys, and as indicated in table 6-2, our sample consists of roughly fifty-two cases involving a top advocate attorney for the government and twenty-one cases involving a top advocate attorney for the private sector. Thus, we did not have enough observations for each top advocate attorney to identify his or her individual specific effect when they represent the government and when they represent the private sector. Thus, we form variables to measure the effect on case outcomes of the *same set of top attorneys* when they represent the government and when they represent the private sector.

16. In some cases, the government or the private party or both were represented by more than one attorney arguing the case. We consider the government or the private party to be represented by a top advocate if at least one of its attorneys was a top advocate.

17. The marginal effect and standard error of the top advocate representing the private sector implied by our probit model are −0.264 (0.120).

18. The marginal effect and standard error of the top advocate representing the federal government implied by our probit model are 0.008 (0.074).

19. Estimates from our model indicate that the federal government is significantly more likely to win in cases involving criminal procedure than in other cases, holding all else constant.

20. In our sample, roughly twenty cases have a top advocate lawyer representing the private sector, and roughly fifty cases have a top advocate lawyer representing the government. But we find that the standard error for the dummy variable for the top advocate lawyer representing the private sector is not relatively large, while the standard error for the dummy variable for the top advocate lawyer representing the government is relatively large. This is the opposite of what one would expect based on the likely power of the estimates.

21. For example, "The Echo Chamber," *A Reuters Special Report*, December 8, 2014, reports that, in just one month, a large trial can generate $1 million or more in fees for a law firm, while the firm's bill for an entire Supreme Court case might range from $50,000 to $500,000.

22. Marcia Coyle, "The Cost of Seeking Supreme Court Review," Law.com, March 25, 2020, www.law.com/supremecourtbrief/2020/03/25/a-doubting-thomas-raises-more-questions-the-cost-of-seeking-review-high-flying-justices-cate-stetson-looks-ahead-to-milestone/.

23. Similarly, McGinnis (1992) characterizes the solicitor general's office as a government bureaucracy that strives to make decisions with minimal interference from other bureaucratic units.

24. The American Lawyer Legal Intelligence database ranks top-revenue-grossing law firms for each year between 1996 and 2014. We obtained employment information for the attorneys in our sample from Martindale Hubble, AVVO, and their websites. We indicate whether the firm that the attorney worked for in the most recent year for which we have employment information for that attorney was in the top 200.

25. We determined where the attorneys in our sample graduated from law school

using information contained in Martindale Hubble, AVVO, and websites of the firms that employed the attorneys, and, in a few instances, from obituaries of the attorneys. In specifications not shown here, we also defined a top law school to be: (1) the top 10 law schools in 2016, and (2) the law schools attended by our top Supreme Court advocates. Those alternative specifications yielded comparable results.

26. In 2016, *U.S. News & World Report* ranked the top 5 law schools as follows: (1) Yale, (2) Harvard and Stanford (tied), and (3) Columbia and Chicago (tied) (http:// grad-schools.usnews.rankingsandreviews.com/best-graduate-schools/top-law-schools/law-rankings).

27. We counted the total number of cases each attorney argued using the Oyez archive of Supreme Court cases.

28. As discussed earlier, data on the case win margins come from the Spaeth Database.

29. In specifications not shown here, we also included variables that measured the years of experience of the private and public sector lawyers, defined as the difference between a lawyer's age during the case before the Supreme Court and age when the lawyer passed the bar examination. Those variables were statistically insignificant and did not affect the estimated coefficients of the top advocates in government and the private sector.

30. The solicitor general's office regularly recruits lawyers from so-called Big Law firms. For example, a Big Law partner and two law firm associates recently filled vacancies in the office just before the 2019 term began.

31. According to an administrative assistant in the office, it currently has a total of fifty-five employees including all the attorneys.

32. U.S. GAO (2015) discusses the substantial time, protracted process, and commitment of resources needed to remove a poor-performing government employee. McGinnis (1992) argues that the solicitor general's office is essentially a procedural organization, where the solicitor general observes the input of his or her workers by reading their briefs and placing great emphasis on whether the briefs cite all relevant Supreme Court precedents and quote extensively from them.

33. As pointed out in chapter 5, the government tends to lose its ablest lawyers, those who decide to work for the private sector, during the beginning of their career.

34. The Supreme Court may also receive *amicus curiae* briefs by interested parties for the most important cases. They may also receive those briefs for other cases.

35. *National Federation of Independent Business v. Sebelius*, 132 S. Ct. 2566 (2012).

36. *FCC v. Fox Television Stations*, 129 S. Ct. 1800 (2009).

37. For those cases in which both the private and government attorneys are top advocates, the effect of the private top advocate attorney on the probability of the government winning the case is measured by the sum of the coefficient for the private attorney is a top advocate (−0.994) and the coefficient for the top government advocate and the top private advocate (1.519), which is positive.

38. As before, top law schools were identified using the 2016 *U.S. News and World Report* survey.

39. To be precise, a statistical test fails to reject the null hypothesis that the effects of a top advocate in government and a top advocate in the private sector on the outcome of an important case, as defined here, are the same.

40. For example, among cases that (1) were argued by non-top government advocates, and (2) involved a private attorney who graduated from a top 3 law school, 47 percent were argued by a government attorney who graduated from a top 3 law school. Similarly, among cases that (1) were argued by non-top government advocates, and (2) *did not* involve a private attorney who graduated from a top 3 law school, 48 percent were argued by a government attorney who graduated from a top 3 law school.

41. For example, if all cases involving high-quality private sector attorneys were ambiguous, and all cases involving lower-quality private attorneys were legally straightforward, we might expect to find muted government attorney quality effects for cases involving lower-quality private attorneys. However, this does not appear to be the case, as we found that the win margin was uncorrelated with our measures of private attorney quality (for example, whether a private attorney graduated from a top 3 law school). As discussed previously, the win margin of a case reflects, in part, the legal ambiguity of a case.

42. Responses by employees of the Office of the Solicitor General to the Office of Personnel Management's Federal Employee Viewpoint Survey (FEVS) may have been able to shed additional light on our findings. However, the office's response rate was so low that results for the solicitor general's office were not published separately from results for several other U.S. Department of Justice entities.

Chapter 7

1. For example, from 1801 to 1940, less than 2 percent of SCOTUS's total rulings were resolved by 5-4 decisions. In contrast, the Roberts court has decided 21.5 percent of its cases by 5-4 rulings, the highest share of any court, and the Rehnquist court decided 20.5 percent of its cases by that margin. The figures are reported in David Paul Kuhn, "The Incredible Polarization and Politicization of the Supreme Court," *The Atlantic*, June 29, 2012.

2. For example, Devins and Baum (2014) report that between 1937 and 2010, one major case (in 1985) broke along party lines, but since 2010, five major decisions have been decided in that manner.

3. Robert Barnes, "The Supreme Court and Political World are more Entangled than either Acknowledges," *Washington Post*, July 17, 2016.

4. Sheldon Whitehouse, "There's a 'Crisis of Credibility' at the U.S. Supreme Court," Law.com, February 19, 2019, www.law.com/newyorklawjournal/2019/02/19/sen-whitehouse-theres-a-crisis-of-credibility-at-the-u-s-supreme-court-389-59002.

5. Carl Hulse, "Political Polarization Takes Hold of the Supreme Court," *New York Times*, July 5, 2018, www.nytimes.com/2018/07/05/us/politics/political-polarization-supreme-court.html.

6. The growing polarity of the Supreme Court is further suggested by Peppers and Giles' (2012) findings that the justices' attendance at the president's State of the Union (SOTU) address has declined in recent decades and that a justice is more likely

to attend the SOTU address if he or she was appointed by the president giving the address. According to the authors, from 1965 (President Johnson's second address) to 1980 (President Carter's last address), 84 percent of the justices attended the SOTU address, on average. From 1982 through 1999, the justices' average attendance declined to 56 percent. And since 2000, only 32 percent of the justices attended the address, with Justice Clarence Thomas claiming that "it has become so partisan and it's very uncomfortable for a judge to sit there," and the late Justice Antonin Scalia describing the annual address as "cheerleading sessions."

7. Justice Roberts' concerns about polarization and partisanship in the Supreme Court are summarized by Rosen (2013) and Professor Geoffrey Stone of the University of Chicago Law School in "Our Politically Polarized Supreme Court?" Huffington Post Blog, September 24, 2014.

8. For example, see Epstein, Landes, and Posner (2013a, b); prediction models of Supreme Court outcomes developed by Ruger et al. (2004) and Katz, Bommarito, and Blackman (2014); and examinations of changes in individual justices' ideological beliefs by Iaryczower and Shum (2012) and Martin and Quinn (2007).

9. Compared with the classic Heckman selection model of the discrete outcome of employment or unemployment and a continuous wage, one can think of the discrete outcome of employment or unemployment and a discrete outcome of earnings above the minimum wage or, in a political context, the choice of whether to run for office and the outcome of the election.

10. One popular definition of a business win focuses on cases that have been coded in the Spaeth Database as being related to "economic activity" and then use Spaeth's ideological classifications of a case as either "conservative" or "liberal" as a proxy for pro- or antibusiness decisions, respectively. Epstein, Landes, and Posner (2013a), however, show that this definition excludes a substantial number of cases that do not fall into the "economic activity" category but nonetheless involved business entities. Even more telling, the authors find that many of those excluded cases were accompanied by an *amicus curiae* brief filed by the Chamber of Commerce, a sure indicator of the business relevance of a case. Epstein, Landes, and Posner also call into question the accuracy of Spaeth's ideological classification of cases when they conduct their own re-analysis of 147 business-related cases. Strikingly, in about 39 percent of the 147 cases reviewed, the authors disagreed with Spaeth's ideological coding. Rates of disagreement were even higher for business cases that did not fall within the "economic activity" classification.

11. Note the dummy captures ideological preferences and not just philosophical disagreement among justices because we control for several other factors on case decisions and because our main analyses explore systematic differences among justices' preferences by assessing them relative to the chief justice's preference.

12. We use Bloomberg BNA's Supreme Court Today's dataset to obtain petitions to the Supreme Court for each year of our sample. That database categorizes petitions according to sixty-four different legal categories. Due to sample size issues, we aggregated those fine-grained classifications into eleven broad topic categories, namely: (1) criminal law, which contains cases related to criminal law, prisons, and racketeering; (2) civil

rights law, which is composed of Bloomberg's civil rights, education, election, and employment discrimination topics; (3) regulatory law, which contains petitions related to agriculture, antitrust, energy, environment, healthcare, international trade, securities, utilities, telecommunications, and transportation; (4) consumer and worker safety law, which contains Bloomberg's consumer credit, consumer protection, deceptive trade, employee benefits, mining, occupational safety, product liability, unfair trade practices, employment/labor, attorney ethnics, and torts topics; (5) private and state business law, which contains petitions related to accounting, banking and finance, contracts, corporate and business law, insurance, partnerships, arbitration, alcoholic beverages, and gambling; (6) intellectual property law, which is composed of Bloomberg's copyrights, patents, and trademarks topics; (7) government authority issues, which contains petitions related to administrative law, agency law, international law, takings, appellate procedure, civil procedure, congressional operations, evidence, judicial appointments, and constitutional law; (8) technology issues, which contains petitions related to cyber law, media, and privacy; (9) other government issues, which is composed of Bloomberg's bankruptcy, government contracts, immigration, infrastructure, maritime, military, Native American, postal services, social security, veterans, and freedom of information topics; (10) tax law, which is composed only of Bloomberg's tax topic; and (11) private nonbusiness, which includes Bloomberg's family law, trusts and estates, and nonprofit organizations topics.

13. "The United States Law Week," Bloomberg Law website, www.bna.com/supreme-court-today-p5946/.

14. Paid cert petitions are also called nonpauper petitions. No one has collected data on pauper (nonpaid) petitions, which represent only about 10 percent of the Supreme Court's docket and tend to be easily resolved by the justices (Posner (2008)). Note that some early-1996 paid cert petitions are also missing from the Bloomberg database. The database does, however, contain the full population of nonpauper SCOTUS petitions submitted in all post-1996 years.

15. To construct our random sample of Bloomberg petitions, we first sorted eligible petitions by the date on which the SCOTUS decided to hear (or not hear) the petition. Only petitions that were either granted or denied a hearing with SCOTUS were eligible for selection. Then, for each year, we selected every tenth petition to include in our sample, meaning that, on average, we sampled between 100 and 300 petitions for each SCOTUS term. Note that the 2,768 randomly selected petitions and the 198 BLD petitions are not mutually exclusive because some randomly selected petitions were also included in the Business Litigant Dataset.

16. Jeffrey L. Fisher, "The Supreme Court's Secret Power," *New York Times*, September 25, 2015, argues that justices' votes on each petition should be announced to increase transparency on why justices pick the cases they do. The absence of this voting information makes it difficult for us to assess whether justices engage in "defensive denials" or other forms of strategic behavior (Corday and Corday 2008).

17. Because we cannot account for individual Supreme Court justices' votes on the thousands of petitions it receives annually and on motions to intervene in lower-court proceedings, we are unable to identify the full extent of ideological polarity on the Su-

preme Court. For example, Biskupic (2019) describes an ideological clash that occurred over a motion when Justice Breyer wrote a dissenting statement signed by his three fellow liberal justices that suggested that the court majority was arbitrarily applying its rules, at least in death penalty cases.

18. More specifically, we include separate dummies for (a) each of the eleven circuit courts of appeals; (b) the District of Columbia circuit court (indicated in the estimations as lower-court dummy 12); and (c) the Federal Patent Court (indicated in the estimations as lower-court dummy 13). The reference category includes petitions from state and lower district courts, as well as any court not explicitly identified by our set of indicator variables.

19. Biskupic, Roberts, and Shiffman (2012) and Lazarus (2008) argue that SCOTUS grants petitions filed by certain top advocate lawyers at a significantly higher rate than they grant petitions filed by other lawyers. While the Bloomberg database provides the names of the lawyers filing a petition, we relied on data published by Bhatia (2012) to identify top Supreme Court advocates. Specifically, Bhatia ranks modern lawyers according to the number of SCOTUS cases they have argued between 2000 and 2010 and provides lifetime numbers of Supreme Court appearances for each of those lawyers. Taken together, the Bloomberg and Bhatia data allowed us to identify petitions filed by lawyers who, as of 2010, had argued at least ten cases before the Supreme Court.

20. Thompson and Wachtell (2009) discuss the close relationship that solicitor generals have with the Supreme Court and the court's requests for their views on petitions.

21. Corday and Corday (2004) discuss how the volume of petitions affects the likelihood of whether the Supreme Court will agree to hear a case. The Supreme Court term begins the first Monday in October and consists of seven argument sessions, during which the justices hear cases and deliver opinions; the May and June lists, during which the court sits only to announce orders and opinions; and the summer recess, during which the court's only duty is to review newly submitted petitions and make preparations for the fall argument sessions. Following Cordray and Cordray (2004), petition decisions announced in July, August, September, and the first Monday of October were assigned to the summer recess; subsequent petition decisions made in October (but after the first Monday) were assigned to the October session, the first of the seven argument sessions. Month dummies were then constructed to identify the six remaining argument sessions (November through April) and the May and June lists.

22. Annual docket size was measured as the total number of petitions filed during the year plus the total number of cases remaining on the docket from the previous year. Note that these counts include both the nonpauper petitions recorded in the Bloomberg dataset and the much smaller number of pauper cases. Data on docket size come from the Federal Judicial Center (www.fjc.gov/history/caseload.nsf/page/caseloads_Sup_Ct_totals).

23. We initially estimate separate dummies for each justice and we then perform estimations where we aggregate and specify liberal or moderate and conservative ideology dummies for each justice. Our derivation also holds for the first approach.

24. Holden, Keane, and Lilley (2017) found that justices are influenced by their

peers. Ideological effects are enhanced by, for example, a conservative judge also affecting other justices' likelihood of voting conservative.

25. Heckman and Singer (1984) propose a nonparametric maximum-likelihood approach that uses a discrete type distribution for the random components in an econometric model. Their approach is difficult to apply to our sample selection model with random coefficients because we show in equation (9) below that the data-likelihood of the sample selection model requires knowledge of both the joint distribution and the conditional and marginal distributions of (v_i, ω_i, η_i). Although we can use a common random component with a discrete type distribution to capture the correlation of (v_i, ω_i, η_i), it is not possible for us to derive marginal and conditional distributions from such a specification. Thus, assuming joint normality provides a tractable and plausible way to identify the sample selection model.

26. The WESML estimator is consistent but not efficient because the shares are determined from data instead of being estimated following an approach developed by Cosslett (1981). However, we found it computationally difficult to simultaneously estimate both the model parameters and the sampling weights.

27. We use the term pseudo-log-likelihood function because we are not taking Cosslett's (1981) approach to obtain efficient estimates by maximum likelihood estimation. Vossmeyer (2015) suggests a Bayesian approach that could be used to estimate the model.

28. Qualitative research, for instance, suggests that the solicitor general's office typically drops a nontrivial number of cert-worthy petitions based on their perceptions of the court's caseload for that year (Griswold 1975). Although the volume of Supreme Court petitions has significantly increased during the past several decades, Posner (2008) points out that the court's annual caseload has sharply decreased. Posner claims that the reason for the decline in the court's caseload is a mystery; nonetheless, the court's desire to hear a smaller number of cases is likely to make its petition decisions more sensitive to its docket size.

29. Once a petition is submitted, the respondents have thirty days to file a brief in opposition. If they choose to submit a brief in opposition, the respondents can file for an extension (typically another thirty days). If the respondents waive their right to file a brief in opposition, or if the thirty-day response period expires, the petition is then circulated among the justices' chamber the next time a conference list of petitions goes out. New conference lists are circulated on a weekly basis, and the court is scheduled to meet on prespecified dates to discuss the petitions on each conference list. If the respondents file a brief in opposition, the court waits approximately ten days in order to allow the petitioner to file a reply, after which time the case is appended to the next conference list. Occasionally, when respondents fail to submit a brief in opposition, the justice will instruct the respondents to prepare and file a brief in opposition within the next thirty days. On rare occasion, the court will also invite the solicitor general to file an *amicus curiae* brief expressing the views of the United States regarding whether the petition should be heard. Decisions on petitions may also be postponed until the subsequent conference if justices need more time to consider the case. Such delays are rare, however, as the average time from submission to disposition of a petition is only

six weeks (Public Information Office of the Supreme Court of the United States 2014). Nelson (2009) provides more details on the petition-review process.

30. The authors hypothesize that the justices may "feel" like they are accepting large numbers of cases (even though their acceptance *rates* are strikingly low), or that the overwhelming volume of cases has a "numbing effect" on the justices and their law clerks. A similar "overload effect" may be contributing to the low grant rates in February. The authors note that the justices consider about 50 percent more petitions in February than in the average session—an increase that they attribute to the abnormally long recess that precedes the February session.

31. Hart (1959), for example, estimated that SCOTUS justices in the late 1950s could spend at most twenty minutes reviewing each nonfrivolous petition, while Chief Justice Hughes reported that his justices were unable to spend more than four minutes discussing each petition at conference (Cordray and Cordray 2004). Finally, Lazarus (2008) explains that the justices do not read a large portion of petitions and, at most, read the memoranda prepared by the clerks.

32. Specifically, Thompson and Wachtell quote Justice Ginsberg as saying: "The Solicitor acts as a true friend of the Court when we call for its views on a case in which the United States is not a party." They also point to the following quote from former solicitor general Rex Lee: "The Solicitor General's office provides the Court from one administration to another with advocacy which is more objective, more dispassionate, more competent, and more respectful of the Court as an institution than it gets from any other lawyer or group of lawyers."

33. The Ninth Circuit has been called the "rogue circuit" due to the high reversal rates of its rulings by the Supreme Court. In addition, Tony Mauro, "Key Patent Dispute Divides Supreme Court Justices," *National Law Journal*, October 15, 2014, reports that SCOTUS has an unspoken distrust of the U.S. Court of Appeals for the Federal Circuit as the ultimate arbiter of patent disputes because this circuit court frequently reverses trial judge findings; thus, SCOTUS steps in to reset the balance.

34. Larger circuits tend to have greater difficulties in maintaining "uniform law" (aka, consistency in decisions across judges) within the circuit, which would account for the observed positive correlation between circuit size and SCOTUS reversals of lower-court rulings (Scott 2006).

35. It is worth noting that the petition-selection model does not control for circuit splits, which occur when appellate courts generate conflicting rulings on a particular legal issue. Although the Supreme Court is substantially more likely to grant cert in cases that create circuit splits, data on circuit splits are sparse, largely because identifying such cases would require reading and comparing thousands of appellate judicial opinions. However, the absence of a circuit split variable does not pose a problem for our model because the lower-court dummies broadly capture a circuit's tendency to diverge from other appellate courts on questions of law. For example, the high reversal rates of Ninth Circuit holdings partially reflect the Ninth Circuit's heightened probability of splitting with other appellate courts on legal issues. In addition, because nearly all cert-worthy cases involve circuit splits, circuit splits are unlikely to be correlated in a meaningful way with Supreme Court rulings on the merits. Thus, omitting circuit

splits from the petition model should not affect the consistency of the estimates in the model.

36. As noted, the systematic difference indicates that the dummies capture ideological preferences, not periodic intellectual disagreements, between justices.

37. The availability of data on justices' votes on petitions could shed additional light on why accounting for selection affects estimates of the justices' ideological preferences. For example, such data may reveal patterns of strategic voting by justices.

38. Generally, the estimates of the petition-selection model for all of the robustness tests did not change much from the estimates we obtained in the base case (table 7-4).

39. The case topic dummies were statistically insignificant in all the petition-selection models that we estimated.

40. Recall that we also pointed out that by comparing the Roberts and Rehnquist courts, we limit the possibility that differences in the types of cases that make it into the SCOTUS pool of petitions are driving our results, because the types of cases being processed by the lower courts during the Rehnquist and Roberts courts are unlikely to be categorically different. Differences in the types of cases processed by the lower courts may arise if we compare the behavior of the Roberts court with the behavior of courts that preceded the Rehnquist court.

41. The most recent Gallop Poll indicated that 50 percent of Americans had a great deal or fair amount of faith in the Supreme Court.

42. Emily Brazen, "Better Judgment," *New York Times Magazine*, June 21, 2015, describes how Justice Oliver Wendell Holmes Jr. was influenced by a Harvard instructor, Harold Laski, to read John Stuart Mill and Adam Smith, and how those works caused him to change his views on freedom of speech. Brazen notes judges rarely change their minds today because they wrap themselves in a mythos of authority and certainty.

43. See Jeffrey Rosen, "The Supreme Court Has a Legitimacy Crisis, But Not for the Reason You Think," *New Republic*, June 11, 2012.

44. In the Supreme Court's two 5-4 decisions on the merits during the 2019 term, Justices Kavanaugh and Roberts joined with conservatives to form a majority. As reported by Barnes (2020), in cases decided during the 2019–2020 term, the two most recent Supreme Court appointees, conservatives Kavanaugh and Gorsuch, agreed most often with Roberts's opinions, while liberal justices Ginsburg and Sotomayor agreed least often with Roberts's opinions. However, liberal justices Kagan and Breyer agreed more often with Roberts's opinions than conservative justice Thomas did, and liberal justice Kagan agreed more often with Roberts's opinions than conservative justice Alito did.

Chapter 8

1. Legal Services Corporation, "The Justice Gap: Measuring the Unmet Civil Legal Needs of Low-income Americans," NORC at the University of Chicago for Legal Services Corporation, 2017, www.lsc.gov/sites/default/files/images/TheJusticeGap-FullReport.pdf.

2. "Civil Justice Initiative: The Landscape of Civil Litigation in State Courts,"

National Center for State Courts, www.ncsc.org/~/media/Files/PDF/Research/ CivilJusticeReport-2015.ashx.

3. Jack Karp, "No Country for Old Lawyers: Rural U.S. Faces a Legal Desert," *Law360*, January 27, 2019, www.law360.com/articles/1121543.

4. "Current and Historical Data," World Justice Project, https://worldjustice project.org/our-work/research-and-data/wjp-rule-law-index-2019/current-historical-data. Hadfield (2010) concludes that compared with other advanced market democracies, the United States devotes fewer legal resources to individuals, including public expenditures, legal aid, judges, and, in some cases, lawyers.

5. "Report on the Future of Legal Services in the United States," ABA, Commission on the Future of Legal Services, 2016, www.americanbar.org/content/dam/aba/ images/abanews/2016FLSReport_FNL_WEB.pdf.

6. Adam Liptak, "An Exit Interview with Richard Posner, Judicial Provocateur," *New York Times*, September 11, 2017, www.nytimes.com/2017/09/11/us/politics/ judge-richard-posner-retirement.html.

7. Mitch (2017) discusses nonprofit sliding-scale law firms, which charge clients according to their income. However, there are only a few dozen of such legal aid organizations in the United States.

8. Adam Feldman, "Empirical SCOTUS: A Class of Their Own: The Supreme Court's Recent Take on Class Actions," SCOTUSblog, August 6, 2019, www .scotusblog.com/2019/08/empirical-scotus-a-class-of-their-own-the-supreme-courts-recent-take-on-class-actions/.

9. *The Economist*, "Lobbying in Trumpland," April 13, 2019, reports that lobbying for corporate America has become even more difficult under the Trump administration because Trump is an outsider, his administration is inefficient, respectable businesses worry about being sullied by association with Trump's entourage or his views, and power in the administration shifts around very quickly.

10. Gibney points out that all major graduate-entrance exams have a math section except the LSAT.

11. Jon Brodkin, "FCC Loses in Court, Judges Say Agency Would Fail 'Intro Statistics Class,'" September 24, 2019, Ars Technica, https://arstechnica.com/tech-policy/2019/09/fcc-ignored-women-and-minorities-in-plan-to-allow-media-mergers-court-rules/.

12. Debra Cassens Weiss, "Should There Be a Duty of Tech Competence for Judges? Survey Raises Questions," *ABA Journal*, May 10, 2019, www.abajournal.com/news/ article/should-there-be-a-duty-of-tech-competence-for-judges-survey-raises-questions.

13. "Barr Blasts His Own DOJ Prosecutors, Equates Them to Preschoolers and 'Headhunters,'" NBC News, September 17, 2020, www.nbcnews.com/politics/justice-department/barr-blasts-his-own-justice-department-prosecutors-accuses-them-being-n1240279.

14. When the antitrust authorities successfully blocked a proposed merger from 1984 to 1996, Crandall and Winston (2003) found that it had no statistically significant effect on reducing industry price-cost margins. The FTC has an in-house admin-

istrative process in which it has rarely lost a case in the past two decades. However, Greene (2014) quotes FTC Commissioner Joshua Wright as saying that the FTC's own decisions are reversed by federal courts of appeal at a much greater rate than those of generalist district court judges with little or no antitrust expertise. Recently, the FTC has lost two cases where it attempted to block hospital mergers in Chicago and Philadelphia.

15. Ideological polarity is also becoming a serious concern in federal courts. Senate Democrats issued a report arguing that Republicans have adopted a long-term strategy of filling those courts with "politicians in robes" to serve the interests of large donors to the Republican Party and indicated that they are considering legislative solutions to counter this influence (Thomsen 2020).

Chapter 9

1. Karen Sloan, "Amid Shrinking Membership, ABA President Touts New Dues Structure and Focus," Law.com, April 30, 2019, www.law.com/2019/04/30/amid-shrinking-membership-aba-president-touts-new-dues-structure-and-focus.

2. ABA, "Report to the House of Delegates," February 2020, www.americanbar.org/content/dam/aba/images/centerforinnovation/r115resandreport.pdf.

3. In June 2020, the Washington Supreme Court sunset the limited license legal technician (LLLT) program such that no new LLLTs will be admitted after July 31, 2021. The Washington state bar has resisted the program.

4. Laura Snyder, "California ATILS (2 of 2): California Dreamin', *Not Just for Lawyers* (blog), September 1, 2019, http://notjustforlawyers.com/atils-comments-part-2/.

5. The Obama administration's Council of Economic Advisors (2015) provided a framework for policymakers to assess occupational licensing, but it has not been used by the Trump administration.

6. Kim Kardashian West has attracted attention from her announcement that she intends to become a lawyer in California without going to law school but rather by apprenticing for a law firm and then passing the California bar exam.

7. It is highly misleading, as some people have asserted, to suggest that unaccredited law schools are an example of how law schools would necessarily evolve in the deregulated environment that we envision.

8. Friley (2017) discusses medical-legal partnerships, which can help medical patients with legal problems. Individuals who graduate from a program in law and medicine could provide and possibly expand the services that such partnerships offer to patients.

9. Rozema (2020) investigated the efficacy of state bar exams to protect the public by estimating the share of lawyers who passed a state bar exam and received a public sanction by state discipline bodies compared with the share of lawyers who obtained diploma privilege by graduating from a certain law school in a state instead of passing a bar exam and receiving a public sanction. Rozema found that lawyers admitted to practice on diploma privilege received public sanctions at similar rates as lawyers admitted to practice after passing a bar exam for the first decade of their careers. Small

differences emerged roughly twenty-five years later because diploma privilege increased the share of lawyers who received a public sanction from 4.5 percent to between 4.6 percent and 6.5 percent. The difference in sanctions, which may actually be negligible, does not reflect actual improvements in the quality of legal services that might help to offset the costs of occupational licensing. Winston and Karpilow (2016) noted that a suspended but not disbarred lawyer in California had accumulated more than one thousand pending bar complaints.

10. Justice Neil Gorsuch's recent hiring of law school professors to clerk for him could be a promising start of justices interacting more intensely with people who may have deep knowledge of a topic that informs decision-making about a case. The goal of expert panels would be to broaden and expand that type of interaction.

11. Ian Schwartz, "Dershowitz: Not Impeachable If President Does Something He Believes Will Help Him Get Elected in the Public Interest," RealClear Politics, January 29, 2020, www.realclearpolitics.com/video/2020/01/29/dershowitz_not_impeach able_if_president_does_something_he_believes_will_help_him_get_elected_in_ the_public_interest.html.

12. The regulated U.S. freight railroad industry supported deregulation because it was earning a rate of return that was below the cost of capital and because deregulation was unlikely to lead to new railroads entering the industry.

INDEX

Page numbers in *italics* represent figures and tables.

ABA. *See* American Bar Association

Affordable Care Act, 173–174

"After the JD" survey (AJD), 19: data to estimate J.D. premium, 20–22, *21*; earnings and sector-choice models, 78–83, *80, 81,* 92, *94–95*; estimating premium, 24–29, *30*; gender balance, 20; racial diversity, 20; respondents' salaries, 21. *See also* Great Recession

age: earnings and, 90; sector choice and, 77, 86, 97

AJD. *See* "After the JD" survey

alcoholism, 69–70

Alternative Business Structure Firm, 184–185

American Bar Association (ABA): approaches to "access to justice crisis," 180; disciplinary action against law schools, 52; dues-paying members, 179; involvement in legal education, 52–53, 169, 171; law school accreditation, 9, 52–53, 169, 182; Model Rules of Professional Conduct, 64; online law courses, 53; prosecution of unauthorized practice of law, 3; regulation of legal profession, 2, 72, 170, 182, 191; Section of Legal Education and Admissions to the Bar, 31, 44, 184. *See also* "After the JD" survey

analytical approach, 4–5: cost-benefit analysis, 4, 174

antitrust actions, reforming, 1, 175, 181

anxiety, 69

Arizona, legal paraprofessional (nonlawyer licensee), 2, 180

Artificial Intelligence: courses in, 56; law firm innovations, 63–64

Atrium (legal software startup), 62

AT&T antitrust case, 175

AVVO, 65, 184

Baccalaureate and Beyond (B&B) survey: data to estimate J.D. premium, 20–22, *21*; estimating premium, 24–28, 29; respondents' salaries, 21

bar examination: decline in first-time pass rates, 10, 63; first-time pass rate, 63; impact of Covid-19 pandemic, 188; jobs requiring bar passage, 45, *45*; passage rate, 31, 44, 46; pass rate effect on salary, 30; pass standard within two years of graduation, 184; school tier, 31; state requirements, 9, 30, 182; states with hardest tests, 31

Barr, William, 175

Barrett, Amy Coney, 130, 131, 132

B&B. *See* Baccalaureate and Beyond survey

Bexar County, Texas, defendants' sentences, 172

Big Data, courses in, 56

billable hours: determinant for making partnership, 33, 66; operations management and, 62

Black lawyers/students: networking at highly selective colleges, 11–12; partnerships, 68. *See also* racial issues

Boies, David, 175

cabinet members, lawyers as, 1

California: bar examination pass rates, 10; client selection and race, 186; nonlawyer legal services, 3, 181; State Bar of California Board of Trustees, 181; Task Force on Access through Innovation in Legal Services, 181

call for the views of the solicitor general (CVSG), 145–146

Catholic University, Columbus School of Law, 66

civil service system, 123, 186

class action lawsuits, 171, 188, 189

clerkships: female applicants, 55; hiring along political lines, 130; judicial, 56–57; Twitter patterns of clerks, 187

client relationships. determinant for making partnership, 33, 66

contract review, 63

"corporate" law schools/law programs, 183

court packing, 130, 173, 187

Covid-19 pandemic: effect on alternatives to legal education, 54–55; prevalence of online courses, 53; strengthening case for deregulation, 7, 187–189

CPS. *See* Current Population Survey

Current Population Survey (CPS), 12, 14, 24

CVSG. *See* call for the views of the solicitor general

Democracy in America (Tocqueville), 1

depression, 65, 69

deregulation of legal profession: educational areas, 182–184; impact of Covid-19 pandemic, 7, 187–189; quality and preparation of policymaking, 6; social benefits of, 189–191; spur competition/innovation, 6, 189–191

Dershowitz, Alan, 189–190

discovery documents, electronic, 63

Dodd-Frank Act, 173

DOJ. *See* U.S. Department of Justice

drug problem. *See* substance abuse

earnings: after Great Recession, 41–43, *43*; age relationship to, 90; bar exam pass rate effect on, 30; before Great Recession, 11, 39; by law school tier, *22, 26, 27*, 28, 36–37; debt-to-earnings ratio, 46–47; during Great Recession, 13, 40–41, *42*; estimating wage trajectories, 37–39, *39*; gender gaps, 67, 90; impact of entry barriers, 15; income regression, 24, *25*; increased, 2; intellectual ability and, 90; law school GPA, 90; lawyer parent effect on, 32–33, 34, *49*; market for lawyers, 12–13, *13, 14*, 172; non-wage benefits, 76–77; parent characteristics and, 90–91; parent citizenship effect on, 85; penalty for government lawyers (*see* public sector lawyers); private practice (*see* private sector lawyers); ranking of law school, 90; salary profiles non-J.D.s vs. J.D.s, 38–39, *40*; sector-choice models, 76–78, 79, 81, 86–87, *88–89*, 90–91, 92, 93, *94–95*, 96; stagnation, 9; years of experience vs. partnership, 38

economic activity, law as basic operating system in, 2, 181

education. *See* law school; legal education

electronic discovery documents, 63

employment: delays in, 46–47, *46*; employment growth rates, 14, *15*; impact of barriers to entry, 2; impact of Great Recession, 9; job connections, 33; jobs requiring bar passage, 45, *45*; law school quality and, 28, *29*, 33, 44, 172; LSAT scores and delayed employment, 46; state of, 30–31

employment practices liability insurance, 68

equity partners: cost of, 60; excess capacity, 63; gender issues, 67; quality of life, 69; vs. nonequity partners, 66–67

executive branch of government, influence on SCOTUS cases, 118, 122, 129

exogeneity condition, 32

father's impact on legal profession choices. *See* parent as lawyer

Federal Communications Commission, 174

federal government: characteristics of lawyers, *101*; earnings penalty, 79, 87; earnings vs. state and local government lawyers, 81; employment of lawyers, 1, 80; *See also* public sector lawyers

Federal Trade Commission, 181

Florida, client selection and race, 186

gender issues: balance in ADJ, 20; compensation growth rates, 67; female law firm equity partners, 67; female law school graduates, 67; female partners, 67; gaps in earnings and promotion, 67, 90; law firm attrition, 69; law firm bias,

68–69, 185; law school inequality, 55; media mergers and diversity, 174–175; sector choice and gender, 77, 79, 86, 96; women as lead counsel, 67

Georgia Supreme Court, 174

gerrymandering, 4, 174

Ginsburg, Ruth Bader, 130

Gorsuch, Neil, 130, 131, 162

Grassley, Charles E., 130

GRE, 24

Great Recession and returns to J.D.: after recession ended, 41–43, *42*, *43*, 78–83, *80*, *81*, 92; before recession, 39–43, 78–83, *80*, *81*; before recession ended, 40–41, 78–83, *80*, *81*; decrease in application, 9; earnings before recession, 11; employment growth rates, 14, *15*; postrecession returns, 43–47; quality of graduates after recession, 11

H&R Block merger, 175

Harvard University, 28, 65

Hispanic students, networking at highly selective colleges, 11–12

income defense industry, 3

insider trading, 176

Institute for the Advancement of the American Legal System, 179

insurance. *See* employment practices liability insurance

J.D. premium, economic value of, 16–19: before Great Recession, 39–43; data to estimate, 19–23; estimating, 24–32; postrecession returns, 43–47; selectivity bias, 32–37

job connections. *See* employment

job security, 77, 90, 92

judges, Republican-appointed, 4

"justice gap," 54

justice ideology. *See* U.S. Supreme Court and justice ideology

Justice Toolbox, 184

Kagan, Elena, 148
Kavanaugh, Brett, 130, 162
Kennedy, Anthony, 130

Latham Watkins, First-Generation Professionals Group, 33
law firms. *See* private law firms
law school: accreditation, 9, 43, 52–53; alternative programs, 53–55, 188; applications to, 9, 44; choice-theoretic framework for value of J.D., 16–19; class size, 44; combined undergraduate and graduate programs, 53, 183; "corporate" schools/programs, 183; cost of, 9; decline in quality of student, 9–10, 44; disciplinary action for enrolling poor quality students, 52; economic return of attending, 5, 9–12, 172, 182; educating policymakers, 56; employment, 14, *15*, 33; enrollment declines, 52; estimating wage trajectories, 37–39; faculty and course quality, 55–57; impact on bar exam passage rates, 31; impact of Covid-19 pandemic, 187–189; importance of parental connections, 33; integrative multidisciplinary degree programs, 183, 186–187; investment decision, 10; J.D. premium, 19–32; market for lawyers, 12–16; minority law professors, 55; online courses, 53, 182; over-production of lawyers, 15–16; postrecession returns, 43–47; preparing students to practice law, 56; ranking and earnings, 90, 93, 96; ranking and employment placement, 33; ranking and sector choice, 77, 79, 82, 86, 97–98, 119, 121, 124, 126; rate of return for type of college, 10; reforming education, 182–183; response to technological trends, 56; returns before Great Recession, 39–43; revenue declines, 52; selectivity bias, 26, 32–37; student's academic ability, 26; tenure standards, 55–56; tier/quality, 10–11, 26, 28, *29*, *30*, 36–37, 41, *42*; trade law schools, 53; tuition costs, 15,

40; undergraduate law programs, 53, 183; vocational schools, 182, 186. *See also* clerkships; legal education; gender issues; racial issues; student loan
LawGeex Artificial Intelligence system, 63–64
lawyer-legislators. *See* public sector lawyers
lawyers: Black lawyers, training and career development of, 190; as cabinet members, 1; career lifecycle, 5, 41; in court system, 1; employment growth, 14, *15*; in federal government, 1; ideological biases, 4; influence on national policy, 1–2; intellectual ability, 79, 92, 98; job satisfaction, 87, 90; market for, 12–16; mental health issues, 65–66, 69–70, 185; minimum lawyer competency, 179; noncognitive skills, 91, 96; online reviews of, 184; over-production of, 15–16; parent as, 32–34; personal goals and sector choice, 78, 79, 82, 83–85, *102*, 169; as presidents, 1; as public officials, 1, 190–191; retirement age, 41; in U.S. Congress, 1; as vice presidents, 1; wages (*see* earnings). *See also* employment; legal education; licensing; parent as lawyer; private sector lawyers; public sector lawyers; student loan; work hours; workplace environment
legal aid, 54, 171. *See also* legal services, affordable access to
legal education: alternatives to, 53–55, 182–183; current state of, 5; deregulation of (*see also* deregulation of legal profession), 182–184; GPA and earnings, 90; GPA and sector choice, 77, 79, 82, 86, 96, 97–98; grades and prediction of partnership, 66; intergenerational transmission of elite education, 86; law school reform, 182–183; market for, 51–57; private and social benefits of, 53–55; private and social costs of, 52–53. *See also* law school; student loan
"legalist" theory of judges' behavior, 134
legal paraprofessional, 2, 180

legal profession: alternative suppliers of
services, 2–3; anticompetitive features,
2; barriers to entry, 2, 5, 15, 54, 64, 72,
172, 181, 188; domination of American
politics and public policymaking, 1;
impact of industry's self-regulation, 2;
lack of competition, 2; lack of innovation, 2; policy reforms to improve field,
179–191; price of services, 2; regulation
of (*see* American Bar Association);
role in American society, 1–2; role in
restricting access to services, 3–4; structural changes, 43. *See also* deregulation
of legal profession
legal research, innovations in, 63–65
legal services: affordable access to,
170–172, 180–181, 185–186, 190 (*see
also* legal aid); competition in, 181,
184–185; impact of Covid-19 pandemic, 187–189
Legal Services Corporation, 3, 171
legal technicians, limited license, 2–3, 180
LegalZoom, 2, 65
liability insurance. *See* employment practices liability insurance
licensed paralegal practitioner. *See* paralegal practitioner, licensed
licensing: free-market outcome, 6–7;
impact of Covid-19 pandemic, 188;
nonlawyer, 2–3, 180–181; opposition
occupational licensing, 2, 63, 181, 182,
183–184; state requirements, 2, 9, 52,
72, 191
limited license legal technician. *See* legal
technicians, limited license
litigation finance, 3
lobbying efforts, 172, 176
local government: characteristics of lawyers, *101*; earnings penalty, 79; earnings
vs. federal government lawyers, 81; employment of lawyers, 81. *See also* public
sector lawyers
Lola v. Skadden, 64
Louisiana, public defender case load, 172
lower-court decisions, 146

low-income Americans, access to legal
services, 3, 170–171
LSAT: GRE in place of, 24; lower scores,
9–10, 44, 45–46

Marshall, John, 131
Martindale-Hubbell, 184
media mergers, 174–175
mental health issues, 65–66, 69–70, 185
#MeToo Movement, 67
Microsoft antitrust case, 175
Minnesota, legal paraprofessional pilot
project, 2, 180
minority lawyers. *See* racial issues

NALP. *See* National Association for Law
Placement
National Association for Law Placement
(NALP), 13, 55
National Center for Education Statistics,
20
networking: Blacks and Hispanics at
highly selective colleges, 11–12; career
advice from lawyer parent, 33; determi-
nant for making partnership, 33, 66
New Mexico, nonlawyer legal services, 3,
180
New York City, NY, corporate law firms,
13
Ninth Circuit Court, 146, 152
N95 mask manufacturers, liability protec-
tion, 189
nonlawyer licensing. *See* licensing,
nonlawyer
North Carolina State Board of Dental
Examiners, 181
*North Carolina State Board of Dental
Examiners v. FTC*, 181
Northwestern University, 53

Occupational Employment Statistics
survey (OES), 14
occupational licensing. *See* licensing
OES. *See* Occupational Employment
Statistics survey

Office of the Solicitor General. *See* U.S.
　Department of Justice Office of the
　Solicitor General
online law courses, 53, 182
online resources: reviews and attorney
　hiring, 184; virtual briefings, 187
Oyez Project, 112

packing the court. *See* court packing
paralegal practitioner, licensed, 2, 180
parent and citizenship, 78, 85, 87
parent as lawyer, 32–34: career advice, 33;
　earnings impact, 32–33, 34, *49*, 90–91;
　employment connections, 33, 85–86;
　father's education level, 20; influence on
　work ethic, 34, 36; sector choice and, 78,
　79; transmission of elite education, 86
partnership, law firm: decision to become
　partner, 31–32; determinants for
　making, 33, 66; earnings, 38; effect of
　decisions, 23; excess partner capac-
　ity, 63; gender issues, 67; geographic
　proximity of school and legal market
　as predictor, 66; information model,
　66; job security, 90; law school grades
　as predictor, 66; promotion to, 66–67;
　racial issues, 68; tournament model, 66
patent examiners, 126–127
Peterson, Nels, 174
*Plaintiff in Chief: A Portrait of Donald
　Trump in 3,500 Lawsuits* (Zirin), 170
policymaking: decrease in efficacy, 3–5,
　190; effects of reforms, 185–187; effects
　of restricting access to legal services,
　4; government performance, 172–176,
　186–187; history of legal profession in,
　1, 190–191; impact of Covid-19 pan-
　demic, 188–189; legal influence on, 1–2
"political science" theory of judges' behav-
　ior, 134
politics, history of legal profession in, 1,
　190–191
presidents, lawyers as, 1
private law firms: cases tried before
　SCOTUS, 107–127; CEO performance

comparison, 62; competition among,
　181, 184–185; "corporate" schools/pro-
　grams, 183; culture of, 59; diversity and
　inclusion in, 68; gender bias, 68–69,
　185; innovation, 63–65; insolvency,
　60; mergers, 63; mismanagement of,
　62; on-the-job training, 56; operations
　management, 61–63; ownership of,
　181, 184, 188; profitability, 60–61, 119;
　racial bias, 68–69, 185; technological
　change, 63–65; workplace environ-
　ment, 65–70, 185. *See also* private sector
　lawyers
private sector lawyers: age and attrition,
　67; characteristics, *81*, 86–87, *88–89*,
　90–91; earnings, 13, *14*, 60–61, 79,
　81–82, 87, *88–89*, 93; intellectual
　ability, 79; law school GPA, 79, 82, 96,
　170; law school ranking, 79, 82, 124,
　126; personal goals, 82, 83–85, 87, *102*;
　student load debt, 80, 96; work hours,
　12, 79, 82, 86, 87, 93. *See also* lawyers;
　private sector law firms
public sector lawyers: age, 77, 97; changes
　in personal goals, *102*; characteristics
　of, *81*, 86–87, *88–89*, 90–91, *101*;
　earnings, 13, *14*, 76–93, 123; earnings
　penalty 73–75, 87, *88–89*, 92, 93,
　96–98, 186; education, 56; education
　debt, 77; gender, 77, 79, 96; government
　attraction and retention of, 96–98,
　97, 99–100; intellectual ability, 79,
　98; job security, 77, 90, 92; law school
　activities, 84; law school GPA, 77, 79,
　82, 96, 97–98; law school ranking,
　77, 79, 82, 93, 96, 97–98, 119, 121,
　124, 126; lawyer-statesman, 3, 5, 7,
　172–174; noncognitive skills, 91, 96;
　parental characteristics, 78, 79, 85, 87;
　personal goals/social impact, 78, 79,
　82, 83–85, 87, 92, 96, *102*; race, 77, 79,
　97; resource constraints, 107–127, *125*,
　170, 174–175, 186; self-selection of gov-
　ernment sector and earnings penalty,
　71–73, 175; student loan debt, 77, 80,

86–87, 96; Trump's criticism of, 175; work hours, 12, 82, 93, 96. *See also* federal government lawyers; lawyers; local government lawyers; state government lawyers; U.S. Department of Justice Office of the Solicitor General

racial issues: client selection and, 185–186; diversity in ADJ, 20; law firm attrition, 69; law firm bias, 68–69, 185; law school inequality, 55; media mergers and diversity, 174–175; minority law professors, 55; partnerships, 67; sector choice and race, 77, 79, 86, 96, 97; training and career development of Black lawyers, 190

racism. *See* racial issues

Recurve, 65

relevancy condition, 32, *48*

Rehnquist, William H., 129

Rehnquist court, 129. *See also* U.S. Supreme Court and justice ideology

Republican party: influence on SCOTUS, 131; judges appointed by, 4

Roberts, John, 4, 5, 129, 131, 132, 158, 162, 174, 177

Roberts court. *See* U.S. Supreme Court and justice ideology

Rocket Lawyer, 180

"rogue circuit." *See* Ninth Circuit Court

Scalia, Antonin, 130, 131, 177

Securities and Exchange Commission, 73, 98

selectivity bias: exogeneity condition, 32; instrumental variables, 32–36; propensity score matching, 36–37; relevancy condition, 32; selection on unobservables, 37

self-selection for government lawyers. *See* public sector lawyers

sexual harassment. *See* gender issues

SIPP. *See* Survey of Income and Program Participation

60 Minutes, 2

social welfare activity: benefits of deregulation, 189–191; decrease in efficacy of public policy, 3–5; increased by reducing barriers to entry, 54; law as basic operating system in, 2; legal profession's self-aggrandizing position, 2–3. *See also* public sector lawyers, personal goals/social impact

Solicitor General. *See* U.S. Department of Justice Office of the Solicitor General

Sotomayor, Sonia, 177

Spaeth, Harold, 110, 134

Spaeth Database, 110–111, 134

Stanford University, 28

state government: characteristics of lawyers, *101*; earnings penalty, 79; earnings vs. federal government lawyers, 81; efforts to improve access to legal services, 180–181; employment of lawyers, 1, 81. *See also* public sector lawyers

stress, 66

student loan: association with LSAT scores, 45–46; debt, 9, 43, 52; debt and sector choice, 77, 80, 86–87, 96; debt-to-earnings ratio, 46–47; federal loan programs, 52

substance abuse, 69–70

Survey of Income and Program Participation (SIPP): data to estimate J.D. premium, 22–23, *23*; estimating premium, 28–29, *30*

Syracuse University, 53

TaxAct merger, 175

tax loopholes, 3

technology, changes in, 63–65, 174–175

tenure standards, 55–56

Tocqueville, Alexis de, 1

trade law schools, 53

Trump, Donald J., 36, 130, 170, 173, 175, 181, 189

Twitter patterns of law clerks, 187

unauthorized practice of law (UPL), 3, 65, 181

undergraduate grades, 15, 29
undergraduate schools, 15, 24, 29: undergraduate law degree, 53, 185
University of Arizona, 180
University of Michigan, 93, 96, *103*, *104–105*
University of Southern California Gould School of Law, First-Generation Professionals Program, 33
UpCounsel, 65
UPL. *See* unauthorized practice of law
U.S. Congress, 1, 129, 173
U.S. Court of Appeals for the Federal Circuit, 146
U.S. Department of Justice (DOJ) Office of the Solicitor General (SG): AT&T antitrust case, 175; call for the views of the solicitor general (CVSG), 145–146; career paths of top advocates, 112–114, *113*, 116–117, 121; case characteristics, 109;   case selection, 114; civil service hiring regulations, 123; H&R Block merger, 175; identification of top advocate, 108, 112–114; invitation to submit brief, 145–146; lawyers in antitrust decisions, 1; Microsoft antitrust case, 175; organizational constraints, 109, 122; participation in petitions, 144–145; as petitioner, 111, 114, 116–121, 126; probability of winning case, 108–109, 111, 114–115, *117*, 121, 124, 126; quality of legal representation, 109–116; resource constraints, 107–109, 170; as respondent, 111, 116–121; robustness tests, 116–118; salaries, 123; sample description, 114–116; staff turnover, 123; TaxAct merger, 175; Trump's criticism of, 175; win margins, 119–120; workplace constraints, 109, 123
U.S. Department of Transportation, lawyers' influence on national policy, 1–2
U.S. Federal Reserve, 2
U.S. News and World Report rankings, 33, 96, 119

U.S. Supreme Court (SCOTUS) and Office of the Solicitor General, 107–127: briefs, importance of, 122; cost of law firm's legal fees, 118; difficulty of case, 118; executive branch's influence on cases, 118, 122; ideological composition, 111; oral arguments, 122; split decision cases, 110–112, *117*, 129
U.S. Supreme Court (SCOTUS) and justice ideology, 109, 129–133, 187: case outcomes, 134–142, 148, *150–151*, 152, 153, *154–157*, 158, *166*, *167*, *168*, *176–177*; case selection, 134–142, 153, *154–157*, 158, 159–161, *167*, *168*; cert petitions, 136–137, 143; econometric model, 137–142; invitation to solicitor general to submit brief, 145–146; justices' lack of technical knowledge, 177; justices' votes, 135, 143–161, *147*, *149*; justices' workload, 143–144; lifetime appointments, 130–131; lower-court decisions, 146; monthly calendar and docket size, 137, 143–144, 153; participation of solicitor general and top advocate, 144–145; petition selection, 133, 134–142, 143–146, 158, *163–165*, *166*; polarization, 129–132, 152, 158, 159–161, 162, 170, 177, 187; politicization, 129–130, 132, 135, 145, 152; probusiness/antibusiness cases, 135, 147–148, 159–161, *160*, 176; Rehnquist court, 129, 132, 134–135, 137, *147*, 148–149, *150–151*, 153, 158–160, *167*, *168;* reversal rates, 146–147; Roberts court, 129, 131, 132, 134–135, 137, 147–149, *147*, *149–151*, 153, 158, 159–161, *167*, *168*
Utah: licensed paralegal practitioner, 2, 180; Supreme Court, 188

vice presidents, lawyers as, 1
Vietnam War, 36
"virtual briefings," 187
vocational law schools, 182, 186

wages. *See* earnings

Warren, Sarah Hawkins, 174

Warren, Elizabeth, 181

Washington, D.C., corporate law firms, 13

Washington State, limited license legal technician, 2, 180

Whitehouse, Sheldon, 130

Wisconsin, Roberts' response to gerrymandering, 4, 174

Women Lawyers on Guard, 68

work ethic, lawyer parent influence on, 34, 36

work hours: public sector vs. private sector lawyers, 12, 82, 87, 93; within public sector, 81

workplace environment, 65–70: constraints on top government advocates, 109, 123; gender law firm bias, 68–69, 185; promotion to partner, 66–67; quality of life, 69–70, 185; racial law firm bias, 68–69, 185; sector choice and workplace location, 78

Yale University, 28

Zirin, James D., 170